INTRODUCTION TO SANSKRIT

Introduction to Sanskrit

THOMAS EGENES

PART ONE

MOTILAL BANARSIDASS PUBLISHERS
PRIVATE LIMITED • DELHI

Reprint: Delhi, 2006, 2008
Third Revised Edition: Delhi, 2003
Second Revised Edition: Delhi, 1996
First Indian Edition: Delhi, 1994

First Published California, 1989

ISBN: 978-81-208-1140-9

MOTILAL BANARSIDASS
41 U.A. Bungalow Road, Jawahar Nagar, Delhi 110 007
8 Mahalaxmi Chamber, 22 Bhulabhai Desai Road, Mumbai 400 026
236, 9th Main III Block, Jayanagar, Bangalore 560 011
203 Royapettah High Road, Mylapore, Chennai 600 004
Sanas Plaza, 1302 Baji Rao Road, Pune 411 002
8 Camac Street, Kolkata 700 017
Ashok Rajpath, Patna 800 004
Chowk, Varanasi 221 001

Printed in India
BY JAINENDRA PRAKASH JAIN AT SHRI JAINENDRA PRESS,
A-45 NARAINA, PHASE-I, NEW DELHI 110 028
AND PUBLISHED BY NARENDRA PRAKASH JAIN FOR
MOTILAL BANARSIDASS PUBLISHERS PRIVATE LIMITED,
BUNGALOW ROAD, DELHI 110 007

CONTENTS

INTRODUCTION

REASONS FOR STUDYING SANSKRIT

There are several reasons to study the subtle and refined language of Sanskrit. The sound, script, grammar, and systematic nature of the language is charming in itself, something of great beauty. The study of Sanskrit creates orderliness within the mind because Sanskrit is a highly systematic language, reflecting the orderliness of nature itself.

Most students who study Sanskrit also have an interest in the content of the Sanskrit literature. This large body of literature is enormously diverse, including such fields as philosophy, science, art, music, phonology, grammar, mathematics, architecture, history, education, and logic (to name just a few). The literature can be understood in greater depth when it is studied in its original language.

Even a little Sanskrit will give you control over English translations of the Sanskrit literature, so you will be able to decide if a crucial word has been mistranslated. While you may not become an expert translator of the Sanskrit literature, you'll find that an introductory knowledge of Sanskrit has great worth. Even a small knowledge of Sanskrit is useful when reading Sanskrit texts in English. And who knows? The study of Sanskrit could lead to something far beyond what you anticipated.

VEDIC AND CLASSICAL SANSKRIT

Sanskrit (**saṃskṛta**) means "perfected," or "put together" ("put," **kṛta** and "together," **saṃ**). Sanskrit is divided into two principal parts: Vedic Sanskrit and Classical Sanskrit. The older language is Vedic Sanskrit, or Vedic, the language of the **Saṃhitā** and

Brāhmaṇa. Vedic Sanskrit begins with the **Ṛk-Saṃhitā.** Classical Sanskrit, which includes several aspects, is the language of the **Bhagavad-Gītā, Rāmāyaṇa,** and the rest of the Sanskrit literature.

This text focuses on the beginning study of Classical Sanskrit, although several of the quotations are in Vedic Sanskrit. Normally, Vedic Sanskrit is studied after Classical Sanskrit is learned.

TEXTS ON SANSKRIT

Over the past several hundred years, few Western scholars have written grammars or introductory textbooks for Sanskrit. In the 17th and 18th centuries, a few introductory materials for Sanskrit were written by Jesuit missionaries living in India. Some 19th Century works are by: Bartholome (1801), Foster (1804), Colebrooke (1805), Carey (1806), Wilkens (1808), Hamilton (1814), Yates (1820), Bopp (1827), Wilson (1841), Monier-Williams (1846), Ballantyne (1862), Benfey (1863), Müller (1866), Kielhorn (1870), Whitney (1879), and Perry (1886). Some 20th Century works are by: MacDonell (1911), Renou (1942), Antoine (1954), Burrow (1955), Tyberg (1964), Gonda (1966), Hart (1972), Coulson (1976), and Goldman (1980).

FEATURES OF THIS TEXT

This text is written to fulfill a need that still remains, which is to make the introductory study of Sanskrit simple, concise, and systematic, thereby making it more accessible and enjoyable for a beginning student. The text is not a complete survey of Sanskrit grammar, or even a primer. It is meant to be a "pre-primer," a step-by-step introduction to the fundamental aspects of the language.

Some of the features of this text are:

- Small, learnable steps
- Sequential organization
- A balance between alphabet, grammar, and vocabulary in each lesson
- As few unnecessary complications as possible
- Gradual integration of **sandhi** rules

After completing this text, you should be able to study any of the above Sanskrit textbooks more comfortably, or begin Part II of this text. Part II will feature the reading of selected verses from the **Bhagavad-Gītā**, accompanied by a more thorough explanation of unfamiliar rules of grammar as they are encountered in the reading. Both volumes together will cover the basic rules of Sanskrit grammar. For college classes, Part I covers the standard material for a one-semester course and Part II for the second semester. After completing Part II, the student should be able to read the **Bhagavad-Gītā** with the aid of a Sanskrit dictionary and a word-by-word English translation.

In this text, each lesson has three sections:

1. Alphabet
2. Grammar
3. Vocabulary

ALPHABET

1. The study of any language begins with the study of the alphabet—both pronunciation and script. From the beginning, the pronunciation of Sanskrit should be relaxed and natural, without straining. One of the texts of **Śikṣā** states that Sanskrit should be

One challenge for the beginning student is learning the rules, called **sandhi** rules, which describe how the sounds of words change in different environments. In the past, students have found these rules demanding, because they cannot be used until they are memorized, and they are difficult to memorize without being used. By introducing **sandhi** in small steps that are easy to master, this text attempts to overcome this problem. Beginning in Lesson 2, the exercises will be given without **sandhi (pada-pāṭha)**, but will also be observed with **sandhi (saṃhitā-pāṭha)**. Beginning in Lesson 8, the **sandhi** rules will be given in chart form, so that the charts can be used temporarily as a quick reference to gain understanding of the general context of the rules. After using the charts for some time, it will be easy to memorize the rules, which begin in Lesson 13.

GRAMMAR

2. The study of grammar is from **Vyākaraṇa**, of which the primary text is the **Aṣṭādhyāyī** of **Pāṇini**. The **Aṣṭādhyāyī** is a concise and complete grammar of Sanskrit, containing about 4,000 **sūtras**, or aphorisms. While **saṃskṛta** means to "put together," **Vyākaraṇa** means to "undo" or to "take apart." It gives the details of the structure of the language.

Many of the grammatical terms are given in Sanskrit. Memorizing these terms will be useful for several reasons. It will give you a better understanding of the tradition from which these rules came. It will allow you to feel more comfortable when studying more advanced Sanskrit textbooks, of which many use these terms. It will increase your vocabulary, which will be useful in many areas, since most of these terms are also found in other areas than grammar.

VOCABULARY

3. According to **Yāska's Nirukta** (the **Vedāṅga** dealing with word meaning), all Sanskrit words can be divided into four categories: verbs (**ākhyāta**), nominals (nouns, pronouns, and adjectives)

(**nāman**), prefixes (**upasarga**), and indeclinables (**nipāta**). Verbs, as well as nominals, are systematically derived from verb roots (**dhātu**), of which there are about 2,000. In this text, the limited vocabulary is aimed at eventually providing you with an entry into the reading of the **Bhagavad-Gītā** and the **Rāmāyaṇa**.

HOW TO STUDY THIS TEXT

Review the alphabet, grammar rules, and vocabulary frequently and in a relaxed state of mind before doing the exercises. Then the exercises will be more enjoyable, with fewer difficult areas. The exercises in this text contain as few idiomatic Sanskrit expressions as possible, so that you will not be overburdened with learning too much at one time. If the exercises seem difficult, you should review more. The answers to the exercises are given in the back of the text (p. 242).

In general, you should review as often as possible during the day, taking a few minutes to bring the material to mind. If there is any hesitation in recall, immediately look at the written form, rather than straining and thus "programming" your mind to forget. The best way to memorize is to speak the words out loud, if possible. Memorization should be easy, comfortable, and frequent.

ACKNOWLEDGEMENTS

The following individuals have kindly offered inspiration and creative suggestions, and have cheerfully assisted in the preparation of this text: Bryan Aubrey, Niels Baumann, Harriet Berman, Laurie Couture, Michael Davis, Carol de Giere, Katherine Doak, Lawrence Eyre, James French, June French, Peter Freund, Elizabeth Goldfinger, Shepley Hansen, Jean Harrison, Monica Hayward, Park Hensley, Jos Hindriks, Sherry Hogue, Jan Houben, Robert Hütwohl, Alicia Isen, Vernon Katz, Lee Keng, John Kremer, John Konhaus, Sara Konhaus, Margaret Lerom, Sherry Levesque, Dawn Macheca, Richard Marsan, Devorah McKay, Meha Mehta, Christine Mosse, Anthony Naylon, Patricia Oates, Dafna O'Neill, Helen Ovens, Craig Pearson, David Reigle, Beatrice Reilly, Beth Reilly, John Roberts, Robert Roney, Frederick Rosenberg, Susan

Rosenfield, William Sands, Peter Scharf, Barney Sherman, Barbara Small, Thomas Stanley, Dale Stephens, Jan Storms, Sheila Terry, Roxie Teague, Susan Tripp, Agnes Maria Von Agris, Douglas Walker, Keith Wegman, Geoffrey Wells, Julan White, and Elinor Wolfe. Many other students who have studied this text have given valuable feedback. Peter Freund and Eric Vautier developed the devanāgarī and transliteration fonts used in this text. My wife, Linda, assisted in editing and offered continuous guidance and support.

The Sanskrit quotations beginning on page 352 (Part One) and the verses from the **Bhagavad Gītā** (Part Two) are from translations by Maharishi Mahesh Yogi.

FOR FURTHER STUDY

- *Sanskrit Manual,* Roderick Buknell, Motilal Banarsidass
- *A Sanskrit-English Dictionary,* Monier Monier-Williams, Motilal Banarsidass
- *The Bhagavad Gītā,* translated by Winthrop Sargeant, State of New York University Press
- *Devavāṇīpraveśikā: Introduction to the Sanskrit Language,* Goldman and Sutherland, University of California, Berkely
- *Sanskrit, An Introduction to the Classical Language,* Michael Coulson, Teach Yourself Books, Hodder and Stoughton
- *A Sanskrit Grammar for Students,* Arthur MacDonell, Motilal Banarsidass
- *Saṃskṛtasubodhinī: A Sanskrit Primer,* Madhav Deshpande, University of Michigan
- *Sanskrit: An Easy Introduction to an Enchanting Language,* Ashok Aklujkar, University of British Columbia
- *Sanskrit Grammar,* William Dwight Whitney, Motilal Banarsidass
- Sanskrit Reader, Charles Lanman, Motilal Banarsidass
- *A Higher Sanskrit Grammar,* M. R. Kale, Motilal Banarsidass
- *A Manual of Sanskrit Phonetics,* C. C. Uhlenbeck, Munshiram
- *A Dictionary of Sanskrit Grammar,* K. V. Abhyankar, Baroda Oriental Institute
- *A Critical Study of Sanskrit Phonetics,* Vidhata Mishra

DEDICATION

This book is dedicated with deep appreciation and gratitude to Maharishi Mahesh Yogi. Maharishi describes Sanskrit as the language of nature, the language of the impulses within pure consciousness, the Self. Maharishi explains how the ancient Vedic rishis of the Himalayas, fathoming the silent depth of their own pure consciousness, cognized these impulses. These cognitions were recorded in the Vedic literature, a vast body of beautiful expressions that embodies the mechanics of evolution in every field of life.

Over the years, Maharishi has emphasized the most significant passages from this literature, of which many are included in the section of this text entitled "Sanskrit Quotations." The knowlege contained in these expressions can be found at the foundation of every culture and tradition.

From the Vedic tradition of India, Maharishi has brought to light practical procedures for experiencing pure consciousness and promoting evolution in daily life—Maharishi's Transcendental Meditation and TM-Sidhi program. This simple, natural program has brought happiness and fultillment to millions of people around the world, and has been verified by more than 500 scientific studies on every continent. Maharishi has provided the means for removing stress and suffering and for unfolding the full potential within every individual—for creating perfect health, progress, prosperity, and permanent peace in the world.

1

LESSON ONE

Alphabet:	The vowels in roman script
	The first six vowels in **devanāgarī**
Grammar:	How a verb is formed
	The singular ending for verbs
Vocabulary:	The verbs √**gam** and √**prach**
	The word for "and"
	How to write simple sentences

ALPHABET: VOWELS

1. In Sanskrit, each letter represents one and only one sound (**varṇa**). In English, the letter "a" may indicate many sounds, but not so in Sanskrit. The alphabet is systematically arranged according to the structure of the mouth.

2. There are two basic divisions to the alphabet:

   a. Vowels (**svara**, or sounded)
   b. Consonants (**vyañjana**, or manifesting)

3. Vowels can be either short (**hrasva**) or long (**dīrgha**). Short vowels are held for one count (**mātrā**), and long vowels are held for two counts. Some vowels are called simple (**śuddha**), and some are called complex (**saṃyukta**).

	SHORT	LONG
Simple	**a**	**ā**
	i	**ī**
	u	**ū**
	ṛ	**ṝ**
	ḷ	
	LONG	LONG
Complex	**e**	**ai**
	o	**au**

4. In Vedic Sanskrit, but rarely in Classical Sanskrit, there are also vowels held for three counts, called **pluta**, which are marked in **devanāgarī** and roman script by the short vowel followed by the numeral 3. For example: **a**3, or **a** times 3. You may also see it marked with a long vowel: **ā**3. **Pāṇini** (1.2.27) compares the three counts to the calling of a rooster: **u ū u**3.

5. Here is the pronunciation of the vowels:

a	like the first "a" in	America
ā	like the "a" in	father
i	like the "ea" in	heat
ī	like the "ee" in	beet
u	like the "u" in	suit
ū	like the "oo" in	pool
ṛ	like the "ri" in	river (usually not rolled)
ṝ	like the "ri" in	reed
ḷ	like the "lry" in	jewelry
e	like the "a" in	gate
ai	like the "ai" in	aisle
o	like the "o" in	pole
au	like the "ou" in	loud

6. The lines and dots are called "diacritics," or "diacritical marks." They are used because the Sanskrit alphabet has more letters than the English alphabet. Diacritics are combined with roman letters to represent new sounds.

7. A vowel by itself, or a consonant or group of consonants followed by a vowel, is called a syllable (**akṣara**).

8. Sanskrit is written in the **devanāgarī** script. The word **devanāgarī** means the "city (**nāgarī**) of immortals (**deva**)." There are no capital letters.

9. The ideal way to learn the script will be to memorize approximately one letter each day, writing it 20 times or so, and putting it on a flash card (**devanāgarī** on the front and roman on the back). Continue to practice regularly with your flash cards throughout the course. Practice for small amounts of time, several times a day.

10. Here are six vowels in **devanāgarī**. The small numbers inside each letter indicate the order in drawing the various parts of the letter. In general, write left to right, top to bottom, writing the bar last. (Alternate forms for **a** and **ā** will be learned in Lesson Seven.)

a 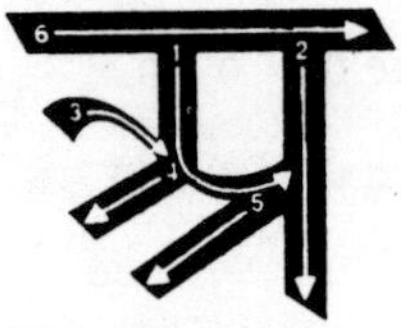

ā 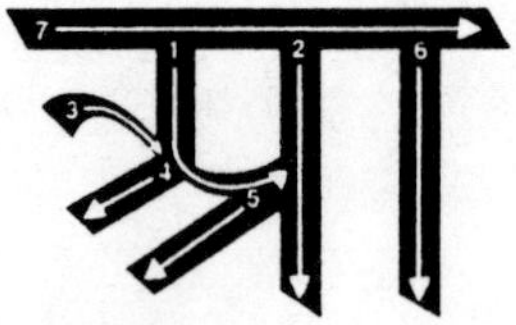

i 

ī 

u 

ū 

GRAMMAR: VERBS

1. Sanskrit roots are divided into ten classes (**gaṇa**) in order to form the present stem. We will study the four classes whose stems end in **a.** The root (**dhātu**), written with √ before it, forms a stem (**aṅga**), and the stem adds an ending (**tiṅ**) to form a verb (**tiṅanta**).

Root	**√gam**	go
Stem	**gaccha**	go
Verb	**gacchati**	he, she, or it goes
	Stem + Ending (**ti**)	

2. Verbs are in three persons (**puruṣa**): third (**prathama**, or first), second (**madhyama**, or middle), and first (**uttama**, or last). (Students in the West have learned these upside down.)

Third person	he, she, or it
Second person	you
First person	I

3. The stem stays the same, but the ending changes for each person. This form is called the present indicative, because it is in the present tense, and it indicates. It is singular (**eka-vacana**).

Third person	**gacchati** (**gaccha + ti**)	she goes, he goes
Second person	**gacchasi** (**gaccha + si**)	you go
First person	**gacchāmi** (**gaccha + a + mi**)	I go

VOCABULARY

1. Here is the vocabulary in Sanskrit and in English. Each verb appears in its root form, followed by the third person singular form. The stem can be found by removing the endings.

SANSKRIT	ENGLISH
√**gam** (root) **gacchati** (3rd per. sing.)	he goes, she goes
ca (indeclinable*)	and (placed after the last word of the series, or after each word) (never first in a sentence or clause)
√**prach** (root) **pṛcchati** (3rd per. sing.)	he asks, she asks

*Some words do not have endings, and so are called "indeclinable" (**avyaya**). Included as indeclinables are: prepositions, adverbs, particles, conjunctions (like **ca**), and interjections. A few nouns (like **svasti**) are also treated as indeclinables.

2. Here are some sample sentences:

gacchāmi	I go. (or) I am going.
pṛcchati gacchāmi ca	He asks and I go.
pṛcchati ca gacchāmi ca	He asks and I go.
gacchasi ca pṛcchasi ca	You go and you ask. (or) You go and ask.

EXERCISES

1. Memorize the vowels and their order in roman script. Learn to pronounce them correctly.

2. Learn to write and recognize the first six vowels in **devanāgarī.**

3. Memorize the forms for the first, second, and third person singular verbs in the present indicative.

4. Memorize the vocabulary.

5. Translate the following sentences into English. Pronounce each sentence several times out loud, both before and after translating. Compare with the correct answers given on page 242.

   a. **pṛcchasi ca gacchati ca**

   b. **gacchāmi pṛcchāmi ca**

   c. **pṛcchati ca gacchati ca**

   d. **gacchasi pṛcchāmi ca**

   e. **pṛcchati pṛcchāmi ca**

   f. **gacchasi ca gacchati ca**

   g. **pṛcchāmi gacchasi ca**

   h. **pṛcchati ca gacchāmi ca**

6. Translate the following sentences into Sanskrit:

   a. I go and I ask.

   b. You ask and he goes.

   c. He asks and you go.

   d. He goes and asks.

   e. You ask.

   f. I ask and you go.

   g. I go and you go

   h. He goes and you go.

2

LESSON TWO

Alphabet:	Most of the consonants and how they are organized The last seven vowels in **devanāgarī**
Grammar:	Verbs in the dual
Vocabulary:	More verbs The word for "where"

ALPHABET: CONSONANTS

1. The first 25 consonants, called stops (**sparśa**), are arranged according to five points of articulation (**sthāna**):

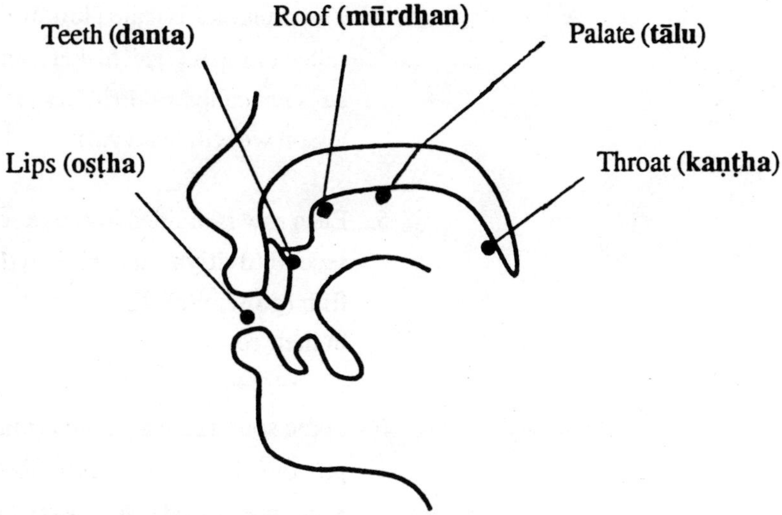

2. Here are the five sets (**varga**), arranged according to point of articulation. For example, all the consonants in the velar row (**ka varga**), are pronounced in the throat. The labial row is pronounced at the lips. The **a** is added for the sake of pronunciation.

	1st	2nd	3rd	4th	5th
Velar (**kaṇṭhya**)	**ka**	**kha**	**ga**	**gha**	**ṅa**
Palatal (**tālavya**)	**ca**	**cha**	**ja**	**jha**	**ña**
Retroflex (**mūrdhanya**)	**ṭa**	**ṭha**	**ḍa**	**ḍha**	**ṇa**
Dental (**dantya**)	**ta**	**tha**	**da**	**dha**	**na**
Labial (**oṣṭhya**)	**pa**	**pha**	**ba**	**bha**	**ma**
		Aspirated		Aspirated	Nasal
			Voiced		

3. Each set of English letters represents one Sanskrit sound. For example, **gh** is one sound. It is the aspirated, voiced velar.

4. The sound **ka** is called **kakāra** ("ka" maker). The sound **ga** is called **gakāra** ("ga" maker), and so on. The only exception is that **ra** is not called **rakāra**, but just **ra** or **repha**, "snarl." (In the next lesson we will learn **ra**.)

5. Each row is divided into five sounds: the first (**prathama**), the second (**dvitīya**), the third (**tṛtīya**), the fourth (**caturtha**), and the fifth (**pañcama**). For example, **ka**, **ca**, **ṭa**, **ta**, and **pa** are all first in their rows.

6. Some sounds are aspirated (**mahā-prāṇa**)—more breath is used in pronouncing these sounds. Some are unaspirated (**alpa-prāṇa**). Some are voiced (**ghoṣavat**)—the vocal chords are used in pronouncing these sounds. Some are unvoiced (**aghoṣa**). The **ṅ**, **ñ**, **ṇ**, **n**, and **m** are called nasals (**anunāsika**).

7. Here is how the consonants are pronounced:

k	like the "k" in	skate
kh	like the "kh" in	bunkhouse
g	like the "g" in	go
gh	like the "gh" in	loghouse
ṅ	like the "n" in	sing
c	like the "c" in	cello
ch	like the "ch" in	charm (using more breath)
j	like the "j" in	just
jh	like the "j" in	just (using more breath)
ñ	like the "n" in	enjoyable

ṭ	like the "t" in	stable (for this group the tongue is touching the hard palate, as in the diagram on page 9.)
ṭh	like the "t" in	table (using more breath)
ḍ	like the "d" in	dynamic
ḍh	like the "dh" in	redhead (using more breath)
ṇ	like the "n" in	gentle

In English, we normally pronounce "t" and "d" somewhere between these two groups (retroflex and dental).

t	like the "t" in	stable (tongue at base of teeth)
th	like the "t" in	table (using breath, tongue at base of teeth)
d	like the "d" in	dynamic (tongue at base of teeth)
dh	like the "dh" in	redhead (using breath, tongue at base of teeth)
n	like the "n" in	gentle (tongue at base of teeth)

p	like the "p" in	spin
ph	like the "ph" in	shepherd
b	like the "b" in	beautiful
bh	like the "bh" in	clubhouse
m	like the "m" in	mother

8. In Vedic Sanskrit, when **ḍa** or **ḍha** have vowels on both sides, they may become **ḷa** or **ḷha.** The example used is that when white has crimson on both sides, the white changes its color slightly. Therefore, when **ḍa** has a vowel on both sides, it changes to **ḷa.** For example, **agnim iḍe** is found in the **Ṛk Saṃhitā** as **agnim iḷe.**

9. Here are the remaining vowels in **devanāgarī**:

ṛ 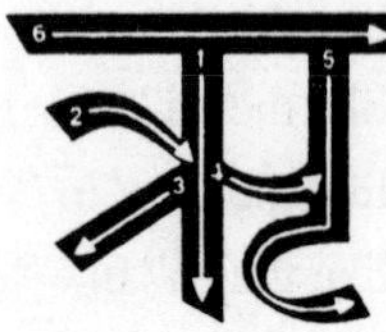 ṝ 

ḷ 

e 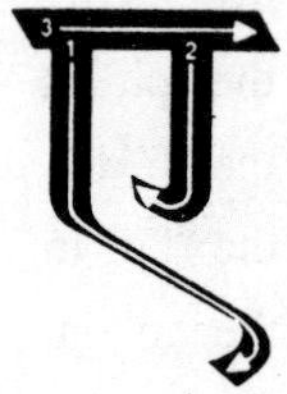 ai 

o 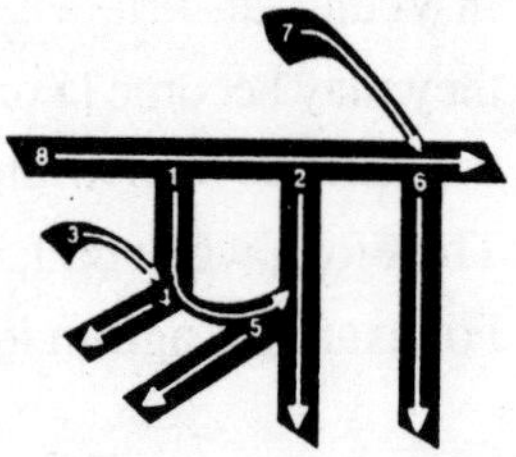 au 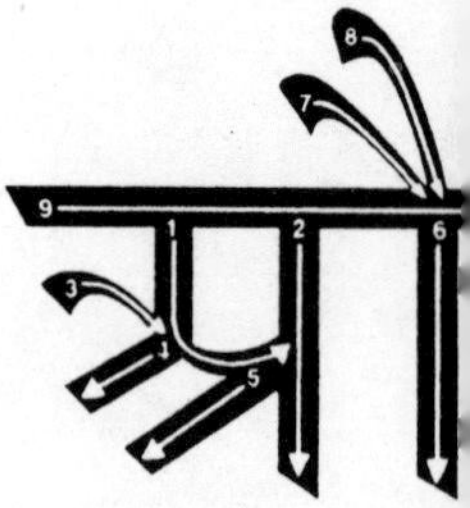

GRAMMAR: DUAL VERBS

1. Unlike English, Sanskrit has dual verbs. The dual **(dvi-vacana)** is formed like this:

Third person	**gacchataḥ** (**gaccha + tas**)	those two go
Second person	**gacchathaḥ** (**gaccha + thas**)	you two go
First person	**gacchāvaḥ** (**gaccha + a + vas**)	we two go

We will learn the pronunciation of **ḥ** in the next lesson. Note that the ending **tas** becomes **taḥ** when it forms a verb. This change is because **sandhi** is applied. (See the following page for an introduction to **sandhi**.)

2. In English, interrogative words usually begin with "wh," such as where, when, etc. In Sanskrit, interrogative words usually begin with **k**. The word for "where" is **kutra**. It is usually placed at the beginning of a sentence. The other words do not need to be rearranged to make a question out of the sentence. For example:

   kutra gacchati
   Where is he going?

3. To translate **kutra gacchati** into English, first write "where" for **kutra** and then write "he goes" for **gacchati**. Literally it would then be translated as "Where he goes?" However, it is important to form correct English sentences. For "Where he goes?" you must write "Where is he going?" or "Where does he go?"

VOCABULARY	SANSKRIT	ENGLISH
	kutra (indeclinable)	where
	√**bhū** (root) **bhavati** (3rd per. sing.)	he is, he becomes (you are, I am)
	√**vas** (root) **vasati** (3rd per. sing.)	he lives
	√**smṛ** (root) **smarati** (3rd per. sing.)	he remembers

SANDHI

Before doing the exercises, we will have an introduction to **sandhi (saṃdhi)**, the rules for how sounds are combined. In English, we say "an apple" but "a pear." The word "the" is often pronounced differently, depending upon the following word. For example, "the house" and "the other house." Some sounds are modified according to their phonetic environment. In Sanskrit, many sounds make these same changes, and unlike English, all of these changes are written. The rules for these changes are called **sandhi**, which means "junction," "putting together," or "combination." **Sandhi** is now an English word and appears in most English dictionaries. The Sanskrit word is **saṃdhi**.

The exercises in Lesson 1 are written the same even after **sandhi** rules have been applied. However, in Lesson 2 the sentences would be written differently if they were to appear in a Sanskrit text. At this point, however, you do not need to learn these rules. Just observe the sentences in parentheses, and notice that these sentences are written slightly differently with **sandhi**.

EXERCISES

1. Learn the five sets of consonants, their order, and their pronunciation. Learn to write the last seven vowels in **devanāgarī**.

2. Be able to identify each consonant by its classification. For example, the aspirated, voiced palatal is **jha**.

3. Learn the dual endings for verbs.

4. Learn the vocabulary.

5. Translate these sentences, using the summary sheet on page 17. Just observe the sentences in parentheses with **sandhi**. (See page 14.) Answers are given on pages 243 and 244.

   a. **kutra vasāvaḥ**
      (kutra vasāvaḥ)
   b. **bhavasi ca bhavāvaḥ ca**
      (bhavasi ca bhavāvaś ca)
   c. **vasāmi smarataḥ ca**
      (vasāmi smarataś ca)
   d. **pṛcchathaḥ ca smarati ca**
      (pṛcchathaś ca smarati ca)
   e. **kutra gacchāvaḥ**
      (kutra gacchāvaḥ)
   f. **kutra bhavāmi**
      (kutra bhavāmi)
   g. **kutra gacchāmi**
      (kutra gacchāmi)

h. **pṛcchāmi ca smarati ca**

(pṛcchāmi ca smarati ca)

i. **vasasi ca gacchāvaḥ ca**

(vasasi ca gacchāvaś ca)

j. **kutra gacchasi**

(kutra gacchasi)

6. Translate the following sentences into Sanskrit:

a. Where are you two going?

b. I live and those two live.

c. We two ask and those two remember.

d. You go and he goes.

e. Where am I going?

f. I am and you two are.

g. Where are you? (Use the singular.)

h. Where is he going?

SUMMARY SHEET

	Singular	Dual
Third	**gacchati** (he, she goes)	**gacchataḥ** (they two go)
Second	**gacchasi** (you go)	**gacchathaḥ** (you two go)
First	**gacchāmi** (I go)	**gacchāvaḥ** (we two go)

VERBS

√gam	**gacchati**	he goes, she goes
√prach	**pṛcchati**	he asks
√bhū	**bhavati**	he is
√vas	**vasati**	he lives
√smṛ	**smarati**	he remembers

INDECLINABLES

kutra	where
ca	and

3

LESSON THREE

Alphabet:	The remaining letters in roman script The first ten consonants in **devanāgarī**
Grammar:	The plural The grammatical terms to describe a verb Accent
Vocabulary:	More verbs

ALPHABET: THE REMAINING LETTERS

1. The previous consonants are sometimes referred to as "stops," because they stop the flow of air. They are formed by "complete contact" (**spṛṣṭa**). The remaining letters are consonants, but they allow more flow of air.

2. There are four consonants, formed by "slight contact" (**īṣat-spṛṣṭa**), called semi-vowels. They are voiced, but not aspirated: They are considered to be between vowels and consonants, and so are called **antaḥstha**, or "in-between":

   ya, ra, la, va

3. The sibilants are formed by "half contact" (**ardha-spṛṣṭa**). They are aspirated, but not voiced. They are called **ūṣman**, or "heated":

   śa, ṣa, sa

4. The aspirate (voiced, but sometimes classified as a sibilant) is:

   ha

5. Here is how these sounds are pronounced:

y	like the "y" in	yes
r	like the "r" in	red
l	like the "l" in	law
v	like the "v" in	victory (but closer to a "w")

ś	like the "sh" in	shine
ṣ	like the "c" in	efficient (similar to the **ś**)
s	like the "s" in	sweet
h	like the "h" in	hero

6. Two additional sounds are the **anusvāra** (**ṃ**) and the **visarga** (**ḥ**), which both follow vowels.

7. The **anusvāra** (**ṃ**) causes the last portion of the vowel before it to be nasal (like the French word "bon"). The **anusvāra** changes its sound according to the following sound. It may sound like the nasal of the set to which the sound following it belongs. For example, **saṃkhyā** is pronounced similar to **saṅkhyā**. In the dictionary, the **anusvāra** is found in the same place as the nasal to which it refers. If the **anusvāra** comes before a semi-vowel or sibilant, it is found in the dictionary before **ka**.

8. The **visarga** (**ḥ**), or **visarjanīya**, is an unvoiced breathing that occurs in many contexts instead of an **s** or **r**. In modern India it is often pronounced, at the end of a line, as an echo of the vowel before it. For example, after an **a** it would be a short **ha**. After an **i** it would be a short **hi**:

   aḥ = **ah**^{a}
   iḥ = **ih**^{i}
   uḥ = **uh**^{u}

   The **jihvāmūlīya** (**ẖ**) is sometimes used in place of a **visarga** before **ka** or **kha**. The **upadhmānīya** (**ḫ**) is sometimes used in place of a **visarga** before **pa** or **pha**. These letters, used more in Vedic Sanskrit, indicate a subtle difference in the breath before **ka** and **pa**, which is like breathing through the throat (**ẖ**) or breathing through the lips (**ḫ**).

9. We have now learned all the letters in their transliterated form (their roman letter equivalents). There are other ways of representing some letters. At times you may see:

śa	as	**sha**	**śānti, shānti**
ṛ	as	**ri**	**ṛk, rik**
ṅ	as	**ñ**	**Śaṅkara, Śañkara**
cha	as	**chha**	**chandas, chhandas**
ca	as	**cha**	**candra, chandra**

10. All the sounds can be classified according to the part of the mouth they come from:

Velar	**a**	**ā**			**ka**	**kha**	**ga**	**gha**	**ṅa**		**ha**
Palatal	**i**	**ī**	**e**	**ai**	**ca**	**cha**	**ja**	**jha**	**ña**	**ya**	**śa**
Retroflex	**ṛ**	**ṝ**			**ṭa**	**ṭha**	**ḍa**	**ḍha**	**ṇa**	**ra**	**ṣa**
Dental	**ḷ**				**ta**	**tha**	**da**	**dha**	**na**	**la**	**sa**
Labial	**u**	**ū**	**o**	**au**	**pa**	**pha**	**ba**	**bha**	**ma**	**va**	

The complex vowels are pronounced at two points of contact: The sounds **e** (which can be said to be composed of **a** and **i**) and **ai** (composed of **ā** and **i**) are both velar and palatal. The sounds **o** (composed of **a** and **u**) and **au** (composed of **ā** and **u**) are both velar and labial. Also, the sound **va** is both dental and labial.

11. Here is the entire alphabet:

VOWELS (svara)		
Simple (śuddha)	a	ā
	i	ī
	u	ū
	ṛ	ṝ
	ḷ	
Complex (saṃyukta)	e	ai
	o	au
Nasalization (anusvāra)		ṃ
Aspiration (visarga)		ḥ

CONSONANTS (vyañjana)					
Velar (kaṇṭhya)	ka	kha	ga	gha	ṅa
Palatal (tālavya)	ca	cha	ja	jha	ña
Retroflex (mūrdhanya)	ṭa	ṭha	ḍa	ḍha	ṇa
Dental (dantya)	ta	tha	da	dha	na
Labial (oṣṭhya)	pa	pha	ba	bha	ma
Semi-vowels (antaḥstha)		ya	ra	la	va
Sibilants (ūṣman)		śa	ṣa	sa	ha

13. Here are the first ten consonants in **devanāgarī** script. Each symbol includes the sound **a.** For example, **ka** and not just **k** is meant by the first symbol.

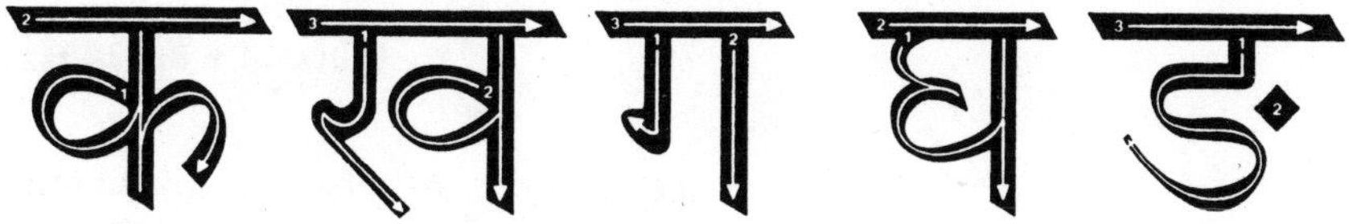

ka kha ga gha ṅa

ca cha ja jha ña

GRAMMAR: THE PLURAL

1. Here is the plural (**bahu-vacana**) for the verb √**gam**:

Third person	**gacchanti** (**gaccha - a + anti**)	they (all) go
Second person	**gacchatha** (**gaccha + tha**)	you (all) go
First person	**gacchāmaḥ** (**gaccha + a + mas**)	we (all) go

Notice that the third person is **gaccha** minus **a** plus **anti.**

2. Now we have the complete conjugation (or verbal paradigm) for the present indicative (**laṭ**):

gacchati	**gacchataḥ**	**gacchanti**
gacchasi	**gacchathaḥ**	**gacchatha**
gacchāmi	**gacchāvaḥ**	**gacchāmaḥ**

he goes	those two go	they all go
you go	you two go	you all go
I go	we both go	we all go
Singular	Dual	Plural

Students of Sanskrit in India memorize these conjugations horizontally. Students in Europe and America have learned them vertically. It would be better to follow the system of India and memorize horizontally (for both verbs and nouns).

3. Here are the standard endings:

	Singular	Dual	Plural
3rd	**ti**	**tas**	**anti**
2nd	**si**	**thas**	**tha**
1st	**mi**	**vas**	**mas**

Note that when a word is formed, final **s** becomes **ḥ** due to **sandhi**.

GRAMMATICAL TERMS

4. Verbs can be classified in four basic ways: tense/mood, voice, person, and number. This is similar to, but slightly different from, how verbs are classified in English. Here is a simplified overview:

Tense/Mood: The tenses and modes are grouped together in the ten **lakāra**, or "**l**" sounds, because they are each abbreviated by **Pāṇini** with a word beginning with the letter "**l**." We have learned the present indicative (abbreviated as **laṭ**). Other tense/moods are the perfect (**liṭ**), the periphrastic future (**luṭ**), the simple future (**lṛṭ**), the subjunctive (**leṭ**), the imperative (**loṭ**), the imperfect (**laṅ**), the optative or potential (**liṅ**), the aorist (**luṅ**), and the conditional (**lṛṅ**).

Voice (**upagraha**): We have learned the active voice (**parasmaipada**), which takes active endings. In Lesson 9 we will learn the middle voice (**ātmanepada**), which takes middle endings. Usually, when the fruit of an action comes back to the agent (**ātman**), the **ātmanepada** is used. When the fruit of an action goes to another person (**para**), the **parasmaipada** is used (although this distinction does not seem to be strictly followed in the literature). Some roots are conjugated in both voices (**ubhayapada**) and some usually in one voice. All the verbs we have learned so far are usually seen in the active voice.

Person: We have learned the three persons (**puruṣa**):

Third (**prathama**)	he, she, or it
Second (**madhyama**)	you
First (**uttama**)	I

Number: We have learned the three numbers (**vacana**):

Singular (**eka**)
Dual (**dvi**)
Plural (**bahu**)

5. Each verb may be classified according to these categories. For example, **gacchati** (he goes), is present indicative, active, third person, singular.

6. Using abbreviations, called parsing codes, we could identify **gacchati** as: pres. indic. act. 3rd per. sing.—present indicative, active, third person, singular. (This isn't as hard as it may seem, since all verbs so far are present indicative and active. All we need to determine is the person and number.)

7. Here are some examples:

gacchāmi	I go	pres. indic. act. 1st per. sing.
bhavanti	they are	pres. indic. act. 3rd per. pl.
pṛcchāvaḥ	we both ask	pres. indic. act. 1st per. dual

ACCENT

1. Accent consists of higher and lower tones (**svara**). There is a raised tone (**udātta**), an unraised tone (**anudātta**), and a "moving" tone (**svarita**). In the **Ṛk Saṃhitā** the **udātta** is unmarked, the **anudātta** is marked by a low horizontal bar, and the **svarita** is marked by a high vertical bar. For example:

   अ॒ग्निमी॑ळे पु॒रोहि॑तं य॒ज्ञस्य॑ दे॒वमृ॒त्विज॑म्

   In classical Sanskrit texts, the accents are not marked.

2. In most Sanskrit dictionaries, a mark is placed over the **udātta** for Vedic words only. For example:

   Mánu
   mádhu
   rátna

3. **Pāṇini** does not give rules for stress accent.

4. For now, an important rule for proper pronunciation is to maintain a clear distinction between the short and long vowels (discussed on pages 2 and 3).

VOCABULARY: MORE VERBS

SANSKRIT	ENGLISH
na	not (placed before the verb)
√**vad** (root) **vadati** (3rd per. sing.)	he says, he speaks
√**sthā** (root) **tiṣṭhati** (3rd per. sing.)	he stands

All vocabulary is given in the order of the Sanskrit alphabet.

An additional rule you'll need to know to do these exercises is that if a member in a series has more than one word (such as **na gacchati**), **ca** usually comes after the first word. For example:

> **gacchāmi na ca gacchati**
> I go and she does not go.

You may also see **ca** at the end of a clause (less often). For example:

> **gacchāmi na gacchati ca**
> I go and she does not go.

EXERCISES

1. Learn the pronunciation and order of the semi-vowels, sibilants, **anusvāra**, and **visarga**. Learn the first ten consonants in **devanāgarī**.

2. Write, in correct order, the entire alphabet (in transliteration, or roman script).

3. Conjugate each verb we have learned, and learn the nine endings.

4. Be able to give the parsing code for each form we have learned.

5. Translate the following sentences into English, using the summary sheet on page 30. Underneath each sentence is the sentence with **sandhi.** Just observe the sentence with the **sandhi.** (Answers are on p. 245.)

a. **vadati na ca vadāmi**
(vadati na ca vadāmi)

b. **vadathaḥ smarataḥ ca**
(vadathaḥ smarataś ca)

c. **na gacchanti**
(na gacchanti)

d. **tiṣṭhāmaḥ gacchāmaḥ ca**
(tiṣṭhāmo gacchāmaś ca)

e. **bhavathaḥ ca vasathaḥ ca**
(bhavathaś ca vasathaś ca)

f. **kutra bhavasi**
(kutra bhavasi)

g. **tiṣṭhanti gacchanti ca**
(tiṣṭhanti gacchanti ca)

h. **na ca pṛcchati na ca vadati**
(na ca pṛcchati na ca vadati)

6. Translate these sentences into Sanskrit. Unless "two" is used, it will be understood that the plural form is intended.

a. Where are they going?

b. We do not speak.

c. He asks and they speak.

d. Where are we standing?

e. Where do those two live?

f. We are not going.

g. I ask and they remember.

h. Where are we?

SUMMARY SHEET

Third	**gacchati** (he, she goes)	**gacchataḥ** (they two go)	**gacchanti** (they all go)
Second	**gacchasi** (you go)	**gacchathaḥ** (you two go)	**gacchatha** (you all go)
First	**gacchāmi** (I go)	**gacchāvaḥ** (we two go)	**gacchāmaḥ** (we all go)
	Singular	Dual	Plural

VERBS

√gam	**gacchati**	he goes
√prach	**pṛcchati**	he asks
√bhū	**bhavati**	he is
√vad	**vadati**	he speaks, he says
√vas	**vasati**	he lives
√sthā	**tiṣṭhati**	he stands
√smṛ	**smarati**	he remembers

INDECLINABLES

kutra	where
ca	and
na	not

4

LESSON FOUR

Alphabet:	Ten more consonants in **devanāgarī**
Grammar:	The nominative case The accusative case
Vocabulary:	Nouns that end in short **a**

ALPHABET

1. Here are ten more consonants to learn:

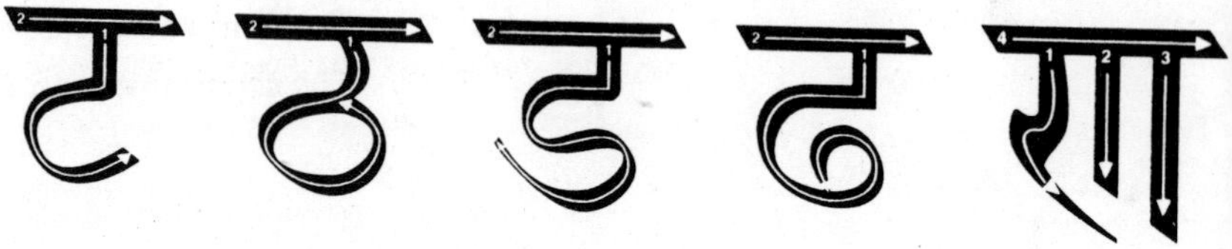

ṭa ṭha ḍa ḍha ṇa

ta tha da dha na

2. There are two additional consonants, **ḷa** and **ḷha**. (See p. 11.)

The **ḷa** is written as: ळ The **ḷha** is written as: ळ्ह

GRAMMAR: NOUNS

1. Sanskrit nouns are formed in a similar way as verbs—the root (**dhātu**) forms a stem (**prātipadika**), and endings (**sup**) are added to form a noun (**subanta**). Nouns are in various cases (**vibhakti**, division), depending upon their role in the sentence.

2. We will learn two cases. The nominative (**prathamā**) is used for naming the subject, as in "<u>Rāma</u> goes." The nominative case is also used for a predicate nominative identified with the subject, as in "<u>Rāma</u> is <u>the king</u>." In India, words are normally cited independently in the nominative, or "naming" case.

   The accusative (**dvitīyā**) is the direct object. The accusative is also the object of motion, as in "He goes <u>to the city</u>."

3. For example, in the sentence, "The man goes to the horse," the word "man" would be in the nominative and the word "horse" would be in the accusative:

   <u>The man</u> goes <u>to the horse</u>.
   (nominative) (accusative)

4. Here is the formation of masculine nouns whose stems end in **a**:

   Stem: **nara** (masculine) man

	Singular (**eka-vacana**)	Dual (**dvi-vacana**)	Plural (**bahu-vacana**)
Nominative	**naraḥ**	**narau**	**narāḥ**
Accusative	**naram**	**narau**	**narān**

Notice that **naraḥ** is formed by **nara** + **s**. The **s** changes to **ḥ** because of **sandhi**.

5. The verb and subject must agree in number in both English and Sanskrit. For example, if the subject is singular, then the verb must also be singular:

The man goes to the horse.	(Subject and verb are singular.)
The men go to the horse.	(Subject and verb are plural.)

6. The direct object need not agree with either the subject or verb. We are learning the rules for the agent construction **(kartari prayoga)**, which is like an active construcition. Here the agent of action **(kartṛ)** is in the nominative, and the object of action **(karman)** is in the accusative.

7. A noun in apposition, such as "Rāma, the boy," is put in the same case as the noun it follows. For example, in the sentence "She speaks to Rāma, the boy," both "Rāma" and "boy" are accusative.

8. The normal word order is:

subject	direct object	verb
naraḥ	**aśvam**	**gacchati** (without **sandhi)**
(**naro**	**'śvaṃ**	**gacchati**) (with **sandhi)**
the man	to the horse	goes

Because **naraḥ** ends in **ḥ**, we know that it is the man who is doing the going and not the horse. While English relies on the order of the words, Sanskrit relies more on the word endings for meaning.

9. Articles, such as "the" or "a," must be put in the English translation as needed.

VOCABULARY

SANSKRIT	ENGLISH
aśvaḥ (masculine)	horse
gajaḥ (masculine)	elephant
naraḥ (masculine)	man
putraḥ (masculine)	son
mṛgaḥ (masculine)	deer
rāmaḥ (masculine)	Rāma
vā (indeclinable)	or (used like **ca**) (never first in sentence or clause)

Nouns will be cited in the nominative case because traditionally that case is used for citing words independently.

Nouns, as well as verbs, may be connected with **ca** and **vā**. When two nominatives are connected with **vā**, the verb agrees with the nominative closest to it, as in English. For example:

> **aśvaḥ gajāḥ vā gacchanti** (without **sandhi**)
> (**aśvo gajā vā gacchanti**) (with **sandhi**)
> The horse or the elephants go.

"He goes" is **gacchati**. "The man, he goes" is **naraḥ gacchati** (with **sandhi**, **naro gacchati**). However, when there is a subject, the "he" is dropped. Therefore, **naraḥ gacchati** (**naro gacchati**) would be translated as "The man goes." Always write English sentences using the rules of correct English.

EXERCISES

1. Continue to learn the consonants in **devanāgarī**.

2. Memorize the singular, dual, and plural forms for the masculine nouns ending with a short **a** (like **nara**) in the nominative and accusative. These should be learned horizontally.

3. Learn the vocabulary and continue reviewing all vocabulary from past lessons.

4. Translate the following sentences into English, using the summary sheet. Translate the verb first, then the nominative, and then the accusative, if any. Continue to observe the **sandhi.**

   a. **narāḥ mṛgam smaranti**
   (narā mṛgaṃ smaranti)

   b. **rāmaḥ aśvau gacchati**
   (rāmo 'śvau gacchati)

   c. **kutra gajāḥ vasanti**
   (kutra gajā vasanti)

   d. **narau rāmam vadataḥ**
   (narau rāmaṃ vadataḥ)

   e. **putraḥ smarati pṛcchati vā**
   (putraḥ smarati pṛcchati vā)

   f. **rāmaḥ mṛgam gacchati**
   (rāmo mṛgaṃ gacchati)

g. **aśvau na vadataḥ**
(**aśvau na vadataḥ**)

h. **rāmaḥ putram vadati**
(**rāmaḥ putraṃ vadati**)

5. Translate the following sentences into Sanskrit:

a. The men speak to the deer. (one deer)

b. Rāma speaks to the horses.

c. The son goes to the horse and stands.

d. Elephants do not remember.

e. Where are the horses standing?

f. Where is the elephant?

g. Rāma speaks and the son remembers.

h. They stand or they go.

i. Where does Rāma stand?

j. Rāma or the son goes.

k. Rāma and the son go.

6. Translate the following sentences into English:

a. **narau putram vadataḥ**
(narau putraṃ vadataḥ)

b. **kutra aśvāḥ ca gajāḥ ca gacchanti**
(kutrāśvāś ca gajāś ca gacchanti)

c. **aśvaḥ mṛgaḥ vā gacchati**
(aśvo mṛgo vā gacchati)

d. **rāmaḥ putrau vadati**
(rāmaḥ putrau vadati)

e. **mṛgaḥ aśvaḥ gajaḥ ca gacchanti**
(mṛgo 'śvo gajaś ca gacchanti)

f. **putrāḥ mṛgān na smaranti**
(putrā mṛgān na smaranti)

g. **kutra narau vasataḥ**
(kutra narau vasataḥ)

h. **rāmam pṛcchāmi**
(rāmaṃ pṛcchāmi)

i. **narau putrān na vadataḥ**
(narau putrān na vadataḥ)

j. **kutra mṛgāḥ bhavanti**
(kutra mṛgā bhavanti)

7. Translate the following sentences into Sanskrit:

a. Where is Rāma going?

b. Rāma is going to the horse.

c. The son does not speak to the horses.

d. The two elephants remember the man.

e. Where do the two deer live?

f. You go to the horse.

g. Where are we standing?

h. The son goes to the horses and the elephants.

i. You are all speaking to the elephant.

j. The elephant does not remember.

SUMMARY SHEET

VERBS

	Singular	Dual	Plural
Third	**gacchati** (he, she goes)	**gacchataḥ** (they two go)	**gacchanti** (they all go)
Second	**gacchasi** (you go)	**gacchathaḥ** (you two go)	**gacchatha** (you all go)
First	**gacchāmi** (I go)	**gacchāvaḥ** (we two go)	**gacchāmaḥ** (we all go)

√gam	**gacchati**	he goes
√prach	**pṛcchati**	he asks
√bhū	**bhavati**	he is
√vad	**vadati**	he speaks, he says
√vas	**vasati**	he lives
√sthā	**tiṣṭhati**	he stands
√smṛ	**smarati**	he remembers

NOUNS

aśvaḥ horse

gajaḥ elephant

naraḥ man

putraḥ son

mṛgaḥ deer

rāmaḥ Rāma

	Singular	Dual	Plural
Nominative (subject)	**naraḥ**	**narau**	**narāḥ**
Accusative (object)	**naram**	**narau**	**narān**

INDECLINABLES

kutra where

ca and

na not

vā or

5

LESSON FIVE

Alphabet: The rest of the alphabet in **devanāgarī**

Grammar: The instrumental and dative cases

Vocabulary: More nouns that end in short **a**

गच्छति   गच्छतः   गच्छन्ति

गच्छसि   गच्छथः   गच्छथ

गच्छामि   गच्छावः   गच्छामः

गच्छति

पृच्छति

ALPHABET

1. Here are the last five stops:

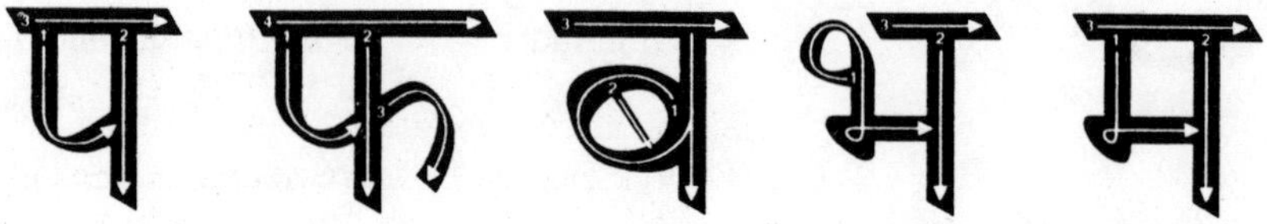

pa pha ba bha ma

2. Here are the semi-vowels:

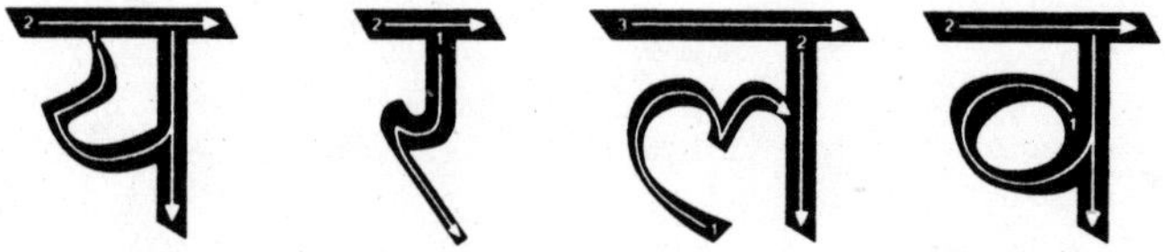

ya ra la va

3. Here are the sibilants and aspirate:

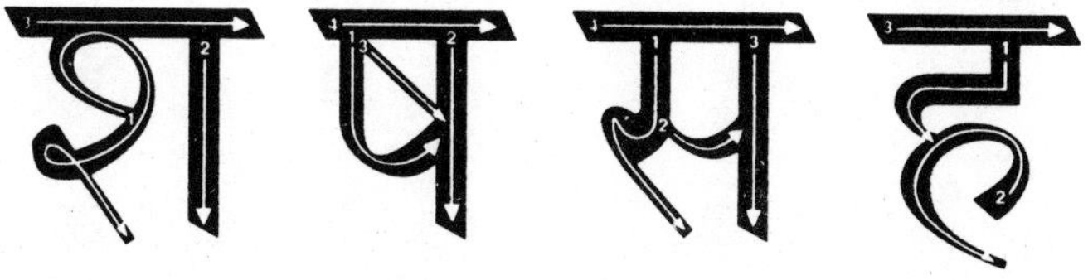

śa ṣa sa ha

4. Here is the **anusvāra** and **visarga** following **a**:

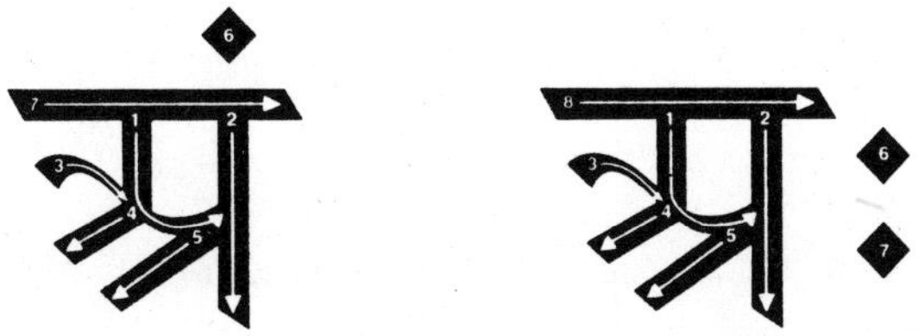

aṃ aḥ

5. Here are the **jihvāmūlīya** (**ẖ**) and **upadhmānīya** (**ḫ**). They are usually written the same way. If followed by **ka** or **kha**, it is a **jihvāmūlīya**. If followed by **pa** or **pha**, it is an **upadhmānīya**:

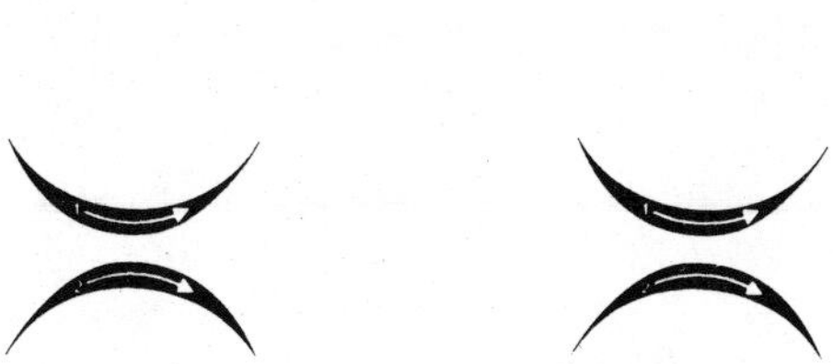

ẖ ḫ

The **upadhmānīya** (**ḫ**) may appear as

6. Here is the entire alphabet in **devanāgarī** script:

Vowels	अ	a	आ	ā
	इ	i	ई	ī
	उ	u	ऊ	ū
	ऋ	ṛ	ॠ	ṝ
	ऌ	ḷ		
	ए	e	ऐ	ai
	ओ	o	औ	au
	अं	aṃ (ṃ)	अः	aḥ (ḥ)

Velar	क ka	ख kha	ग ga	घ gha	ङ ṅa
Palatal	च ca	छ cha	ज ja	झ jha	ञ ña
Retroflex	ट ṭa	ठ ṭha	ड ḍa	ढ ḍha	ण ṇa
Dental	त ta	थ tha	द da	ध dha	न na
Labial	प pa	फ pha	ब ba	भ bha	म ma
Semi-vowels	य ya	र ra	ल la	व va	
Sibilants	श śa	ष ṣa	स sa	ह ha	

GRAMMAR: INSTRUMENTAL AND DATIVE

1. We will now learn two new cases: the instrumental (**tṛtīyā**) and the dative (**caturthī**).

2. The instrumental is used for accompaniment. For example:

   gajena saha rāmaḥ gacchati (without **sandhi**)
   (**gajena saha rāmo gacchati**) (with **sandhi**)
   Rāma goes with the elephant.
   (instrumental)

   The word **saha**, "together," is sometimes used after the instrumental to indicate accompaniment.

3. The instrumental is also used to express instrumentality, or "by means of." (Although this usage is derived from the first, it is used more frequently.) For example:

   I write with a pen.
   (instrumental)

4. The dative is used for the indirect object. It shows "purpose." For example:

   rāmaḥ putrāya aśvam gacchati (without **sandhi**)
   (**rāmaḥ putrāyāśvaṃ gacchati**) (with **sandhi**)
   Rāma goes to the horse for the son.
   (dative)

   rāmaḥ putrāya pustakam paṭhati (without **sandhi**)
   (**rāmaḥ putrāya pustakaṃ paṭhati**) (with **sandhi**)
   Rāma reads the book to the son.
   (dative)

5. Here is how they are formed:

Stem: **nara** (masculine) man

	Singular	Dual	Plural
Instrumental	**nareṇa***	**narābhyām**	**naraiḥ**
Dative	**narāya**	**narābhyām**	**narebhyaḥ**

*"with the elephant" is **gajena** (See below.)

6. We will learn the following **sandhi** rule in more detail in Lesson 11. For now, when a word contains an **r** or **ṛ**, it often changes the following **n** to **ṇ**. For example: **nareṇa, putreṇa, mṛgeṇa, rāmeṇa.** But **aśvena, gajena.**

7. The word order is not rigid in Sanskrit. Usually the instrumental goes near the word most closely associated with it, and the dative goes before the verb. (More will be said about word order later.)

8. The verbs **vadati** (he says) and **pṛcchati** (he asks) often take a "double accusative": the object talked about and the person addressed. Usually the person addressed is placed closer to the verb. The context will give you the correct meaning. For example:

   rāmaḥ mṛgam putram vadati (without **sandhi**)
   (**rāmo mṛgaṃ putraṃ vadati**) (with **sandhi**)
   Rāma speaks to the son about the deer.

VOCABULARY

SANSKRIT	ENGLISH
tatra (indeclinable)	there
nṛpaḥ (mas.)	king
bālaḥ (mas.)	boy
vīraḥ (mas.)	hero
saha (indeclinable)	with, together (sometimes used after the instrumental as a marker of accompaniment)

Remember that word order is less rigid in Sanskrit than in English. Even more than English, words can be placed in several different orders and still be correct.

EXERCISES

1. Learn the alphabet in **devanāgarī**.

2. Learn the forms for the instrumental and dative. By now you have learned four cases.

3. Learn the vocabulary and keep up with all past vocabulary.

4. Translate the following sentences. (Remember that more than one word order will still be correct in Sanskrit as well as English.)

   a. **kutra vīrāḥ tiṣṭhanti**
   (kutra vīrās tiṣṭhanti)

   b. **bālau gajena saha tatra bhavataḥ**
   (bālau gajena saha tatra bhavataḥ)

   c. **nṛpaḥ aśvam gacchati**
   (nṛpo 'śvaṃ gacchati)

   d. **aśvena saha vīraḥ nṛpān gacchati**
   (aśvena saha vīro nṛpān gacchati)

   e. **mṛgeṇa saha rāmaḥ vasati**
   (mṛgeṇa saha rāmo vasati)

   stays

   f. **gajaiḥ saha bālāḥ gacchanti**
   (gajaiḥ saha bālā gacchanti)

   g. **narāḥ putram vadanti**
   (narāḥ putraṃ vadanti)

h. **vīrāḥ mṛgān rāmam pṛcchanti** (same as 5b. below)
(vīrā mṛgān rāmaṃ pṛcchanti)

i. **tatra bālaḥ nṛpāya gacchati**
(tatra bālo nṛpāya gacchati)

5. Translate the following sentences into Sanskrit:

a. The boys go to the horses.

b. The son asks the king about the deer. (double accusative)

c. The king remembers the man.

d. The hero lives with the son.

e. The boy asks the king and the king remembers.

f. There are no elephants with the son.

g. Where does Rāma live?

h. The king or the hero speaks to the boy.

i. The hero goes for the boy.

j. The elephants are there with the horses.

k. I remember the king.

l. You are going there with the boy.

6. Translate the following sentences into English:

a. **aśvaiḥ saha vīraḥ gacchati**
(aśvaiḥ saha vīro gacchati)

b. **tatra nṛpāya narāḥ gacchanti**
(tatra nṛpāya narā gacchanti)

c. **vīrau tiṣṭhataḥ vadataḥ ca**
(vīrau tiṣṭhato vadataś ca)

d. **mṛgāḥ tatra vasanti**
(mṛgās tatra vasanti)

e. **kutra bālābhyām saha nṛpaḥ gacchati**
(kutra bālābhyāṃ saha nṛpo gacchati)

f. **rāmaḥ aśvam putram pṛcchati**
(rāmo 'śvaṃ putraṃ pṛcchati)

g. **tatra gajāḥ na tiṣṭhanti**
(tatra gajā na tiṣṭhanti)

h. **vīraḥ nṛpam bālam vadati**
(vīro nṛpaṃ bālaṃ vadati)

i. **mṛgaiḥ aśvaiḥ ca saha gajaḥ vasati**
(mṛgair aśvaiś ca saha gajo vasati)

j. **kutra tiṣṭhāmaḥ**
(kutra tiṣṭhāmaḥ)

7. Translate the following sentences into Sanskrit:

a. The king lives there with the two boys.

b. Where are you going with the elephants?

c. The man goes there for the horse.

d. The boy does not remember the king.

e. I am speaking to the king about the two elephants.

f. The king goes to the horse for the son.

g. Where are we standing?

h. The man asks the boy about the horse.

i. Rāma goes there for the man.

j. Where are all the deer?

SUMMARY SHEET VERBS

	Singular	Dual	Plural
Third	**gacchati** (he, she goes)	**gacchataḥ** (they two go)	**gacchanti** (they all go)
Second	**gacchasi** (you go)	**gacchathaḥ** (you two go)	**gacchatha** (you all go)
First	**gacchāmi** (I go)	**gacchāvaḥ** (we two go)	**gacchāmaḥ** (we all go)

√gam	**gacchati**	he goes
√prach	**pṛcchati**	he asks
√bhū	**bhavati**	he is
√vad	**vadati**	he speaks, he says
√vas	**vasati**	he lives
√sthā	**tiṣṭhati**	he stands
√smṛ	**smarati**	he remembers

NOUNS

aśvaḥ	horse	Nominative (subject)	**naraḥ**	**narau**	**narāḥ**
gajaḥ	elephant	Accusative (object)	**naram**	**narau**	**narān**
naraḥ	man	Instrumental (with)	**nareṇa***	**narābhyām**	**naraiḥ**
nṛpaḥ	king	Dative (for)	**narāya**	**narābhyām**	**narebhyaḥ**
putraḥ	son		Singular	Dual	Plural
bālaḥ	boy				
mṛgaḥ	deer				
rāmaḥ	Rāma				
vīraḥ	hero				

***gajena, bālena** (See page 46.)

INDECLINABLES

kutra	where
ca	and
tatra	there
na	not
vā	or
saha	with, together (used after instrumental)

6

LESSON SIX

Alphabet:	How vowels are formed when they follow consonants
Grammar:	The ablative and the genitive The use of **iti**
Vocabulary:	More nouns in **a**

ALPHABET: VOWELS AFTER CONSONANTS

1. Words are formed by putting letters together. The vowel characters learned so far are used only when they are the first letter of a word. For example, **eka** (one) is written:

   एक **eka**

2. A consonant without a vowel following it is written with a short stroke (**virāma**) beneath it. For example:

क	**ka**	प	**pa**
क्	**k**	प्	**p**

3. When a vowel follows a consonant, the vowel is written in contracted form. The **a** is replaced by other vowels. Here are the vowel forms:

ga	ग	**gā**	गा
gi	गि	**gī**	गी
gu	गु	**gū**	गू

gṛ	गृ	gṝ	गॄ
ge	गे	gai	गै
go	गो	gau	गौ

4. Note that the sign for the **i** is written before the consonant, even though the **i** is sounded after the consonant. When written by hand, the curved line on top should touch the vertical line of the consonant. For example:

गि

Often, due to typesetting, the **i** will not touch at all. For example:

गि

5. These vowel signs may follow all consonants, including the semi-vowels, sibilants, and aspirate. For example:

च	चा	चि	ची	चु	चू	चृ	चॄ
ca	**cā**	**ci**	**cī**	**cu**	**cū**	**cṛ**	**cṝ**
चे	चै	चो	चौ				
ce	**cai**	**co**	**cau**				

ज	जा	जि	जी	जु	जू	जृ	जॄ
ja	**jā**	**ji**	**jī**	**ju**	**jū**	**jṛ**	**jṝ**
जे	जै	जो	जौ				
je	**jai**	**jo**	**jau**				

6. Sometimes these signs are put in different places. For example:

   ru is written: रु

   rū is written: रू

   hṛ is written: हृ

   We will learn more of these forms in the next lesson.

7. Here are more examples of how words are formed by putting letters together:

गज	वीर	वसति
gaja	**vīra**	**vasati**

GRAMMAR: ABLATIVE AND GENITIVE

1. Now we will learn the ablative (**pañcamī**) and genitive (**ṣaṣṭhī**) cases (**vibhakti**).

2. The ablative is used for origin or source. It usually means "from." It is also used for comparison. For example:

gajāt āgacchati
(gajād āgacchati)
He comes from the elephant.
(ablative)

One learns from practice. (ablative)
He is taller than she. (ablative)

3. The genitive is used for possession. For example:

narasya aśvaḥ
(narasyāśvaḥ)
the horse of the man.
(genitive)

4. The genitive is always used in relation to the noun which follows it. For example:

rāmasya putraḥ the son of Rāma (or Rāma's son)
(rāmasya putraḥ)

amṛtasya putrāḥ sons of immortality
(amṛtasya putrāḥ)

5. The genitive is sometimes used as a substitute for other cases, such as the dative, instrumental, ablative, and locative.

6. Here is the formation of the ablative and genitive:

Stem: **nara** (masculine) man

	Singular	Dual	Plural
Ablative	**narāt**	**narābhyām**	**narebhyaḥ**
Genitive	**narasya**	**narayoḥ**	**narāṇām***

***gajānām, bālānām** (See page 46.)

ITI

7. Now we will learn the use of **iti**. This important particle is used at the end of a quotation. For example:

aśvaḥ gacchati iti rāmaḥ vadati
(aśvo gacchatīti rāmo vadati)
"The horse goes," says Rāma.

Notice that **iti** is a convenient point to break the sentence down into smaller, more manageable parts.

8. When translating from English to Sanskrit, indirect quotations must first be turned into direct quotations before **iti** can be used. For example:

He says that he is going. (indirect quotation)
"I am going," he says. (direct quotation)
gacchāmi iti vadati
(gacchāmīti vadati)

Notice that the change from an indirect quotation to a direct quotation changes the clause from "he is going" to "I am going."

VOCABULARY

SANSKRIT	ENGLISH
atra (indeclinable)	here
ā + √gam (root) **āgacchati** *	he comes
iti (indeclinable)	indicates the end of a quotation
grāmaḥ (mas.)	village

*Note that **ā** is a verb prefix. It changes the meaning of **gacchati** from "he goes" to "he comes."

EXERCISES

1. Learn to recognize and write the **devanāgarī** for vowels that follow consonants.

2. Learn the forms for the ablative and genitive.

3. Write the following words in **devanāgarī:**

a. **iti**	g. **bhavāvaḥ**	m. **ṛṣi**
b. **nara**	h. **vadasi**	n. **devatā**
c. **rāma**	i. **nṛpaḥ**	o. **guṇa**
d. **gaja**	j. **na**	p. **jaya**
e. **vīra**	k. **vā**	q. **guru**
f. **vasati**	l. **ca**	r. **deva**

4. Translate the following sentences into English, using the summary sheet. Remember to read each sentence out loud several times.

   a. **bālasya gajaḥ grāmam gacchati**
   (bālasya gajo grāmaṃ gacchati)

   b. **rāmasya putraḥ aśvam gacchati**
   (rāmasya putro 'śvaṃ gacchati)

   c. **atra aśvaḥ bhavati iti nṛpaḥ vadati**
   (atrāśvo bhavatīti nṛpo vadati)

   d. **grāmāt putraḥ āgacchati**
   (grāmāt putra āgacchati)

e. **kutra gajāḥ tiṣṭhanti iti nṛpaḥ pṛcchati**
(kutra gajās tiṣṭhantīti nṛpaḥ pṛcchati)

f. **bālaḥ nṛpasya grāmam gacchati**
(bālo nṛpasya grāmaṃ gacchati)

g. **atra vīrāḥ vasanti iti narāḥ vadanti**
(atra vīrā vasantīti narā vadanti)

h. **kutra gacchasi iti rāmaḥ pṛcchati**
(kutra gacchasīti rāmaḥ pṛcchati)

5. Translate the following sentences into Sanskrit:

a. "I live here," the son says.

b. The horses and elephants are coming from the village.

c. "Do you remember the men?" the king asks the boy.

d. Rāma says that he is going to the village.

e. "I am going to the village for the boy," says Rāma.

f. Where does the hero go?

g. "The hero goes to the village," says the king.

h. The son of the king lives here.

i. The king's sons come from the village.

j. The man speaks to Rāma about the elephants.

6. Translate the following sentences into English:

a. **narau grāmāt āgacchataḥ**
(narau grāmād āgacchataḥ)

b. **atra bhavāmi iti bālaḥ nṛpam vadati**
(atra bhavāmīti bālo nṛpaṃ vadati)

c. **kutra vasasi iti vīraḥ putram pṛcchati**
(kutra vasasīti vīraḥ putraṃ pṛcchati)

d. **rāmeṇa saha atra vasāmi iti putraḥ vadati**
(rāmeṇa sahātra vasāmīti putro vadati)

e. **narasya putrāḥ tatra tiṣṭhanti**
(narasya putrās tatra tiṣṭhanti)

f. **atra vīrasya gajaḥ bhavati**
(atra vīrasya gajo bhavati)

g. **rāmam smarasi iti bālāḥ naram pṛcchanti**
(rāmaṃ smarasīti bālā naraṃ pṛcchanti)

h. **kutra grāmaḥ bhavati iti naraḥ putram pṛcchati**
(kutra grāmo bhavatīti naraḥ putraṃ pṛcchati)

i. **grāmaḥ tatra bhavati iti putraḥ naram vadati**
(grāmas tatra bhavatīti putro naraṃ vadati)

j. **gajāya grāmam gacchāmi iti naraḥ vadati**
(gajāya grāmaṃ gacchāmīti naro vadati)

7. Translate the following sentences into Sanskrit:

a. "Where are you going?" the king asks the boy.

b. "I am going to the horse," the boy says.

c. The king of the villages speaks to the men.

d. The two boys are coming from the horse and the elephant.

e. The boy lives with Rāma.

f. "Here are the sons of Rāma," says the hero.

g. The king says that the boys are standing there.

h. "I am going to the village," says the son of the hero.

i. The two horses are coming here together with the two deer.

j. The king's two horses are there.

SUMMARY SHEET

	Singular	Dual	Plural
Third	**gacchati** (he, she goes)	**gacchataḥ** (they two go)	**gacchanti** (they all go)
Second	**gacchasi** (you go)	**gacchathaḥ** (you two go)	**gacchatha** (you all go)
First	**gacchāmi** (I go)	**gacchāvaḥ** (we two go)	**gacchāmaḥ** (we all go)

VERBS

ā + √gam	**āgacchati**	he comes
√gam	**gacchati**	he goes
√prach	**pṛcchati**	he asks
√bhū	**bhavati**	he is
√vad	**vadati**	he speaks, he says
√vas	**vasati**	he lives
√sthā	**tiṣṭhati**	he stands
√smṛ	**smarati**	he remembers

NOUNS

aśvaḥ	horse
gajaḥ	elephant
grāmaḥ	village
naraḥ	man
nṛpaḥ	king
putraḥ	son
bālaḥ	boy
mṛgaḥ	deer
rāmaḥ	Rāma
vīraḥ	hero

	Singular	Dual	Plural
Nom. (subject)	**naraḥ**	**narau**	**narāḥ**
Acc. (object)	**naram**	**narau**	**narān**
Inst. (with)	**nareṇa***	**narābhyām**	**naraiḥ**
Dat. (for)	**narāya**	**narābhyām**	**narebhyaḥ**
Abl. (from)	**narāt**	**narābhyām**	**narebhyaḥ**
Gen. (of, 's)	**narasya**	**narayoḥ**	**narāṇām***

***gajena, gajānām** (See page 46.)

INDECLINABLES

atra	here
iti	end of quote
kutra	where
ca	and
tatra	there
na	not
vā	or
saha	with, together

7

LESSON SEVEN

Alphabet:	Conjunct consonants
Grammar:	The locative and vocative
Vocabulary:	More nouns in **a**

ALPHABET: CONJUNCT CONSONANTS

1. We will now learn how to write two or more consonants without a vowel coming between them. To write **tva**, remove the vertical line from the **t**. For example:

tava	तव	**tva**	त्व

2. Here are examples of other clusters of consonants that are written side by side:

tma	त्म	**ṣya**	ष्य
sya	स्य	**tya**	त्य
bhya	भ्य	**nta**	न्त
nti	न्ति	**ṣṭa**	ष्ट

3. Some clusters are written on top of each other. For example:

dva	द्व	**dda**	द्द
ṅga	ङ्ग	**ddho**	द्धो

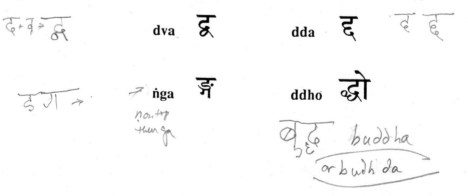

4. Consonant conjuncts are read left to right and top to bottom. They will be learned most easily by close observation to their formation as we continue with the exercises.

5. When the semi-vowel **r** comes immediately before another consonant, the **r** takes the form of a small hook above the consonant. For example:

rpa	र्प	**rmya**	र्म्य
ryā	र्या	**rgo**	र्गो

Notice that the **r** is placed as far to the right as possible.

6. When **r** immediately follows a consonant, the **r** takes the form of a small slanted stroke, written near the bottom of the vertical line (**daṇḍa**, meaning "stick"), if there is a vertical line. For example:

pra	प्र	**bra**	ब्र
sra	स्र	**gra**	ग्र
mra	म्र	**dra**	द्र

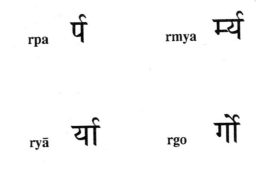

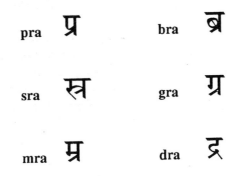

7. Some forms are completely different than the two letters that make them up. These must be learned:

tra	त्र	**jña**	ज्ञ
ddhya	द्ध्य	**śva**	श्व (or) श्व
dya	द्य	**kta**	क्त (or) क्त
tta	त्त	**kṣa**	क्ष (or) क्ष
hma	ह्म	**kra**	क्र (or) क्र
hṇa	ह्ण	**hva**	ह्व

The ’ represents a missing **a**. It is written in **devanāgarī** as ऽ

For example: वेदोऽहम् **vedo ’ham**

8. A vertical line (**daṇḍa**) is used as a period at the end of a sentence. It is also used to mark the halfway part of a verse. Two vertical lines mark the end of a paragraph or the end of a verse. For example:

रामो गच्छति ।

9. There are other ways of forming certain letters, which you should be able to recognize:

a	अ	or	अ
ā	आ	or	आ
ṛ	ऋ	or	ऋ
ṝ	ॠ	or	ॠ
jha	झ	or	झ
ṇa	ण	or	ण

GRAMMAR: LOCATIVE AND VOCATIVE

1. Now we will learn the locative (**saptamī**) and vocative (**saṃbodhana**—"awakening," "arousing").

2. The locative case is used to express location. For example:

grāme vasati	**gaje tiṣṭhati** (same with **sandhi**)
He lives in the village.	He stands on the elephant.
(locative)	(locative)

3. The vocative is used for address. The vocative often, but not always, begins a sentence. For example:

rāma atra āgacchasi
(**rāma atrāgacchasi**)
O Rāma, you are coming here.
(vocative)

Indian grammarians do not consider the vocative a true case (**vibhakti**) like the seven other cases, but a modification of the nominative, or naming case.

4. Here is the formation of the locative and vocative:

Stem: **nara** (masculine) man

	Singular	Dual	Plural
Locative	**nare**	**narayoḥ**	**nareṣu**
Vocative	**nara**	**narau**	**narāḥ**

5. Like verbs, there is a parsing code, or way of classifying nouns. They are classified according to:

Gender (**liṅga**):	Masculine (**puṃ-liṅga**)	(mas.)
	Feminine (**strī-liṅga**)	(fem.)
	Neuter (**napuṃsaka-liṅga**)	(n.)
Case (**vibhakti**):	Nominative (**prathamā**)	(nom.)
	Accusative (**dvitīyā**)	(acc.)
	Instrumental (**tṛtīyā**)	(inst.)
	Dative (**caturthī**)	(dat.)
	Ablative (**pañcamī**)	(abl.)
	Genitive (**ṣaṣṭhī**)	(gen.)
	Locative (**saptamī**)	(loc.)
	Vocative (**saṃbodhana**)	(voc.)
Number (**vacana**):	Singular (**eka-vacana**)	(sing.)
	Dual (**dvi-vacana**)	(dual)
	Plural (**bahu-vacana**)	(pl.)

6. The word **naraḥ** would be classified as masculine, nominative, singular. Its parsing code would be mas. nom. sing.

   The word **narān** would be classified as masculine, accusative, plural. Its parsing code would be mas. acc. pl.

7. Here is the entire short **a** masculine declension:

Stem: **nara** (masculine) man

	Singular	Dual	Plural
Nominative	नरः	नरौ	नराः
(subject)	**naraḥ**	**narau**	**narāḥ**
Accusative	नरम्	नरौ	नरान्
(object)	**naram**	**narau**	**narān**
Instrumental	नरेण	नराभ्याम्	नरैः
(with)	**nareṇa***	**narābhyām**	**naraiḥ**
Dative	नराय	नराभ्याम्	नरेभ्यः
(for)	**narāya**	**narābhyām**	**narebhyaḥ**
Ablative	नरात्	नराभ्याम्	नरेभ्यः
(from)	**narāt**	**narābhyām**	**narebhyas**
Genitive	नरस्य	नरयोः	नराणाम्
(of, 's)	**narasya**	**narayoḥ**	**narāṇām***
Locative	नरे	नरयोः	नरेषु
(in, on)	**nare**	**narayoḥ**	**nareṣu**
Vocative	नर	नरौ	नराः
(O)	**nara**	**narau**	**narāḥ**

***gajena, gajānām** (See p. 46.)

VOCABULARY

SANSKRIT		ENGLISH
आचार्यः	**ācāryaḥ** (mas.)	teacher
चन्द्रः	**candraḥ** (mas.)	moon
चिन्त्	√**cint** (root) **cintayati**	he thinks
पश्	√**paś** (root) **paśyati**	he sees
	(√**dṛś** is also considered to be the root.)	
विना	**vinā** (indeclinable)	without (used like **saha**)
शिष्यः	**śiṣyaḥ** (mas.)	student
सूर्यः	**sūryaḥ** (mas.)	sun

EXERCISES

1. Learn the examples given for consonant conjuncts. Put these words into roman letters (transliterate them):

a. पुराण	e. गच्छति	i. अश्व
b. गन्धर्व	f. चन्द्र	j. पुत्रस्य
c. छन्दः	g. ज्योतिष	k. शिष्यः
d. व्याकरण	h. कल्प	l. तिष्ठन्ति

2. Learn the forms for the locative and vocative.

3. Parse the following words and give their meaning:

a. **narāḥ**	f. **mṛgeṇa**
b. **hastau**	g. **gajaiḥ**
c. **bālānām**	h. **vīrān**
d. **nṛpāt**	i. **grāmeṣu**
e. **rāmāya**	j. **ācāryāya**

4. Translate the following sentences into English. (Use the summary sheet.) Cover the **devanāgarī** with a sheet of paper, write it yourself, and then compare:

a. शिष्यः चन्द्रम् सूर्यम् च पश्यति ।

śiṣyaḥ candram sūryam ca paśyati
(śiṣyaś candraṃ sūryaṃ ca paśyati)

b. राम गजाः ग्रामे तिष्ठन्ति ।

rāma gajāḥ grāme tiṣṭhanti
(rāma gajā grāme tiṣṭhanti)

c. वीरः ग्रामे वसति इति आचार्यः शिष्यम् वदति ।

vīraḥ grāme vasati iti ācāryaḥ śiṣyam vadati
(vīro grāme vasatīty ācāryaḥ śiṣyaṃ vadati)

d. कुत्र चन्द्रः भवति इति पुत्रः पृच्छति ।

kutra candraḥ bhavati iti putraḥ pṛcchati
(kutra candro bhavatīti putraḥ pṛcchati)

e. तत्र गजे बालौ तिष्ठतः ।

tatra gaje bālau tiṣṭhataḥ
(tatra gaje bālau tiṣṭhataḥ)

f. पुत्र कुत्र चन्द्रः भवति इति वीरः बालम् पृच्छति ।

putra kutra candraḥ bhavati iti vīraḥ bālam pṛcchati
(putra kutra candro bhavatīti vīro bālaṃ pṛcchati)

g. आचार्यस्य शिष्यः तिष्ठति वदति च ।

ācāryasya śiṣyaḥ tiṣṭhati vadati ca
(ācāryasya śiṣyas tiṣṭhati vadati ca)

h. रामेण विना वीराः ग्रामात् आगच्छन्ति ।

rāmeṇa vinā vīrāḥ grāmāt āgacchanti
(rāmeṇa vinā vīrā grāmād āgacchanti)

i. ग्रामे वसामि इति वीरस्य बालः चिन्तयति ।

grāme vasāmi iti vīrasya bālaḥ cintayati
(grāme vasāmīti vīrasya bālaś cintayati)

5. Translate the following sentences into Sanskrit:

   a. The king tells the hero that the boys are going to the village.

   b. Without the king, the boys come.

   c. In the hand of the hero is the son.

   d. "Where am I?" thinks the boy.

   e. He asks the son of the hero where the men are.

   f. The teacher tells the student that the sun is not the moon.

   g. The king lives in the village.

   h. There are the elephants of the king.

6. Translate the following sentences into English:

   a. रामेण विना बालः ग्रामम् गच्छति ।

   rāmeṇa vinā bālaḥ grāmam gacchati
   (rāmeṇa vinā bālo grāmaṃ gacchati)

b. कुत्र नृपस्य गजाः भवन्ति ।

kutra nṛpasya gajāḥ bhavanti
(kutra nṛpasya gajā bhavanti)

c. अत्र भवामि इति बालः नरम् वदति ।

atra-here

atra bhavāmi iti bālaḥ naram vadati
(atra bhavāmīti bālo naraṃ vadati)

d. सूर्येण विना चन्द्रम् न पश्यसि ।

sūryeṇa vinā candram na paśyasi
(sūryeṇa vinā candraṃ na paśyasi)

e. आचार्यः शिष्यान् वदति ।

ācāryaḥ śiṣyān vadati
(ācāryaḥ śiṣyān vadati)

f. चन्द्रम् पश्यामि इति बालः चिन्तयति ।

candram paśyāmi iti bālaḥ cintayati
(candraṃ paśyāmīti bālaś cintayati)

g. अत्र ग्रामाणाम् नृपः आगच्छति ।

atra grāmāṇām nṛpaḥ āgacchati
(atra grāmāṇāṃ nṛpa āgacchati)

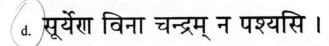

h. नृपः वीरस्य अश्वम् पश्यति ।

nṛpaḥ vīrasya aśvam paśyati
(nṛpo vīrasyāśvaṃ paśyati)

i. कुत्र सूर्यः चन्द्रः च भवतः इति बालः पृच्छति ।

kutra sūryaḥ candraḥ ca bhavataḥ iti bālaḥ pṛcchati
(kutra sūryaś candraś ca bhavata iti bālaḥ pṛcchati)

j. शिष्याः नरम् न स्मरन्ति ।

śiṣyāḥ naram na smaranti
(śiṣyā naraṃ na smaranti)

7. Translate the following sentences into Sanskrit, writing first in roman script and then in **devanāgarī**:

a. "Where are you going?" the boy asks the king's son.

b. The two deer are in the village.

c. The teacher speaks to the hero's son.

d. The king sees the sun and the moon.

e. Without the sun we do not see the moon.

f. The hero is on the elephant of the king.

g. "We live in the villages," the boys say.

h. Rāma goes from the horses to the elephants.

i. "Where are we going?" the boy asks the king.

j. The teacher lives in the village with the students.

8. Transliterate the following:

1. ऋषि   *rishi*   13. चित्तवृत्ति

2. आसन   *asana*   14. अविद्या

3. अहंकार   *augur*   15. अव्यक्त

4. गुण   *guna*   16. धारणा

5. ज्ञान   17. आत्मन्

6. कुरुक्षेत्र   *Ee tra*   18. आनन्द

7. कर्म   *karma*   19. अष्टाङ्गयोग   *asta anga yoga*
                                          8 body yoga

8. ध्यान   20. तत्त्वमसि   *tattva masi*

9. दर्शन   21. नामरूप

10. दुःख   22. उपनिषद्   *Upanisad*

11. वेद   23. नित्य

12. चित्त   24. धर्म

SUMMARY SHEET

	Singular	Dual	Plural
Third	**gacchati** (he, she goes)	**gacchataḥ** (they two go)	**gacchanti** (they all go)
Second	**gacchasi** (you go)	**gacchathaḥ** (you two go)	**gacchatha** (you all go)
First	**gacchāmi** (I go)	**gacchāvaḥ** (we two go)	**gacchāmaḥ** (we all go)

VERBS

ā + √gam	**āgacchati**	he comes
√gam	**gacchati**	he goes
√cint	**cintayati**	he thinks
√paś (**√dṛś**)	**paśyati**	he sees
√prach	**pṛcchati**	he asks
√bhū	**bhavati**	he is
√vad	**vadati**	he speaks, he says
√vas	**vasati**	he lives
√sthā	**tiṣṭhati**	he stands
√smṛ	**smarati**	he remembers

NOUNS

aśvaḥ	horse
ācāryaḥ	teacher
gajaḥ	elephant
grāmaḥ	village
candraḥ	moon
naraḥ	man
nṛpaḥ	king
putraḥ	son
bālaḥ	boy
mṛgaḥ	deer
rāmaḥ	Rāma
vīraḥ	hero
śiṣyaḥ	student
sūryaḥ	sun
hastaḥ	hand

	Singular	Dual	Plural
Nom. (subject)	**naraḥ**	**narau**	**narāḥ**
Acc. (object)	**naram**	**narau**	**narān**
Inst. (with)	**nareṇa***	**narābhyām**	**naraiḥ**
Dat. (for)	**narāya**	**narābhyām**	**narebhyaḥ**
Abl. (from)	**narāt**	**narābhyām**	**narebhyaḥ**
Gen. (of, 's)	**narasya**	**narayoḥ**	**narāṇām***
Loc. (in, on)	**nare**	**narayoḥ**	**nareṣu**
Voc. (O)	**nara**	**narau**	**narāḥ**

***gajena, gajānām** (See page 46.)

INDECLINABLES

atra	here
iti	end of quote
kutra	where
ca	and
tatra	there
na	not
vā	or
vinā	without (used like **saha**)
saha	with

8

LESSON EIGHT

Alphabet: The **sandhi** rules for combining vowels

Grammar: Neuter nouns in short **a**

Vocabulary: Neuter nouns

ALPHABET: VOWEL SANDHI

1. The word "**sandhi**" means "combination" or "junction point." The rules of **sandhi** insure that sounds will combine in a pleasing, euphonic way. **Pāṇini** (1.4.109) also refers to these junction points as **saṃhitā**, or "togetherness." There are two types of **sandhi** rules:

    a. External **sandhi**, or changes at the junction between words
    b. Internal **sandhi**, or changes within a word

2. The **sandhi** rules involve sound changes so that the flow of the language is smooth. As mentioned in Lesson 2, "an apple" is smoother to pronounce than "a apple." "The house" is pronounced differently than "the other house." These are examples of external **sandhi**. The **sandhi** rules of Sanskrit exist because the Sanskrit tradition has been primarily an oral tradition, and because its grammatical insights were so sophisticated. (The term **sandhi** has been adopted by modern linguists to describe sound modifications between words in any language.)

3. Don't allow the **sandhi** rules to overwhelm you. There are many rules to learn, but with practice you will gradually assimilate them. We will begin our study of the external **sandhi** rules using charts, and then after we have used the rules for some time, we will memorize them. There will be three charts, because external **sandhi** can be divided into three groups:

    a. Vowel **sandhi (svara-sandhi)** Lesson Eight
    b. Final **ḥ sandhi (visarga-sandhi)** Lesson Nine
    c. Consonant **sandhi (hal-sandhi)** Lesson Ten

4. The chart on page 89 describes what happens if a word ends with a vowel and the next word begins with a vowel. For example, if one word ends with a short **i**, and the next word begins with an **a**, then the two combine (**sandhi**) to form **ya**:

गच्छति + अश्वम् would be written **गच्छत्यश्वम्**

gacchati + aśvam would be written **gacchaty aśvam**

एव + अवशिष्यते = एवावशिष्यते

eva + avaśiṣyate = evāvaśiṣyate

ब्रह्म + अस्मि = ब्रह्मास्मि

brahma + asmi = brahmāsmi

भव + अर्जुन = भवार्जुन

bhava + arjuna = bhavārjuna

5. On the following page is the chart describing the **sandhi** change if the first word ends in a vowel (the vowels at the top of the chart) and the second word begins in a vowel (the vowels in the right column). If a vowel has ≚ above it, then it refers to a short or a long vowel.

6. This chart need not be memorized. It should be used in the exercises, and the rules will be memorized later, once the patterns of change are more clear.

VOWEL SANDHI

FINAL VOWELS

ā̆	**ī̆**	**ū̆**	**ṛ**	**e**	**ai**	**au**	INITIAL VOWELS
ā	ya	va	ra	e	ā a	āva	**a**
ā	yā	vā	rā	a ā	ā ā	āvā	**ā**
e	ī	vi	ri	a i	ā i	āvi	**i**
e	ī	vī	rī	a ī	ā ī	āvī	**ī**
o	yu	ū	ru	a u	ā u	āva	**u**
o	yū	ū	rū	a ū	ā ū	āvū	**ū**
ar	yṛ	vṛ	ṝ	a ṛ	ā ṛ	āvṛ	**ṛ**
ai	ye	ve	re	a e	ā e	āve	**e**
ai	yai	vai	rai	a ai	ā ai	āvai	**ai**
au	yo	vo	ro	a o	ā o	āvo	**o**
au	yau	vau	rau	a au	ā au	āvau	**au**

7. Here are some examples:

i + ū = yū

ṛ + i = ri

i + u = yu

गच्छति + इति = गच्छतीति

gacchati + iti = gacchatīti

Additional examples are given on pages 167–170.

8. Remember that the apostrophe (') represents the missing letter **a.** It is called **avagraha**, meaning "separation." It is written in **devanāgarī** as:

ऽ

ग्रामे + अत्र = ग्रामेऽत्र

grāme + atra = grāme 'tra

9. Once the **sandhi** rules have been applied, there is no further application of **sandhi** rules. The **sandhi** rules are only applied once.

10. In this text, words are always separated in transliteration (roman script), unless two vowels have formed one long vowel, such as **i + i = ī**. In **devanāgarī** script, words involving vowel **sandhi** are joined except when there is a space (hiatus) between the vowels in the chart. Until you learn more **sandhi** rules, all other words should be kept separated. For example:

गच्छति + इति = गच्छतीति
gacchati + iti = gacchatīti

गच्छति + अश्वम् = गच्छत्यश्वम्
gacchati + aśvam = gacchaty aśvam

11. In vowel **sandhi**, often a vowel will be replaced by the semi-vowel that corresponds to it. For example, **i** will be replaced b **y**. According to **Pāṇini**, the change from the corresponding semi-vowel to the vowel is called **samprasāraṇa** ("spreading out," "extension") because the semi-vowel "spreads out" to form the vowel:

	Vowels		Semi-vowels
Palatal	**i**	**ī**	**y**
Retroflex	**ṛ**	**ṝ**	**r**
Dental	**ḷ**		**l**
Labial	**u**	**ū**	**v**

12. Some vowels (**pragṛhya**) are not subject to **sandhi**. They are:

a. The vowels **i**, **u**, and **e** when they are dual endings.

b. The final vowel of an interjection (usually a vocative). For example, **rāma āgacchanti** (Rāma, they come.) needs no **sandhi**.

13. The rules for this lesson are written out in Lesson 13. We will memorize them at that time.

GRAMMAR: NEUTER NOUNS

1. All the nouns that we have studied so far have been **masculine.** Now we will study the neuter nouns that end in short **a.**

2. Here is the formation of the neuter short **a** nouns:

Stem: **phala** (neuter) fruit

	Singular	Dual	Plural
Nominative	फलम् **phalam**	फले **phale**	फलानि **phalāni**
Accusative	फलम् **phalam**	फले **phale**	फलानि **phalāni**
Instrumental	फलेन **phalena**	फलाभ्याम् **phalābhyām**	फलैः **phalaiḥ**
Dative	फलाय **phalāya**	फलाभ्याम् **phalābhyām**	फलेभ्यः **phalebhyaḥ**
Ablative	फलात् **phalāt**	फलाभ्याम् **phalābhyām**	फलेभ्यः **phalebhyaḥ**
Genitive	फलस्य **phalasya**	फलयोः **phalayoḥ**	फलानाम् **phalānām**
Locative	फले **phale**	फलयोः **phalayoḥ**	फलेषु **phaleṣu**
Vocative	फल **phala**	फले **phale**	फलानि **phalāni**

VOCABULARY

SANSKRIT		ENGLISH
अमृतम्	**amṛtam** (n.)	immortality, an immortal
कथम्	**katham** (ind.)	how (used like **kutra**)
ज्ञानम्	**jñānam** (n.)	knowledge
पठ्	√**paṭh** (root) **paṭhati**	he reads
पुस्तकम्	**pustakam** (n.)	book
फलम्	**phalam** (n.)	fruit
वनम्	**vanam** (n.)	forest
शास्त्रम्	**śāstram** (n.)	scripture
सत्यम्	**satyam** (n.)	truth
सूक्तम्	**sūktam** (n.)	hymn

Notice that neuter nouns are also given in their nominative singular form. For example, **amṛta** (stem form) is listed as **amṛtam** (nominative form).

Notice that the neuter nouns decline like the masculine nouns, except in the nominative, accusative, and vocative.

EXERCISES

1. We had learned that **ṛ** or **r** changes the following **n** to **ṇ**. This change will not occur if a **t** comes between, because the **t** changes the position of the tongue. Therefore: **amṛtāni, amṛtena, amṛtānām**. But: **śāstrāṇi, śāstreṇa, śāstrāṇām**. This **sandhi** rule will be studied in more detail in Lesson 11.

2. Put the following words together, using correct **sandhi** rules, and then write the final form in **devanāgarī**:

   a. **putreṇa atra** f. **devau āgacchataḥ**

   b. **saha ācāryaḥ** g. **nare atra**

   c. **tatra iti** h. **vane iti**

   d. **iti atra** i. **phalāni iti**

   e. **iti ācāryaḥ** j. **smarati atra**

3. Write in roman script and take out the **sandhi**:

   a. गच्छतीति f. नृपस्याश्वः

   b. गजावागच्छतः g. अश्वेऽत्र

   c. पृच्छत्यागच्छति च h. कुत्राश्वः

   d. गच्छामीति i. कुत्रेति

   e. हस्त इति j. गच्छत्यत्र

4. In the following exercises, remember that the subject and the predicate nominative are put in the nominative case, since they both refer to the same subject. (See page 33.) For example:

   rāmaḥ putraḥ bhavati
   (rāmaḥ putro bhavati)
   Rāma is the son.

   In this text, the predicate nominative is usually placed after the subject, although other word orders are equally common. (See 5b, c; 6a, f, g.)

5. In the following sentences, cover up the roman script and transliterate each sentence (write in roman script). Then cover the **devanāgarī** and write in **devanāgarī**. Then take out any **sandhi**. Only the **sandhi** rules learned so far have been applied—that is, only when one word ends in a vowel and the next word begins in a vowel. Finally, translate into English:

   a. रामः ग्रामात् वनम् गच्छति ।

   rāmaḥ grāmāt vanam gacchati
   (rāmo grāmād vanaṃ gacchati)

   b. अमृतम् ज्ञानस्य फलम् भवति ।

   amṛtam jñānasya phalam bhavati
   (amṛtaṃ jñānasya phalaṃ bhavati)

c. ज्ञानम् सत्यम् भवतीति बालाः शास्त्रे पठन्ति ।

jñānam satyam bhavatīti bālāḥ śāstre paṭhanti
(jñānaṃ satyaṃ bhavatīti bālāḥ śāstre paṭhanti)

d. अमृतस्य पुत्राः भवथेत्याचार्यः शिष्यान् वदति ।

amṛtasya putrāḥ bhavathety ācāryaḥ śiṣyān vadati
(amṛtasya putrā bhavathety ācāryaḥ śiṣyān vadati)

e. कथम् आचार्याः सूक्तानि स्मरन्ति ।

katham ācāryāḥ sūktāni smaranti
(katham ācāryāḥ sūktāni smaranti)

f. शास्त्रेषु सत्यम् पश्यामीति रामः वदति ।

śāstreṣu satyam paśyāmīti rāmaḥ vadati
(śāstreṣu satyaṃ paśyāmīti rāmo vadati)

g. कुत्र सूक्तानाम् ज्ञानम् भवतीति वीरः पुत्रम् पृच्छति ।

kutra sūktānām jñānam bhavatīti vīraḥ putram pṛcchati
(kutra sūktānāṃ jñānaṃ bhavatīti vīraḥ putraṃ pṛcchati)

h. नृपः बालाय पुस्तकम् पठति ।

nṛpaḥ bālāya pustakam paṭhati
(nṛpo bālāya pustakaṃ paṭhati)

6. Translate the following sentences into Sanskrit. First write them without **sandhi**, then with (vowel) **sandhi**, and finally in **devanāgarī.**

   a. The elephant is not the king of the forest.

   b. How do you see the moon?

   c. Rāma thinks that he sees the deer.

   d. The fruit is in the hands of the boy.

   e. How does the king live without Rāma?

   f. Rāma is the king.

g. The king is Rāma.

h. The hero lives in the village of the immortals.

7. Translate the following sentences into English. First write in roman script, then take out the **sandhi**, and finally write in English:

a. कथम् सूर्येण विना नराः नृपम् पश्यन्ति ।

(कथं सूर्येण विना नरा नृपं पश्यन्ति ।)

b. शिष्यानाम् आचार्यः पुस्तकम् पठति ।

(शिष्यानामाचार्यः पुस्तकं पठति ।)

c. अत्र वने फलानि भवन्तीति बालः वीरम् वदति ।

(अत्र वने फलानि भवन्तीति बालो वीरं वदति ।)

d. मृगः वने वसति गजः च ग्रामे वसति ।

(मृगो वने वसति गजश्च ग्रामे वसति ।)

(When a phrase or clause is joined by **ca**, it usually takes the second position. See p. 28.)

e. ज्ञानम् पुस्तकेन भवतीत्याचार्यः वदति ।

(ज्ञानं पुस्तकेन भवतीत्याचार्यो वदति ।)

f. पुस्तकेन विना शिष्यः ज्ञानम् स्मरति ।

(पुस्तकेन विना शिष्यो ज्ञानं स्मरति ।)

g. राम कुत्र मृगेण सह गच्छसीति पुत्रः पृच्छति ।

(राम कुत्र मृगेण सह गच्छसीति पुत्रः पृच्छति ।)

h. नरः बालाय पुस्तकम् पठति ।

(नरो बालाय पुस्तकं पठति ।)

8. Translate the following sentences into Sanskrit. Translate, put in the vowel **sandhi**, and write in **devanāgarī**:

a. Where do you read the knowledge of immortality?

b. How does Rāma go to the forest without the horses?

c. "The hymns are in the book," the teacher tells the students.

d. Rāma sees the truth and speaks the truth.

e. "I see the sun and the moon," says the son of the king.

f. Without knowledge, there are no teachers or students.

g. The hero speaks to the boys about immortality.

h. The horses, elephants, and boys come from the village.

9. Transliterate the following:

1. पुराण
2. राम
3. पुरुष
4. प्रकृति
5. प्रज्ञा
6. सीता
7. सुखम्
8. संयम
9. संसार
10. संस्कार
11. संस्कृत
12. सत्यम्
13. रामराज्य
14. रामायण
15. शिष्य
16. स्थितप्रज्ञ
17. भगवद्गीता
18. समाधि
19. योग
20. बुद्ध
21. महाभारत
22. प्रज्ञापराध
23. वेदान्त
24. वेदलीला

SUMMARY SHEET

VERBS

	Singular	Dual	Plural
Third	**gacchati** (he, she goes)	**gacchataḥ** (they two go)	**gacchanti** (they all go)
Second	**gacchasi** (you go)	**gacchathaḥ** (you two go)	**gacchatha** (you all go)
First	**gacchāmi** (I go)	**gacchāvaḥ** (we two go)	**gacchāmaḥ** (we all go)

ā + √gam	**āgacchati**	he comes
√gam	**gacchati**	he goes
√cint	**cintayati**	he thinks
√paṭh	**paṭhati**	he reads
√paś (√dṛś)	**paśyati**	he sees
√prach	**pṛcchati**	he asks
√bhū	**bhavati**	he is
√vad	**vadati**	he speaks, he says
√vas	**vasati**	he lives
√sthā	**tiṣṭhati**	he stands
√smṛ	**smarati**	he remembers

MASCULINE NOUNS

	Singular	Dual	Plural
Nom. (subject)	**naraḥ**	**narau**	**narāḥ**
Acc. (object)	**naram**	**narau**	**narān**
Inst. (with)	**nareṇa***	**narābhyām**	**naraiḥ**
Dat. (for)	**narāya**	**narābhyām**	**narebhyaḥ**
Abl. (from)	**narāt**	**narābhyām**	**narebhyaḥ**
Gen. (of, 's)	**narasya**	**narayoḥ**	**narāṇām***
Loc. (in, on)	**nare**	**narayoḥ**	**nareṣu**
Voc. (O)	**nara**	**narau**	**narāḥ**

***gajena, gajānām** (See page 46.)

MASCULINE NOUNS

aśvaḥ	horse	**rāmaḥ**	Rāma
ācāryaḥ	teacher	**vīraḥ**	hero
gajaḥ	elephant	**śiṣyaḥ**	student
grāmaḥ	village	**sūryaḥ**	sun
candraḥ	moon	**hastaḥ**	hand
naraḥ	man		
nṛpaḥ	king		
putraḥ	son		
bālaḥ	boy		
mṛgaḥ	deer		

NEUTER NOUNS

	Singular	Dual	Plural
Nom. (subject)	**phalam**	**phale**	**phalāni***
Acc. (object)	**phalam**	**phale**	**phalāni***
Inst. (with)	**phalena***	**phalābhyām**	**phalaiḥ**
Dat. (for)	**phalāya**	**phalābhyām**	**phalebhyaḥ**
Abl. (from)	**phalāt**	**phalābhyām**	**phalebhyaḥ**
Gen. (of, 's)	**phalasya**	**phalayoḥ**	**phalānām***
Loc. (in, on)	**phale**	**phalayoḥ**	**phaleṣu**
Voc. (O)	**phala**	**phale**	**phalāni***

***śāstrāṇi, śāstreṇa, śāstrāṇām**

NEUTER NOUNS
(given in nominative form)

amṛtam	immortality
jñānam	knowledge
pustakam	book
phalam	fruit
vanam	forest
śāstram	scripture
satyam	truth
sūktam	hymn

INDECLINABLES

atra	here
iti	end of quote
katham	how (used like **kutra**)
kutra	where
ca	and
tatra	there
na	not
vā	or
vinā	without + acc
saha	with + Instr

THE MONKEY AND THE CROCODILE

Translate the following, using the vocabulary on the next page. Words not given you should already know.

1. तत्र गङ्गायाम् कुम्भीरः भवति ।

   (तत्र गङ्गायां कुम्भीरो भवति ।)

2. वानरः तटे वसति ।

   (वानरस्तटे वसति ।)

3. वानरः फलानि कुम्भीराय निक्षिपति ।

   (वानरः फलानि कुम्भीराय निक्षिपति ।)

4. कुम्भीरः फलानि खादति ।

   (कुम्भीरः फलानि खादति ।)

5. भार्या वानरस्य हृदयम् इच्छति ।

   (भार्या वानरस्य हृदयमिच्छति ।)

6. हृदयम् वृक्षे भवतीति वानरः वदति ।

(हृदयं वृक्षे भवतीति वानरो वदति ।)

7. कश्चित् हृदयम् चोरयतीति वानरः वदति ।

(कश्चिद्धृदयं चोरयतीति वानरो वदति ।)

8. एवम् कुम्भीरः वानरः च मित्रे तिष्ठतः ।

(एवं कुम्भीरो वानरश्च मित्रे तिष्ठतः ।)

VOCABULARY (IN ORDER OF APPEARANCE)

1. **gaṅgā** (fem. noun) Ganges. This follows the feminine declension for long **ā**. The locative is **gaṅgāyām**, "in the Ganges."
   kumbhīraḥ (mas. noun) crocodile

2. **vānaraḥ** (mas. noun) monkey
   taṭaḥ (mas. noun) bank (of the river)

3. **nikṣipati** (3rd per. sing. verb) he throws down

4. **khādati** (3rd per. sing. verb) he eats

5. **bhāryā** (fem. noun) wife. This, again, follows the feminine declension for long **ā**. The stem, as well as the nominative, is **bhāryā**.

hṛdayam (neuter noun) heart. The **ṛ** is written next to the **h.** (See Lesson 6, page 57.)
icchati (3rd per. sing. verb) she wants (to eat)

6. **vṛkṣaḥ** (mas. noun) tree

7. **kaḥ** (mas. pronoun) who
cit (ind.) (makes **kaḥ** indefinite)
kaścit someone
corayati (3rd per. sing. verb) he steals

8. **evam** (ind.) therefore
mitram (neuter noun) friend (Here it is used in the nom. dual.)
tiṣṭhati (3rd per. sing. verb) he remains, or stands as (Here used in the dual.)

(The story will become more clear when it is studied in detail in Lesson 11.)

9

LESSON NINE

Aphabet: The **sandhi** rules for final **ḥ**

Grammar: The middle voice and "have"

Vocabulary: Verbs in the middle voice

ALPHABET: SANDHI RULES FOR FINAL ḥ

1. The following chart describes the changes that take place when the first word ends in **ḥ** (which was originally **s**). There are three categories: **aḥ**, **āḥ**, and **ḥ** preceded by any other vowel.

FINAL LETTERS OF FIRST WORD

Any vowel **r** Any vowel **ḥ** (except **aḥ** and **āḥ**)	**āḥ**	**aḥ**	INITIAL LETTER OF SECOND WORD	
The **ḥ** or **r** becomes				
r	**ā**	**a** (2)	**vowels**	(a)
r	**ā**	**o**	**g/gh**	
r	**ā**	**o**	**j/jh**	
r	**ā**	**o**	**ḍ/ḍh**	
r	**ā**	**o**	**d/dh**	(b)
r	**ā**	**o**	**b/bh**	
r	**ā**	**o**	**nasals (n/m)**	
r	**ā**	**o**	**y/v**	
-(1)	**ā**	**o**	**r**	
r	**ā**	**o**	**l**	
r	**ā**	**o**	**h**	
ḥ	**āḥ**	**aḥ**	**k/kh**	
ś	**āś**	**aś**	**c/ch**	
ṣ	**āṣ**	**aṣ**	**ṭ/ṭh**	
s	**ās**	**as**	**t/th**	
ḥ	**āḥ**	**aḥ**	**p/ph**	(c)
ḥ	**āḥ**	**aḥ**	**ś**	
ḥ	**āḥ**	**aḥ**	**ṣ/s**	
ḥ	**āḥ**	**aḥ**	**end of line**	

(1) The **ḥ** disappears, and if **i** or **u** precedes, it becomes **ī** or **ū**.
The **r** disappears, and if **a**, **i**, or **u** precedes, it becomes **ā**, **ī**, or **ū**.

(2) Except that **aḥ** + **a** = **o '** For example:

रामः + अत्र = रामोऽत्र

rāmaḥ + **atra** = **rāmo 'tra**

2. If the first word ends in **aḥ**, then use the third column. If the first word ends in **āḥ**, then use the middle column. If the first word ends in any other vowel before the **ḥ** or any vowel before the **r** (including **ar** or **ār**), then use the first column.

3. Here are some examples:

Without **sandhi**	With **sandhi**
रामः गच्छति **rāmaḥ gacchati**	रामो गच्छति **rāmo gacchati**
वीराः गच्छन्ति **vīrāḥ gacchanti**	वीरा गच्छन्ति **vīrā gacchanti**
रामः पश्यति **rāmaḥ paśyati**	रामः पश्यति **rāmaḥ paśyati**
वीराः पश्यन्ति **vīrāḥ paśyanti**	वीराः पश्यन्ति **vīrāḥ paśyanti**

Additional examples are given on pages 183–187.

4. Final **s** should be treated as **ḥ**. For example, **rāmas** follows the same rules as **rāmaḥ**. Either would become **rāmo** before **gacchati**.

5. After these **sandhi** rules have been applied, if the first word ends in a vowel (including **ḥ**), then there is a break between words in **devanāgarī**. For now, words that do not follow the **sandhi** rules presented in Lessons 8 and 9 should be kept separate.

In this text, when writing in roman script, words are usually separated, unless the **sandhi** change is a result of two vowels joining together, such as **bhavārjuna**. For example:

Without **sandhi**	With **sandhi**
रामः चिन्तयति **rāmaḥ cintayati**	रामश्चिन्तयति **rāmaś cintayati**
रामः तिष्ठति **rāmaḥ tiṣṭhati**	रामस्तिष्ठति **rāmas tiṣṭhati**
गच्छति इति **gacchati iti**	गच्छतीति **gacchatīti**
भव अर्जुन **bhava arjuna**	भवार्जुन **bhavārjuna**

6. Notice that the chart is divided into three groups on the right side: (a), (b), and (c). These three groups are determined by the first letter of the second word. The groups are:

   (a) Vowels
   (b) Voiced consonants
   (c) Unvoiced consonants (The end of the line is considered to be unvoiced.)

7. The following chart (described in more detail in Lesson 14) puts the **sandhi** changes into these three groups. It gives the same information as the first chart, but in a more conceptual form, so that later on it will be easier to memorize. Each group represents the first letter of the second word:

a	**ā**	
i	**ī**	
u	**ū**	(a)
ṛ	**ṝ**	Vowels
ḷ		
e	**ai**	
o	**au**	

ḥ		**ka**	**kha**	I	**ga**	**gha**	**ṅa**	
ś		**ca**	**cha**	I	**ja**	**jha**	**ña**	
ṣ		**ṭa**	**ṭha**	I	**ḍa**	**ḍha**	**ṇa**	
s		**ta**	**tha**	I	**da**	**dha**	**na**	
ḥ		**pa**	**pha**	I	**ba**	**bha**	**ma**	
				I	**ya**	**ra**	**la**	**va**
ḥ	**śa**	**ṣa**	**sa**	I	**ha**			
ḥ	end of line			I				
	(c) Unvoiced consonant				(b) Voiced consonant			

(a) If the second word begins in a vowel:
 aḥ becomes **a** (except **aḥ** + **a** = **o '**)
 āḥ becomes **ā**
 vowel **ḥ** becomes **r**

(b) If the first letter of the second word is a voiced consonant:
 aḥ becomes **o**
 āḥ becomes **ā**
 vowel **ḥ** becomes **r** (except before a word beginning in **r**)

(c) If the first letter of the second word is an unvoiced consonant, the **ḥ** changes to the letter in the far left column.

GRAMMAR: MIDDLE VERBS

1. Now we will learn the middle endings (**ātmanepada**). For the middle voice, the fruit of action is said to go to the agent (**ātman**). For the active voice, the fruit of action goes to someone else (**para**). Many verbs usually take active endings, many usually take middle endings and some verbs take both endings.

2. Here is the formation of the middle verb √**bhāṣ** (to speak):

	Singular	Dual	Plural
Third	**bhāṣate**	**bhāṣete**	**bhāṣante**
Second	**bhāṣase**	**bhāṣethe**	**bhāṣadhve**
First	**bhāṣe**	**bhāṣāvahe**	**bhāṣāmahe**

Note that the present middle endings are listed on p. 316.

3. Although most of the verbs we have learned (before √**bhāṣ**) are usually seen with active endings, they occasionally take middle endings also (in situations where the fruit of action goes more to the agent). One verb, √**cint**, regularly takes both active and middle endings, and so is classified as **ubhayapada**. (See p. 25.) Verbs that regulary take both endings will be listed like this: **cintayati -te**.

"HAVE"

4. There is no verb for "have" in Sanskrit. "Have" is formed with the genitive and √**bhū**. For example:

वीरस्य पुत्रो भवति ।

vīrasya putro bhavati

Of the hero a son is. (becomes)

The hero has a son.

VOCABULARY

SANSKRIT		ENGLISH
एव	**eva** (ind.)	only, ever
गृहम्	**gṛham** (n.)	house
जलम्	**jalam** (n.)	water
जि	√**ji** (active) **jayati**	he conquers
दुःखम्	**duḥkham*** (n.)	suffering
भाष्	√**bhāṣ** (middle) **bhāṣate**	he speaks
मन्	√**man** (middle) **manyate**	he thinks
लभ्	√**labh** (middle) **labhate**	he obtains
सुखम्	**sukham** (n.)	happiness
सेव्	√**sev** (middle) **sevate**	he serves

*When the **ḥ** occurs in the middle of a word, it is pronounced as a breath of air.

EXERCISES   1. Put in the correct **sandhi** for the following phrases:

      o   a. रामः गच्छति   e. रामः इति

      ā   b. बालाः आगच्छन्ति   f. देवाः स्मरन्ति

   ava   c. वीरौ आगच्छतः   g. पुत्रः पश्यति

             d. शिष्यः अत्र   h. अश्वः वदति

2. Take out the **sandhi** in the following phrases:

             a. रामो गच्छति   e. अश्वा आगच्छन्ति

             b. कुत्रागच्छसि   f. रामः पुत्रश्च

 iḥ any vowel th no reason for r̥r̥ gaje virāḥ

             c. सूर्यश्चन्द्रश्च   g. गजैः सह

             d. गजैर्वीरिः   h. फलयोर्जलम्

                   hero ē elephants (x2)   *phaloyoḥ jalam*

3. Translate the following sentences into English. Take out the
   sandhi (for vowels and final **ḥ**), and then translate:

       a. वीरस्य बालो भवति ।
          vīrasya bālo bhavati

       (वीरस्य बालो भवति ।)

b. सुखम् ज्ञानस्य फलम् भवति ।
sukham jñānasya phalam bhavati

(सुखं ज्ञानस्य फलं भवति ।)

c. शिष्या गृहात् जलम् आचार्याय लभन्ते ।
śiṣyā gṛhāt jalam ācāryāya labhante

(शिष्या गृहाज्जलमाचार्याय लभन्ते ।)

d. रामस्तत्र जलाय गच्छतीति वीरो वदति ।
rāmas tatra jalāya gacchatīti vīro vadati

(रामस्तत्र जलाय गच्छतीति वीरो वदति ।)

e. शिष्य आचार्यम् सेवते ।
śiṣya ācāryam sevate

(शिष्य आचार्यं सेवते ।)

f. शिष्या ज्ञानम् आचार्यात् लभन्ते ।
śiṣyā jñānam ācāryāt labhante

(शिष्या ज्ञानमाचार्याल्लभन्ते ।)

g. राम कथम् दुःखम् जयसि ।
rāma katham duḥkham jayasi
(राम कथं दुःखं जयसि ।)

h. पुत्रो गृहात् नृपस्याश्वेषु गच्छति ।
putro gṛhāt nṛpasyāśveṣu gacchati
(पुत्रो गृहान्नृपस्याश्वेषु गच्छति ।)

i. अमृतम् सुखस्य फलम् भवतीति चिन्तयते ।
amṛtam sukhasya phalam bhavatīti cintayate
(अमृतं सुखस्य फलं भवतीति चिन्तयते ।)

j. आचार्यो ज्ञानस्य पुस्तकम् शिष्याय पठति ।
ācāryo jñānasya pustakam śiṣyāya paṭhati
(आचार्यो ज्ञानस्य पुस्तकं शिष्याय पठति ।)

4. Translate the following sentences into Sanskrit. First write in roman, then **devanāgarī**, and then write again with the (vowel and final **ḥ**) **sandhi**:

a. The water is in Rāma's hands.

b. The boy reads the book.

c. The hero stands ever in the house of the king.

d. The boys obtain the fruits from the forest.

e. "You conquer suffering with knowledge," the teacher says.

f. From the fruit the boy obtains water. (Use singular for "fruit.")

g. "I see truth in the sun and the moon," says Rāma.

h. Without knowledge there is suffering.

i. "I do not come from the village," the king's son says.

j. The hero and the boy live in the forest.

SUMMARY SHEET

	Singular	Dual	Plural
Third	**gacchati** (he, she goes)	**gacchataḥ** (they two go)	**gacchanti** (they all go)
Second	**gacchasi** (you go)	**gacchathaḥ** (you two go)	**gacchatha** (you all go)
First	**gacchāmi** (I go)	**gacchāvaḥ** (we two go)	**gacchāmaḥ** (we all go)

VERBS PRIMARILY TAKING ACTIVE ENDINGS **(parasmaipada)**

ā + √gam	**āgacchati**	he comes
√gam	**gacchati**	he goes
√ji	**jayati**	he conquers
√paṭh	**paṭhati**	he reads
√paś (√dṛś)	**paśyati**	he sees
√prach	**pṛcchati**	he asks
√bhū	**bhavati**	he is
√vad	**vadati**	he speaks, he says
√vas	**vasati**	he lives
√sthā	**tiṣṭhati**	he stands
√smṛ	**smarati**	he remembers

	Singular	Dual	Plural
Third	**bhāṣate** (he speaks)	**bhāṣete** (they two speak)	**bhāṣante** (they all speak)
Second	**bhāṣase** (you speak)	**bhāṣethe** (you two speak)	**bhāṣadhve** (you all speak)
First	**bhāṣe** (I speak)	**bhāṣāvahe** (we two speak)	**bhāṣāmahe** (we all speak)

VERBS PRIMARILY TAKING MIDDLE ENDINGS (**ātmanepada**)

√**bhāṣ**	**bhāṣate**	he speaks
√**man**	**manyate**	he thinks
√**labh**	**labhate**	he obtains
√**sev**	**sevate**	he serves

VERB REGULARLY TAKING BOTH ENDINGS (**ubhayapada**)

√**cint**	**cintayati -te**	he thinks

MASCULINE NOUNS

	Singular	Dual	Plural
Nom. (subject)	**naraḥ**	**narau**	**narāḥ**
Acc. (object)	**naram**	**narau**	**narān**
Inst. (with)	**nareṇa***	**narābhyām**	**naraiḥ**
Dat. (for)	**narāya**	**narābhyām**	**narebhyaḥ**
Abl. (from)	**narāt**	**narābhyām**	**narebhyaḥ**
Gen. (of, 's)	**narasya**	**narayoḥ**	**narāṇām***
Loc. (in, on)	**nare**	**narayoḥ**	**nareṣu**
Voc. (O)	**nara**	**narau**	**narāḥ**

***gajena, gajānām** (See page 46.)

aśvaḥ	horse	**vīraḥ**	hero
ācāryaḥ	teacher	**śiṣyaḥ**	student
gajaḥ	elephant	**sūryaḥ**	sun
grāmaḥ	village	**hastaḥ**	hand
candraḥ	moon		
naraḥ	man		
nṛpaḥ	king		
putraḥ	son		
bālaḥ	boy		
mṛgaḥ	deer		
rāmaḥ	Rāma		

NEUTER NOUNS

	Singular	Dual	Plural
Nom. (subject)	**phalam**	**phale**	**phalāni***
Acc. (object)	**phalam**	**phale**	**phalāni***
Inst. (with)	**phalena***	**phalābhyām**	**phalaiḥ**
Dat. (for)	**phalāya**	**phalābhyām**	**phalebhyaḥ**
Abl. (from)	**phalāt**	**phalābhyām**	**phalebhyaḥ**
Gen. (of, 's)	**phalasya**	**phalayoḥ**	**phalānām***
Loc. (in, on)	**phale**	**phalayoḥ**	**phaleṣu**
Voc. (O)	**phala**	**phale**	**phalāni***

***śāstrāṇi, śāstreṇa, śāstrāṇām**

amṛtam	immortality	**satyam**	truth
gṛham	house	**sukham**	happiness
jalam	water	**sūktam**	hymn
jñānam	knowledge		
duḥkham	suffering		
pustakam	book		
phalam	fruit		
vanam	forest		
śāstram	scripture		

INDECLINABLES

atra	here
iti	end of quote
eva	only, ever
katham	how (used like **kutra**)
kutra	where
ca	and
tatra	there
na	not
vā	or
vinā	without
saha	with

RĀMĀYAṆA

Translate the following, using the vocabulary given afterward:

1. अयोध्यायाम् दशरथो नाम नृपो वसति ।

(अयोध्यायां दशरथो नाम नृपो वसति ।)

2. दशरथस्य चत्वारः पुत्रा भवन्ति ।

(दशरथस्य चत्वारः पुत्रा भवन्ति ।)

3. पुत्रा रामो भरतो लक्ष्मणः शत्रुघ्नो भवन्ति ।

(पुत्रा रामो भरतो लक्ष्मणः शत्रुघ्नो भवन्ति ।)

4. रामः सुन्दरः शान्तो वीरश्च भवति ।

(रामः सुन्दरः शान्तो वीरश्च भवति ।)

5. नृपो रामे स्निह्यति ।

(नृपो रामे स्निह्यति ।)

6. रामो मिथिलाम् लक्ष्मणेन सह गच्छति ।

(रामो मिथिलां लक्ष्मणेन सह गच्छति ।)

Sītā

7. तत्र रामः सीताम् पश्यति ।

(तत्र रामः सीतां पश्यति ।)

8. सीतायाम् स्निह्यामीति रामो वदति ।।

(सीतायां स्निह्यामीति रामो वदति ।।)

VOCABULARY

1. **ayodhyā** (fem.) the city of Ayodhyā (The locative is **ayodhyāyām**, "in Ayodhyā.")
   daśarathaḥ (mas. noun) Daśaratha, the king of Ayodhyā
   nāma (ind.) by name

2. **catvāraḥ** (nom.) four (used as an adjective)

3. **bharataḥ, lakṣmaṇaḥ, śatrughnaḥ** names of Rāma's brothers

4. **sundara** (adjective) beautiful
   śānta (adjective) peaceful
   vīra strong (here an adjective—strong like a hero)

5. **snihyati** (3rd per. sing. verb) he loves (used with locative)

6. **mithilā** (fem.) city of Mithilā (The accusative is **mithilām**.)

7. **sītā** (fem.) Sītā (The accusative is **sītām**.)

8. The locative of **sītā** is **sītāyām**.

10

LESSON TEN

Alphabet: The remaining **sandhi** rules

Grammar: Pronouns and adjectives
The verb √**as**

Vocabulary: Adjectives and particles

ALPHABET: REMAINING SANDHI RULES

1. Here is the chart for the **sandhi** rules for final **t, n, and m:**

FINAL LETTER OF FIRST WORD: t	n	m	INITIAL LETTER OF SECOND WORD:
d	**n**[1]	**m**	**vowels**
d	**n**	**ṃ**	**g/gh**
j	**ñ**	**ṃ**	**j/jh**
ḍ	**ṇ**	**ṃ**	**ḍ/ḍh**
d	**n**	**ṃ**	**d/dh**
d	**n**	**ṃ**	**b/bh**
n	**n**	**ṃ**	**nasals (n/m)**
d	**n**	**ṃ**	**y/v**
d	**n**	**ṃ**	**r**
l	**ṃl**	**ṃ**	**l**
d(dh)[3]	**n**	**ṃ**	**h**
t	**n**	**ṃ**	**k/kh**
c	**ṃś**	**ṃ**	**c/ch**
ṭ	**ṃṣ**	**ṃ**	**ṭ/ṭh**
t	**ṃs**	**ṃ**	**t/th**
t	**n**	**ṃ**	**p/ph**
c(ch)[4]	**ñ(ch)**[2]	**ṃ**	**ś**
t	**n**	**ṃ**	**ṣ/s**
t	**n**	**m**	**end of line**

1. If the vowel before **n** is short, **n** becomes **nn**.

2. The following **ś** may become **ch**.

3. The following **h** becomes **dh**.

4. The following **ś** becomes **ch**.

Examples for this chart can be found on:

p. 196 (for final **m**)
pps. 205–207 (for final **n**)
pps. 218 and 219 (for final **t**)

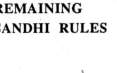

2. Many of the changes on this chart occur because the last letter of the first word is "getting ready" to say the first letter of the next word. This rule, which often involves a change of voicing, is called "regressive assimilation." The prior sound is assimilated.

3. There are a few additional rules, which are used less often. They are discussed in Lesson 18.

4. There are no **sandhi** changes if the first word ends in a vowel (excluding **ḥ** and **ṃ**) and the second word begins with a consonant.

5. At one time the manuscripts didn't have any breaks between words, sentences, or paragraphs in the written script. Fortunately, modern editions have introduced some spaces between words. Words are separated in **devanāgarī** as much as possible without changing how they are written and without adding a **virāma**.

6. Here are the cases that result in a break between words. After the **sandhi** has been applied, there is a break in the **devanāgarī** between words when the first word ends in a vowel, which includes **ḥ** or **ṃ**. For example:

रामः गच्छति = रामो गच्छति (vowel)

रामः पृच्छति = रामः पृच्छति (ḥ)

रामम् गच्छामि = रामं गच्छामि (ṃ)

rāmaḥ gacchati = **rāmo gacchati** (vowel)
rāmaḥ pṛcchati = **rāmaḥ pṛcchati** (ḥ)
rāmam gacchāmi = **rāmaṃ gacchāmi** (ṃ)

7. If the first word ends in a vowel and the second word begins in a vowel and together they form a new vowel (**bhava + arjuna = bhavārjuna**), then there can be no break in **devanāgarī** or roman script. (See point 10 on page 90.)

GRAMMAR: PRONOUNS

1. Pronouns (**sarva-nāman**) decline exactly the same way that nouns decline. This table does not give, however, the endings, but the entire first person pronoun (I, we two, we, etc.):

Stems: **mad** (singular) I; **asmad** (plural) we. Both are any gender.

	Singular	Dual	Plural
Nom. I, we	अहम् **aham**	आवाम् **āvām**	वयम् **vayam**
Acc. me, us	माम् मा **mām (mā)**	आवाम् नौ **āvām (nau)**	अस्मान् नः **asmān (naḥ)**
Inst. with me, us	मया **mayā**	आवाभ्याम् **āvābhyām**	अस्माभिः **asmābhiḥ**
Dat. for me, us	मह्यम् मे **mahyam (me)**	आवाभ्याम् नौ **āvābhyām (nau)**	अस्मभ्यम् नः **asmabhyam (naḥ)**
Abl. from me, us	मत् **mat**	आवाभ्याम् **āvābhyām**	अस्मत् **asmat**
Gen. my, our	मम मे **mama (me)**	आवयोः नौ **āvayoḥ (nau)**	अस्माकम् नः **asmākam (naḥ)**
Loc. on me, us	मयि **mayi**	आवयोः **āvayoḥ**	अस्मासु **asmāsu**

2. The Sanskrit words in parentheses are sometimes used. For example, **mā** is sometimes used instead of **mām** (except beginning a sentence).

3. Here is the second person pronoun (you):

Stems: **tvad** (singular) you; **yuṣmad** (plural) you. Both are any gender.

	Singular	Dual	Plural
Nom.	त्वम्	युवाम्	यूयम्
you	**tvam**	**yuvām**	**yūyam**
Acc.	त्वाम् त्वा	युवाम् वाम्	युष्मान् वः
you	**tvām (tvā)**	**yuvām (vām)**	**yuṣmān (vaḥ)**
Inst.	त्वया	युवाभ्याम्	युष्माभिः
with you	**tvayā**	**yuvābhyām**	**yuṣmābhiḥ**
Dat.	तुभ्यम् ते	युवाभ्याम् वाम्	युष्मभ्यम् वः
for you	**tubhyam (te)**	**yuvābhyām (vām)**	**yuṣmabhyam (vaḥ)**
Abl.	त्वत्	युवाभ्याम्	युष्मत्
from you	**tvat**	**yuvābhyām**	**yuṣmat**
Gen.	तव ते	युवयोः वाम्	युष्माकम् वः
your	**tava (te)**	**yuvayoḥ (vām)**	**yuṣmākam (vaḥ)**
Loc.	त्वयि	युवयोः	युष्मासु
on you	**tvayi**	**yuvayoḥ**	**yuṣmāsu**

ADJECTIVES

4. Adjectives (**viśeṣaṇa**) are considered nominals (**subanta**), or noun forms. They are declined like nouns. They are usually placed before the noun that they modify and agree with it in number, case, and gender. For example, the adjective for "beautiful" is **sundara**:

सुन्दरो गजो गच्छति ।
sundaro gajo gacchati (with **sandhi**)
The beautiful elephant goes.

If a genitive is also modifying a noun, the genitive goes closest to the noun. For example:

सुन्दरो नृपस्य गजो गच्छति ।
sundaro nṛpasya gajo gacchati (with **sandhi)**
The beautiful elephant of the king goes.

सुन्दरस्य नृपस्य गजो गच्छति ।
sundarasya nṛpasya gajo gacchati (with **sandhi**)
The elephant of the beautiful king goes.

√AS

5. One of the most common roots in Sanskrit is √**as**, which means "to be." We have had another root, √**bhū**, which also means "to be," but √**as** is more common. It is used to mean "there is" and as a copula. For example:

There is the horse. अश्वोऽस्ति
aśvo 'sti

Rāma is the king. रामो नृपोऽस्ति
rāmo nṛpo 'sti

Possibility –
asti - Declaration
bhavati - Location

6. Here is the present indicative (**laṭ**) for √**as**. These are not the endings, but the entire verb:

	Singular	Dual	Plural
Third	अस्ति **asti**	स्तः **staḥ**	सन्ति **santi**
Second	असि **asi**	स्थः **sthaḥ**	स्थ **stha**
First	अस्मि **asmi**	स्वः **svaḥ**	स्मः **smaḥ**

Note how closely this is related to the endings for the active verbs. Note also that the singular forms begin with **a**, and the dual and plural begin with **s**.

7. This verb is often understood. That is, the verb is meant, but is not written in the sentence. For example:

रामो नृपोऽस्ति ।
rāmo nṛpo 'sti
Rāma is the king.

or

नृपो रामः ।
nṛpo rāmaḥ
Rāma is the king.

Notice that when the verb is understood, the predicate nominative (king) is sometimes placed before the subject (Rāma).

8. Often this verb begins the sentence. For example:

अस्ति नृपो दशरथो ग्रामे ।
asti nṛpo daśaratho grāme
There is a king, Daśaratha, in the village.

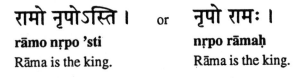

VOCABULARY

SANSKRIT		ENGLISH
अतीव	**atīva** (ind.)	very
	Sometimes ati (not iti)	
अपि	**api** (ind.)	also, too (placed after the word it is associated with)
अस्	√**as** (root) **asti** (3rd per. sing.)	he, she, or it is
अस्मद्	**asmad** (plural pro.)	we
अहो	**aho** (ind.)	aha! hey!
एवम्	**evam** (ind.)	thus, in this way
कुपित	**kupita** (adj.)	angry
त्वद्	**tvad** (sing. pro.)	you
धार्मिक	**dhārmika** (adj.)	virtuous
नाम	**nāma** (ind.)	by name (placed after the word it is associated with)
पुनर्	**punar** (ind.)	again
भीत	**bhīta** (adj.)	afraid
मद्	**mad** (sing. pro.)	I
युष्मद्	**yuṣmad** (plural pro.)	you
सुन्दर	**sundara** (adj.)	beautiful

EXERCISES

1. Put in the correct **sandhi**, write in **devanāgarī**, and translate:

   a. **mama putraḥ gacchati**

   b. **tava gajaḥ mat tvām gacchati**

   c. **mama hastau pustakeṣu staḥ**

   d. **aham nṛpaḥ asmi**

   e. **vayam aśve tiṣṭhāmaḥ**

   f. **tvam mama pustakam paṭhasi**

   g. **rāmaḥ tava nṛpaḥ asti**

   h. **yūyam gṛhe stha**

   i. **asmākam nṛpaḥ kupitaḥ asti**

   j. **tvayā saha aham gacchāmi**

   k. **dhārmikaḥ nṛpaḥ bhītaḥ asti**

   l. **sundaraḥ tvam**

2. Take out the **sandhi** and translate the following:

   a. नृपस्य पुत्रोऽस्ति ।

b. अहो रामः पुनर्वदति ।

c. अहमतीव भीतो भवामि ।

d. आचार्या अपि पुस्तकानि पठन्ति ।

e. अस्ति नृपो रामो नाम वने ।

f. कथं तव गृहं गच्छामीति शिष्यः पृच्छति ।

g. वीरो मम ग्रामं जयति ।

h. पुत्रः सुन्दरात्फलाज्जलं लभते ।

i. सुखेन विना दुःखमस्ति ।

j. सुन्दरो गज इति पुत्रो मन्यते ।

3. Translate the following sentences, writing them first without **sandhi** (in **devanāgarī**) and then with **sandhi** (in **devanāgarī**):

   a. The student is not afraid of the teacher. (Use ablative for teacher.)

   b. You obtain knowledge from the scriptures.

   c. "The boy is there," says the hero to the teacher.

   d. I ask the teacher about the deer.

   e. "Where are you going?" the boy asks.

   f. Again the hero comes to my house.

   g. Your teacher speaks the truth.

   h. Our horses are standing in the village.

   i. There is a king, Rāma by name, in our village.

   j. How do I obtain the king's horses from you?

SUMMARY SHEET

Third	**gacchati** (he, she goes)	**gacchataḥ** (they two go)	**gacchanti** (they all go)
Second	**gacchasi** (you go)	**gacchathaḥ** (you two go)	**gacchatha** (you all go)
First	**gacchāmi** (I go)	**gacchāvaḥ** (we two go)	**gacchāmaḥ** (we all go)
	Singular	Dual	Plural

VERBS PRIMARILY TAKING ACTIVE ENDINGS (**parasmaipada**)

ā + √gam	**āgacchati**	he comes
√gam	**gacchati**	he goes
√ji	**jayati**	he conquers
√paṭh	**paṭhati**	he reads
√paś (**√dṛś**)	**paśyati**	he sees
√prach	**pṛcchati**	he asks
√bhū	**bhavati**	he is
√vad	**vadati**	he speaks, he says
√vas	**vasati**	he lives
√sthā	**tiṣṭhati**	he stands
√smṛ	**smarati**	he remembers

	Singular	Dual	Plural
Third	**bhāṣate** (he speaks)	**bhāṣete** (they two speak)	**bhāṣante** (they all speak)
Second	**bhāṣase** (you speak)	**bhāṣethe** (you two speak)	**bhāṣadhve** (you all speak)
First	**bhāṣe** (I speak)	**bhāṣāvahe** (we two speak)	**bhāṣāmahe** (we all speak)

VERBS PRIMARILY TAKING MIDDLE ENDINGS (**ātmanepada**)

√bhāṣ	**bhāṣate**	he speaks
√man	**manyate**	he thinks
√labh	**labhate**	he obtains
√sev	**sevate**	he serves

VERB REGULARLY TAKING BOTH ENDINGS (**ubhayapada**)

√cint	**cintayati -te**	he thinks

THE VERB **√as**

	Singular	Dual	Plural
Third	**asti**	**staḥ**	**santi**
Second	**asi**	**sthaḥ**	**stha**
First	**asmi**	**svaḥ**	**smaḥ**

Charts for pronouns are listed on pages 307-311.

MASCULINE NOUNS

	Singular	Dual	Plural
Nom. (subject)	**naraḥ**	**narau**	**narāḥ**
Acc. (object)	**naram**	**narau**	**narān**
Inst. (with)	**nareṇa***	**narābhyām**	**naraiḥ**
Dat. (for)	**narāya**	**narābhyām**	**narebhyaḥ**
Abl. (from)	**narāt**	**narābhyām**	**narebhyaḥ**
Gen. (of, 's)	**narasya**	**narayoḥ**	**narāṇām***
Loc. (in, on)	**nare**	**narayoḥ**	**nareṣu**
Voc. (O)	**nara**	**narau**	**narāḥ**

***gajena, gajānām** (See page 46.)

aśvaḥ	horse	**vīraḥ**	hero
ācāryaḥ	teacher	**śiṣyaḥ**	student
gajaḥ	elephant	**sūryaḥ**	sun
grāmaḥ	village	**hastaḥ**	hand
candraḥ	moon		
naraḥ	man		
nṛpaḥ	king		
putraḥ	son		
bālaḥ	boy		
mṛgaḥ	deer		
rāmaḥ	Rāma		

NEUTER NOUNS

	Singular	Dual	Plural
Nom. (subject)	**phalam**	**phale**	**phalāni***
Acc. (object)	**phalam**	**phale**	**phalāni***
Inst. (with)	**phalena***	**phalābhyām**	**phalaiḥ**
Dat. (for)	**phalāya**	**phalābhyām**	**phalebhyaḥ**
Abl. (from)	**phalāt**	**phalābhyām**	**phalebhyaḥ**
Gen. (of, 's)	**phalasya**	**phalayoḥ**	**phalānām***
Loc. (in, on)	**phale**	**phalayoḥ**	**phaleṣu**
Voc. (O)	**phala**	**phale**	**phalāni***

***śāstrāṇi, śāstreṇa, śāstrāṇām**

amṛtam	immortality	**satyam**	truth
gṛham	house	**sukham**	happiness
jalam	water	**sūktam**	hymn
jñānam	knowledge		
duḥkham	suffering		
pustakam	book		
phalam	fruit		
vanam	forest		
śāstram	scripture		

ADJECTIVES

kupita	angry
dhārmika	virtuous
bhīta	afraid
sundara	beautiful

INDECLINABLES

atīva	very
atra	here
api	also, too (placed after the word it is associated with)
aho	aha! hey!
iti	end of quote
eva	only, ever
evam	thus, in this way
katham	how
kutra	where
ca	and
tatra	there
na	not
nāma	by name (placed after the word it is associated with)
punar	again
vā	or
vinā	without
saha	with

11

LESSON ELEVEN

Alphabet: Internal **sandhi** rules

Grammar: Feminine nouns in **ā** and third person pronouns

Vocabulary: Feminine nouns

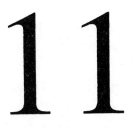

ALPHABET: INTERNAL SANDHI

1. We will learn only two internal **sandhi** rules at this time. These need not be memorized, but are mainly for recognition.

2. The first rule is that **s** changes to **ṣ** if immediately preceded by any vowel but **a** or **ā**, or preceded by **k** or **r**. The rule does not apply if the **s** is final or followed by an **r**. It applies even if an **anusvāra** (**ṃ**) or **visarga** (**ḥ**) comes between the vowel, **k**, or **r**—and the **s**. This rule is clearer in chart form:

any vowel (but **a** or **ā**), **k**, or **r**	in spite of intervening **ṃ** or **ḥ**	changes **s** to **ṣ**	unless final or followed immediately by **r**

3. If the sound following the **s** is **t**, **th**, or **n**, it is also retroflexed. For example:

sthā becomes **tiṣṭhati**

4. The second rule is that **n** changes to **ṇ** if preceded anywhere in the same word by **r**, **ṛ**, **ṝ**, or **ṣ**. Certain sounds may interrupt the process. Study this chart:

r **ṛ** **ṝ** or **ṣ**	unless **c**, **ch**, **j**, **jh**, **ñ**, **ṭ**, **ṭh**, **ḍ**, **ḍh**, **ṇ**, **t**, **th**, **d**, **dh**, **l**, **ś**, **s** interferes	changes **n** to **ṇ**	if followed by vowels, **m**, **y**, **v**, or **n**

5. Retroflex sounds, such as **r**, **ṛ**, **ṝ**, and **ṣ**, leave the tongue in a retroflexed position. Unless certain sounds interfere, such as retroflex sounds of the releasing type, like **ṭ**, or sounds from the row above or below, then **n** becomes retroflexed. (The **ka varga** and **pa varga** don't seem to move the tongue enough to change out of the retroflex position.) For example:

   rāmeṇa (The **r** changes the **n** to **ṇ**.)
   putreṇa (The **r** changes the **n** to **ṇ**.)
   putrāṇām (The **r** changes the **n** to **ṇ**.)

6. In this chart, the sounds which could interfere are in bold. They are all the consonants in three rows except for **ya**:

ka	kha	ga	gha	ṅa	ha	
ca	**cha**	**ja**	**jha**	**ña**	ya	**śa**
ṭa	**ṭha**	**ḍa**	**ḍha**	**ṇa**	ra	ṣa
ta	**tha**	**da**	**dha**	na	**la**	**sa**
pa	pha	ba	bha	ma	va	

7. If another **n** immediately follows the **n**, they both become **ṇṇ**.

GRAMMAR: FEMININE NOUNS IN Ā

1. There are standard endings to nouns, and it will help to compare all future declensions with the standard endings. Some declensions follow these endings more closely than other declensions. The standard endings are the same for all genders, except the neuter nominative and neuter accusative, which are **m**, **ī**, and **i**.

	mas/fem	n	mas/fem	n	mas/fem	n
Nom.	**s**	**m**	**au**	**ī**	**as**	**i**
Acc.	**am**	**m**	**au**	**ī**	**as**	**i**
Inst.	**ā**		**bhyām**		**bhis**	
Dat.	**e**		**bhyām**		**bhyas**	
Abl.	**as**		**bhyām**		**bhyas**	
Gen.	**as**		**os**		**ām**	
Loc.	**i**		**os**		**su**	
	Singular		Dual		Plural	

These endings are generally applied to most stems using **sandhi** rules. For example, the masculine nominative plural standard ending is **as**. When **as** is added to **nara**, the word for "men" becomes **narās** (**narāḥ** with **sandhi**). These standard endings are listed by **Pāṇini** in a **sūtra** (4.1.2) that begins with **su** and ends with **p**. **Pāṇini** therefore calls the nominal endings **sup**.

2. On the following page is the declension for feminine nouns ending with **ā** in their stem form:

Stem: **senā** (feminine) army

	Singular	Dual	Plural
Nom.	सेना **senā**	सेने **sene**	सेनाः **senāḥ**
Acc.	सेनाम् **senām**	सेने **sene**	सेनाः **senāḥ**
Inst.	सेनया **senayā**	सेनाभ्याम् **senābhyām**	सेनाभिः **senābhiḥ**
Dat.	सेनायै **senāyai**	सेनाभ्याम् **senābhyām**	सेनाभ्यः **senābhyaḥ**
Abl.	सेनायाः **senāyāḥ**	सेनाभ्याम् **senābhyām**	सेनाभ्यः **senābhyaḥ**
Gen.	सेनायाः **senāyāḥ**	सेनयोः **senayoḥ**	सेनानाम् **senānām**
Loc.	सेनायाम् **senāyām**	सेनयोः **senayoḥ**	सेनासु **senāsu**
Voc.	सेने **sene**	सेने **sene**	सेनाः **senāḥ**

3. Feminine nouns must have feminine adjectives. Masculine and neuter adjectives normally are declined like **nara** and **phala**. If the noun is feminine, the adjective is declined like **ā** or **ī** stems. (The feminine stem ending in **ī** will be studied in Lesson 13.) The dictionary will indicate how the feminine adjective is formed. For example:

kupita mf(ā)n **bhīta** mf(ā)n
dhārmika mf(ī)n **sundara** mf(ī)n

If the dictionary entry is marked (mfn), the word is an adjective, and the feminine adjective is usually formed with **ā.**

THIRD PERSON PRONOUNS

4. While the first and second person pronoun have only one declension, the third person pronoun has three declensions—one for each gender:

Stem: **tad** (masculine) he

	Singular	Dual	Plural
Nom. (he, they)	सः **saḥ**	तौ **tau**	ते **te**
Acc. (him, them)	तम् **tam**	तौ **tau**	तान् **tān**
Inst. (with him, them)	तेन **tena**	ताभ्याम् **tābhyām**	तैः **taiḥ**
Dat. (for him, them)	तस्मै **tasmai**	ताभ्याम् **tābhyām**	तेभ्यः **tebhyaḥ**
Abl. (from him, them)	तस्मात् **tasmāt**	ताभ्याम् **tābhyām**	तेभ्यः **tebhyaḥ**
Gen. (his, their)	तस्य **tasya**	तयोः **tayoḥ**	तेषाम् **teṣām**
Loc. (on him, them)	तस्मिन् **tasmin**	तयोः **tayoḥ**	तेषु **teṣu**

5. With **sandhi**, **saḥ**, the masculine nominative singular, drops the final **ḥ** before all consonants and all vowels but **a**. It usually appears as **sa**. At the end of a line, it appears as **saḥ**, and before **a** it appears as **so** (and the **a** is dropped). For example:

स गच्छति		सोऽत्र	
sa gacchati	He goes.	**so 'tra**	He is here.

6. Here is the neuter third person pronoun:

Stem: **tad** (neuter) it

	Singular	Dual	Plural
Nom.	तत्	ते	तानि
(it)	**tat**	**te**	**tāni**
Acc.	तत्	ते	तानि
(it—object)	**tat**	**te**	**tāni**
Inst.	तेन	ताभ्याम्	तैः
(with it)	**tena**	**tābhyām**	**taiḥ**
Dat.	तस्मै	ताभ्याम्	तेभ्यः
(for it)	**tasmai**	**tābhyām**	**tebhyaḥ**
Abl.	तस्मात्	ताभ्याम्	तेभ्यः
(from it)	**tasmāt**	**tābhyām**	**tebhyaḥ**
Gen.	तस्य	तयोः	तेषाम्
(of it, its)	**tasya**	**tayoḥ**	**teṣām**
Loc.	तस्मिन्	तयोः	तेषु
(on it)	**tasmin**	**tayoḥ**	**teṣu**

7. Notice that the nominative and accusative are the only forms in which the neuter differs from the masculine.

8. Here is the feminine third person pronoun:

Stem: **tad** (feminine) she

	Singular	Dual	Plural
Nom. (she, they)	सा **sā**	ते **te**	ताः **tāḥ**
Acc. (her, them)	ताम् **tām**	ते **te**	ताः **tāḥ**
Inst. (with her, them)	तया **tayā**	ताभ्याम् **tābhyām**	ताभिः **tābhiḥ**
Dat. (for her, them)	तस्यै **tasyai**	ताभ्याम् **tābhyām**	ताभ्यः **tābhyaḥ**
Abl. (from her, them)	तस्याः **tasyāḥ**	ताभ्याम् **tābhyām**	ताभ्यः **tābhyaḥ**
Gen. (her, their)	तस्याः **tasyāḥ**	तयोः **tayoḥ**	तासाम् **tāsām**
Loc. (on her, them)	तस्याम् **tasyām**	तयोः **tayoḥ**	तासु **tāsu**

9. The third person pronoun can act as a pronoun or a demonstrative pronoun meaning "that." For example:

स गच्छति ।

sa gacchati

He goes. ("He" is a pronoun.)

स नरो गच्छति ।

sa naro gacchati

That man goes. ("That" is a demonstrative pronoun.)

The demonstrative pronoun is usually referred to in English as a demonstrative adjective. In Sanskrit, it is called a pronoun.

10. The demonstrative pronoun goes in front of the noun it is used with and corresponds to the noun in case, gender, and number. For example:

स बालो गच्छति ।

sa bālo gacchati

That boy goes.

बालस्तं ग्रामं गच्छति ।

bālas taṃ grāmaṃ gacchati

The boy goes to that village.

IVA

11. The word "**iva**" indicates "like" or "as if." For example:

नृप इव बालो वदति ।

nṛpa iva bālo vadati.

The boy speaks like a king.

VOCABULARY

SANSKRIT		ENGLISH
अविद्या	**avidyā** (fem.)	ignorance
इव	**iva** (ind.)	as if, like (used after verbs, nouns or adjectives)
कथा	**kathā** (fem.)	story
कन्या	**kanyā** (fem.)	girl
कुपिता	**kupitā** (fem. adj.)	angry
छाया	**chāyā** (fem.)	shadow
पुत्रिका	**putrikā** (fem.)	daughter
प्रजा	**prajā** (fem.)	child, subject (of a king)
बाला	**bālā** (fem.)	girl
भार्या	**bhāryā** (fem.)	wife
भीता	**bhītā** (fem. adj.)	afraid
माला	**mālā** (fem.)	garland
विद्या	**vidyā** (fem.)	knowledge
सीता	**sītā** (fem.)	Sītā (wife of Rāma)
सेना	**senā** (fem.)	army

EXERCISES

1. Write in **devanāgarī**, with correct internal and external **sandhi,** and translate. Use the vocabulary list and tables located in the back of the text.

a. **rāmena saha**

b. **śāstrāni**

c. **phale aśve staḥ**

d. **saḥ gacchati**

e. **saḥ bālaḥ āgacchati**

f. **bālaḥ mām āgacchati**

g. **sā bālā mām āgacchati**

h. **tām gacchati**

i. **saḥ bālaḥ gacchati**

j. **sā bālā gacchati**

k. **saḥ bālaḥ iva gacchāmi**

l. **aho rāma**

m. **tasmin vane saḥ vasati**

n. **sītāyāḥ mālā**

2. Take out the **sandhi** and translate the following:

a. सा सेना नृपं जयति ।

b. राम इव बालो धार्मिकोऽस्ति ।

c. तव प्रजा कथां पठति ।

d. गजस्य च्छायायां प्रजास्तिष्ठन्ति । (Notice that **ch** becomes **cch** after a short vowel. See p. 230 #5.)

e. नृपस्य पुत्रिका सीतास्ति ।

f. स आचार्यस्य भार्यां सेवते ।

g. नृपस्य पुत्रिका ।

h. विद्यया शिष्योऽमृतं लभते ।

i. सा बालेव सीता गृहं गच्छति ।

3. Translate the following into Sanskrit, including **sandhi**, and then write in **devanāgarī**:

   a. There is a girl, Sītā by name, in that village.

   b. The daughter of the virtuous king is very afraid.

   c. "He tells me again," that subject says.

   d. "Aha! I remember that story!" the girl says.

   e. With knowledge, you obtain immortality; with ignorance, you obtain suffering.

   f. Like those girls, Sītā reads books.

   g. "Where is our daughter?" the hero asks his wife.

h. The wife of Rāma is Sītā.

i. The hero obtains a garland and thus obtains a wife.

j. "Without Sītā, I am as if without the sun," Rāma says.

THE MONKEY AND THE CROCODILE

4. Translate the following story. The vocabulary is given afterward:

a. अस्ति गङ्गायां कुम्भीरः ।

b. वानरस्तस्य मित्रं गङ्गायास्तटे वसति ।

c. प्रतिदिनं वानरः पक्वानि फलानि निक्षिपति ।

d. कुम्भीरः फलानि खादति ।

e. वानरस्य हृदयं मिष्टमस्तीति कुम्भीरस्य भार्या वदति ।

f. भार्या हृदयं खादितुमिच्छति ।

g. अहो वानर मम गृहमागच्छेति कुम्भीरो वानरं वदति ।

h. एवमस्त्विति वानरो वदति ।

i. तस्य पृष्ठे कुम्भीरो वानरं वहति ।

j. गङ्गाया मध्ये कुम्भीरः सत्यं वदति ।

k. मम हृदयं वृक्षे भवतीति वानरो भाषते ।

l. पुनर्मां तत्र नयेति वानरो भाषते ।

m. कुम्भीरो वानरं गङ्गायास्तटं नयति ।

n. वानरो वृक्षमुच्छलति ।

o. वानरो वृक्षस्य बिले पश्यति ।

p. कश्चिन्मम हृदयं चोरयति स्मेति वानरो वदति ।

q. एवं कुम्भीरो वानरश्च मित्रे तिष्ठतः ।

VOCABULARY

a. **gaṅgā** (fem., ā declension) Ganges
kumbhīraḥ (mas.) crocodile

b. **mitram** (n.) friend
vānaraḥ (mas.) monkey. Appears first as an appositional (his friend, a monkey)
taṭaḥ (mas.) bank (of the river)

c. **pratidinam** (ind.) everyday
pakva mf(ā)n (adj.) ripe
nikṣipati (3rd per. sing.) he throws down

d. **khādati** (3rd per. sing.) he eats

e. **hṛdayam** (n.) heart
miṣṭa mf(ā)n (adj.) sweet
bhāryā (fem., **ā** declension) wife

f. **khāditum** (infinitive—treated like an accusative) to eat
icchati (3rd per. sing.) he wants (**khāditum icchati** = he wants to eat)

g. **āgaccha** (2nd per. sing. imperative)

h. **evam astu** (ind.) O.K., so let it be

i. **pṛṣṭham** (n.) back
vahati (3rd per. sing.) he carries

j. **madhyam** (n.) middle

k. **vṛkṣaḥ** (mas.) tree

l. **nayati** (3rd per. sing.) he takes, he carries. Second person imperative is **naya** (combined with **iti** is **nayeti**).

n. **ucchalati** (3rd per. sing.) he jumps up

o. **bilam** (n.) hole

p. **kaḥ** (mas. pronoun) who
cit (ind.) (makes **kaḥ** indefinite)
kaścit someone
corayati (3rd per. sing.) he steals
sma (ind.) makes verb before it in past tense

q. **tiṣṭhati** (3rd per. sing.) he remains

12

LESSON TWELVE

Alphabet: Numerals; cardinal and ordinal numbers

Grammar: Nouns in **i** and the gerund

Vocabulary: Nouns in **i**

ALPHABET: NUMBERS

1. Here are the numerals (**saṃkhyā**) and cardinal numbers from one to ten. Alternate forms for some numerals are given in parentheses.

NUMERALS		CARDINAL NUMBERS		
Arabic	**devanāgarī**	English	Sanskrit	
1.	१	one	एक	**eka**
2.	२	two	द्वि	**dvi**
3.	३	three	त्रि	**tri**
4.	४	four	चतुर्	**catur**
5.	५ (५)	five	पञ्च	**pañca**
6.	६	six	षष्	**ṣaṣ**
7.	७	seven	सप्त	**sapta**
8.	८ (८)	eight	अष्ट	**aṣṭa**
9.	९ (९)	nine	नव	**nava**
10.	१०	ten	दश	**daśa**

2. The **devanāgarī** numerals combine just like Arabic numerals (since Arabic numerals were formed from Sanskrit). For example:

11	११
12	१२
13	१३
20	२०

eka daśa

3. For now, we will not use the cardinal numbers (**eka, dvi, etc.**) as part of the sentences, since their declensions are complex. At the end of each sentence in the exercises, we will use the numerals (१, २, ३, etc.).

4. Here are the ordinal numbers:

First	**prathama**	Sixth	**ṣaṣṭha**
Second	**dvitīya**	Seventh	**saptama**
Third	**tṛtīya**	Eighth	**aṣṭama**
Fourth	**caturtha** (or **turīya**)	Ninth	**navama**
Fifth	**pañcama**	Tenth	**daśama**

5. The ordinal numbers will be used in the exercises, because their declensions are easier than the cardinal numbers. The ordinal numbers are used like adjectives, going before the noun they modify and agreeing with it in gender and case. The number will be singular.

6. The ordinal numbers follow the short **a** declension for the masculine and neuter. Here are the feminine stems. (The feminine **ī** will be learned in Lesson 13.)

First	**prathamā**	Sixth	**ṣaṣṭhī**
Second	**dvitīyā**	Seventh	**saptamī**
Third	**tṛtīyā**	Eighth	**aṣṭamī**
Fourth	**caturthī** (or **turīyā**)	Ninth	**navamī**
Fifth	**pañcamī**	Tenth	**daśamī**

Compare the **devanāgarī** numerals with other scripts:

COMPARATIVE TABLE OF NUMERALS

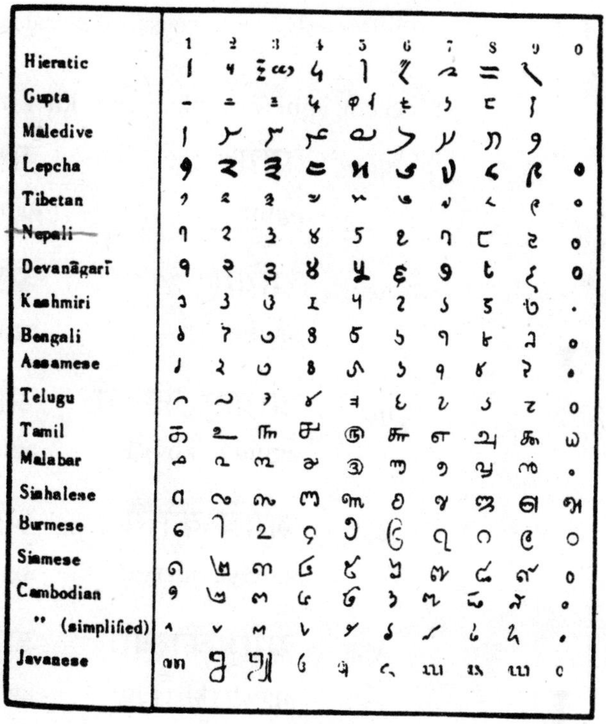

7. Compare the cardinal numbers with numbers from several Romance languages:

English	Sanskrit	Italian	French	Spanish
one	**eka**	uno	un	uno
two	**dvi**	due	deux	dos
three	**tri**	tre	trois	tres
four	**catur**	quattro	quatre	cuatro
five	**pañca**	cinque	cinq	cinco
six	**ṣaṣ**	sei	six	seis
seven	**sapta**	sette	sept	siete
eight	**aṣṭa**	otto	huit	ocho
nine	**nava**	nove	neuf	nueve
ten	**daśa**	dieci	dix	diez

GRAMMAR: NOUNS IN I

1. Here are the masculine and feminine declensions for **i** nouns. They differ only in the accusative plural and the instrumental singular.

Stem: **agni** (masculine) fire; **kīrti** (feminine) glory

	Singular	Dual	Plural
Nom.	अग्निः **agniḥ**	अग्नी **agnī**	अग्नयः **agnayaḥ**
Acc.	अग्निम् **agnim**	अग्नी **agnī**	अग्नीन् कीर्तीः **agnīn / kīrtīḥ**
Inst.	अग्निना कीर्त्या **agninā / kīrtyā**	अग्निभ्याम् **agnibhyām**	अग्निभिः **agnibhiḥ**
Dat.	अग्नये कीर्त्यै **agnaye (kīrtyai)**	अग्निभ्याम् **agnibhyām**	अग्निभ्यः **agnibhyaḥ**
Abl.	अग्नेः कीर्त्याः **agneḥ (kīrtyāḥ)**	अग्निभ्याम् **agnibhyām**	अग्निभ्यः **agnibhyaḥ**
Gen.	अग्नेः कीर्त्याः **agneḥ (kīrtyāḥ)**	अग्न्योः **agnyoḥ**	अग्नीनाम् **agnīnām**
Loc.	अग्नौ कीर्त्याम् **agnau (kīrtyām)**	अग्न्योः **agnyoḥ**	अग्निषु **agniṣu**
Voc.	अग्ने **agne**	अग्नी **agnī**	अग्नयः **agnayaḥ**

2. The singular dative, ablative, genitive, and locative have an optional feminine form. For example, the feminine dative singular is **kīrtaye** or **kīrtyai**. The feminine instrumental singular is **kīrtyā** only.

THE GERUND

3. Now we will study the gerund, which is a participle. A participle is formed from a verb, but does not take verb endings (**tiṅ**). The gerund (**ktvānta**) indicates prior action. The sentence, "Rāma speaks and goes," could be formed with a gerund. It would be: "Having spoken, Rāma goes." "Having spoken" is the gerund.

   uditvā rāmo gacchati
   <u>Having spoken</u>, Rāma goes.
   (gerund)

4. Because the gerund continues the action, it is sometimes called a continuative or conjunctive participle.

5. The gerund is used with only one subject.

6. The gerund has the meaning of doing something first, whether the main verb is past, present, or future. A series of gerunds may be used, but they must always be followed by a main verb. Each gerund follows in time the one before it, and the main verb comes last in time, as well as position in the sentence. For example:

   gajaṃ dṛṣṭvā jalaṃ labdhvā rāmo gacchati
   Having seen the elephant, having obtained water, Rāma goes.

7. There are several alternative translations:

   Seeing the elephant, obtaining water, Rāma goes.
   After seeing the elephant and after obtaining water, Rāma goes.
   After having seen the elephant and after having obtained water, Rāma goes.

8. Everything that goes with the gerund, such as the accusative, is usually placed immediately before it. (See the example in #6.)

9. The gerund is easy to recognize because it is not declined. It is sometimes called the absolutive, because it stays in the same form. It is usually formed from the root by adding **-tvā** to the end (called **ktvā** by Pāṇini). If there is a prefix, **-ya** is added at the end **(lyap)**.

10. Here are the forms for the gerund (√**as** has no gerund):

Root	3rd Per. Sing.	Gerund	
ā + √gam	**āgacchati**	**āgamya**	having come
		(also **āgatya**)	
√gam	**gacchati**	**gatvā**	having gone
√cint	**cintayati -te**	**cintayitvā**	having thought
√ji	**jayati**	**jitvā**	having conquered
√dṛś (paś)	**paśyati**	**dṛṣṭvā**	having seen
√paṭh	**paṭhati**	**paṭhitvā**	having read
√prach	**pṛcchati**	**pṛṣṭvā**	having asked
√bhāṣ	**bhāṣate**	**bhāṣitvā**	having said
√bhū	**bhavati**	**bhūtvā**	having been
√man	**manyate**	**matvā**	having thought
√labh	**labhate**	**labdhvā**	having obtained
√vad	**vadati**	**uditvā**	having said
√vas	**vasati**	**uṣitvā**	having lived
√sev	**sevate**	**sevitvā**	having served
√sthā	**tiṣṭhati**	**sthitvā**	having stood
√smṛ	**smarati**	**smṛtvā**	having remembered

VOCABULARY

SANSKRIT		ENGLISH
अग्निः	**agniḥ** (mas.)	fire
अतिथिः	**atithiḥ** (mas.)	guest
ऋषिः	**ṛṣiḥ** (mas.)	seer, sage
कविः	**kaviḥ** (mas.)	poet
कीर्तिः	**kīrtiḥ** (fem.)	glory, fame
भूमिः	**bhūmiḥ** (fem.)	earth
शान्तिः	**śāntiḥ** (fem.)	peace
सिद्धः	**siddhaḥ** (mas.)	one who attains perfection
सिद्धा	**siddhā** (fem.)	one who attains perfection
सिद्धिः	**siddhiḥ** (fem.)	perfection, attainment, proof

EXERCISES

1. Translate the following sentences. Use the vocabulary and tables listed at the end of the text.

a. अग्निं दृष्ट्वा गृहादश्वो गच्छति ।१।

b. शिष्यो ग्रामे वसति ।२।

c. ऋषयः शास्त्राणां सूक्तानि पश्यन्ति ।३।

d. नृपो दशममतिथिं सेवते ।४।

e. ग्रामं जित्वा वीरः कीर्तिं लभते ।५।

f. सिद्धो ग्रामे वसति ।६।

g. अहो राम कुत्र गच्छसीति द्वितीयो वीरः पृच्छति ।७।

h. पुस्तकं पठित्वा कविस्तच्चिन्तयति ।८।

i. सत्येन सह शान्तिरागच्छति ।९।

j. भूमौ वसाम इति प्रजा वदन्ति ।१०।

2. Write the following sentences in Sanskrit:

   a. After conquering the army, the hero obtains fame on earth.

   b. Like Sītā and Rāma, the student goes to the forest.

   c. After serving her third guest, Sītā speaks to Rāma.

   d. In the story, Rāma obtains fame.

   e. The hero does not conquer ignorance.

   f. The king, Rāma by name, is very virtuous.

   g. "How do you obtain perfection?" the second student asks.

   h. Having lived in the forest with his wife, the king, Rāma by name, goes to the village.

   i. Having obtained peace, perfection, and glory, the seer goes to the beautiful forest.

   j. Thus having seen his wife on the elephant, the hero goes to her.

13 LESSON THIRTEEN

Alphabet:	The **sandhi** rules for combining vowels
Grammar:	Feminine nouns in ī Relative-correlative clauses
Vocabulary:	Nouns in ī Relative and correlative adverbs

ALPHABET: VOWEL SANDHI

1. The following chart shows the changes that vowels often undergo. These changes are called **guṇa** and **vṛddhi** changes:

	guṇa	**vṛddhi**	Corresponding Semi-vowel
a	**a**	**ā**	
ā	**ā**	**ā**	
i, ī	**e**	**ai**	**y**
u, ū	**o**	**au**	**v**
ṛ	**ar**	**ār**	**r**
ḷ	**al**	**āl**	**l**

2. This important chart will help you understand how vowels combine in both internal and external **sandhi**. Later on, it will help you understand how roots are strengthened (by **guṇa** or **vṛddhi**) to form verbs and nominals. For example:

Root	**guṇa**	**vṛddhi**
√vid	**veda**	**vaidya**
√div	**deva**	**daivika**
√yuj	**yoga**	**yaugika**
√dhṛ	**dharma**	**dhārmika**

3. Memorize the above chart and then memorize the **sandhi** rules for combining vowels that follow:

4. SIMILAR VOWELS

ā̆ + ā̆ = ā   **राम + अश्वः = रामाश्वः**

rāma + aśvaḥ = rāmāśvaḥ

ī̆ + ī̆ = ī   गच्छति + इति = गच्छतीति
gacchati + iti = gacchatīti

ū̆ + ū̆ = ū   गुरु + उप = गुरूप
guru + upa = gurūpa

ṛ + ṛ = ṝ   पितृ + ऋषि = पितॄषि
pitṛ + ṛṣi = pitṝṣi

These rules apply first. Then the following rules apply.

5. DISSIMILAR VOWELS

ī̆ + vowel = yvowel ("vowel" means any short or long vowel)

गच्छति + अश्वम् =
गच्छत्यश्वम्
gacchati + aśvam =
gacchaty aśvam

ū̆ + vowel = vvowel   गुरु + अश्वम् = गुर्वश्वम्
guru + aśvam = gurv aśvam

ṛ + vowel = rvowel   पितृ + अत्र = पित्रत्र
pitṛ + atra = pitr atra

6. **e + a = e '**

ग्रामे + अत्र = ग्रामेऽत्र
grāme + atra = grāme 'tra

e + vowel = **a** vowel

ग्रामे + इति = ग्राम इति
grāme + iti = grāma iti

7. **ai** + vowel = **ā** vowel

तस्मै + अत्र = तस्मा अत्र
tasmai + atra = tasmā atra

An **o** seldom occurs in a final position before **sandhi** is applied.

au + vowel = **āv**vowel

गजौ + इति = गजाविति
gajau + iti = gajāv iti

8. FINAL "a" FOLLOWED BY DISSIMILAR VOWELS

ă + ĭ = e

तत्र + इति = तत्रेति
tatra + iti = tatreti

ă + ŭ = o

कठ + उपनिषद् = कठोपनिषद्
kaṭha + upaniṣad = kaṭhopaniṣad

ă + ṛ = ar

सत्य + ऋतम् = सत्यर्तम्
satya + ṛtam = satya rtam

ă̄ + e, ai = ai तत्र + एव = तत्रैव
tatra + eva = tatraiva

ă̄ + o, au = au अत्र + ओकः = अत्रौकः
atra + okaḥ = atraukaḥ

9. Some vowels (**pragṛhya**) are not subject to **sandhi**. They are:

   a. the letters **ī**, **ū**, and **e**, when they serve as dual endings. For example, **bāle āgacchataḥ** (The two girls come.) needs no **sandhi**.

   b. the final vowel of an interjection (usually a vocative). For example, **aho aśva** (O horse!) needs no **sandhi**.

GRAMMAR: NOUNS IN Ī

1. Here is the declension for feminine nouns ending with ī in their stem form:

Stem: **nadī** (feminine) river

	Singular	Dual	Plural
Nom.	नदी **nadī**	नद्यौ **nadyau**	नद्यः **nadyaḥ**
Acc.	नदीम् **nadīm**	नद्यौ **nadyau**	नदीः **nadīḥ**
Inst.	नद्या **nadyā**	नदीभ्याम् **nadībhyām**	नदीभिः **nadībhiḥ**
Dat.	नद्यै **nadyai**	नदीभ्याम् **nadībhyām**	नदीभ्यः **nadībhyaḥ**
Abl.	नद्याः **nadyāḥ**	नदीभ्याम् **nadībhyām**	नदीभ्यः **nadībhyaḥ**
Gen.	नद्याः **nadyāḥ**	नद्योः **nadyoḥ**	नदीनाम् **nadīnām**
Loc.	नद्याम् **nadyām**	नद्योः **nadyoḥ**	नदीषु **nadīṣu**
Voc.	नदि **nadi**	नद्यौ **nadyau**	नद्यः **nadyaḥ**

RELATIVE-CORRELATIVE CLAUSES

2. Now we will learn about relative and correlative clauses. In English, the sentence "I see where the king lives," contains two separate clauses: "I see" and "where the king lives." The sentence contains a subordinate, or relative clause ("where the king lives"), and an independent or correlative clause ("I see"). For example:

I see where the king lives.

correlative relative

3. In Sanskrit, the relative clause usually goes first and the correlative goes second. The relative clause is introduced by a relative adverb (indeclinable) and the correlative clause by a correlative adverb.

Where the king lives, there I see.

relative clause correlative clause

Where the king lives, there I see.

relative adverb correlative adverb

yatra nṛpo vasati tatra ahaṃ paśyāmi

relative clause correlative clause

yatra nṛpo vasati tatra ahaṃ paśyāmi

relative adverb correlative adverb

4. Here are the relative adverbs and their correlative partners (none are declined):

yataḥ	since, when	**tataḥ**	therefore
yatra	where	**tatra**	there
yathā	since	**tathā**	so, therefore
yadā	when	**tadā**	then
yadi	if	**tadā**	then

5. Here are some examples:

When he goes, then I remember.
yadā gacchati tadā smarāmi

I go if you go. (becomes)
If you go, then I go.
yadi gacchasi tadā gacchāmi

You obtain fruit where the forest is. (becomes)
Where the forest is, there you obtain fruit.
yatra vanam asti tatra phalāni labhase

6. There is also a relative-correlative pronoun, **yad** and **tad** ("who" and "he"). This construction would be used to translate this sentence:

The man who goes is the king.
|________|
relative clause

7. In Sanskrit, the relative clause contains the relative pronoun **yad,** and the correlative clause contains the correlative pronoun **tad.** Sometimes the correlative pronoun may be omitted. The pronoun **yad** follows the declension of **tad** (See p.177.):

who man goes, he is the king

|_____________| |_____________|

relative clause correlative clause

yo naro gacchati sa nṛpo 'sti

|_______________| |_____________|

relative clause correlative clause

8. Both "who" (**yo**) and "he" (**sa**) refer back to the man, who is called the antecedent. In English, the antecedent goes directly before the relative pronoun (who). In Sanskrit, the antecedent usually follows the relative pronoun (who) or the correlative pronoun (he):

who man goes, he is the king

yo naro gacchati sa nṛpo 'sti

|____|

antecedent

or

who goes, that man is the king

yo gacchati sa naro nṛpo 'sti

|____|

antecedent

9. The relative and correlative pronouns take the gender and number of the antecedent. The case of the antecedent depends upon its role in each clause. Study the following examples:

I see the man who is going. (becomes)
which man is going, him I see
yo naro gacchati taṃ paśyāmi

|____|
antecedent

|______________| |_____________|
relative clause correlative clause

or

who is going, that man I see
yo gacchati taṃ naraṃ paśyāmi

|____|
antecedent

|__________| |____________________|
relative clause correlative clause

The king sees the elephant on which I stand. (becomes)
on which elephant I stand, him the king sees
yasmin gaje tiṣṭhāmi taṃ nṛpaḥ paśyati

|____|
antecedent

|____________________| |____________________|
relative clause correlative clause

or

on which I stand, that elephant the king sees

yasmiṃs tiṣṭhāmi taṃ gajaṃ nṛpaḥ paśyati

antecedent

relative clause correlative clause

10. Notice that the relative pronoun (**yad**) and the correlative pronoun (**tad**) agree with each other in gender and number, but may differ in case. Like the antecedent, the relative word and the correlative word take a case (**vibhakti**) that is determined by their role in the clause. Study the following examples:

I see the man with whom Rāma goes.
(becomes)
with which man Rāma goes, him I see

येन नरेण सह रामो गच्छति तमहं पश्यामि ।

yena nareṇa saha rāmo gacchati tam ahaṃ paśyāmi

or

with whom Rāma goes, that man I see

येन रामो गच्छति तं नरमहं पश्यामि ।

yena rāmo gacchati taṃ naram ahaṃ paśyāmi

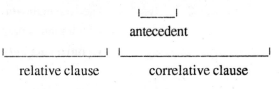

Rāma lives in the village from which I am coming.
(becomes)
from which village I am coming, in it Rāma lives

यस्माद्ग्रामादागच्छामि तस्मिन्रामो वसति ।
yasmād grāmād āgacchāmi tasmin rāmo vasati

or
from which I am coming in that village Rāma lives

यस्मादागच्छामि तस्मिन्ग्रामे रामो वसति ।
yasmād āgacchāmi tasmin grāme rāmo vasati

11. The pronoun **yad** follows the same declension as **tad** (mas., n., fem.), except that the masculine nominative singular follows normal **sandhi** rules, and therefore appears as **yaḥ**, **yo**, etc. Observe, for example, the masculine:

Stem: **yad** (masculine) who, what, which

Nom. (who)	यः	यौ	ये
Acc. (whom)	यम्	यौ	यान्
Inst. (with whom)	येन	याभ्याम्	यैः
Dat. (for whom)	यस्मै	याभ्याम्	येभ्यः
Abl. (from whom)	यस्मात्	याभ्याम्	येभ्यः
Gen. (whose)	यस्य	ययोः	येषम्
Loc. (on whom)	यस्मिन्	ययोः	येषु

VOCABULARY

SANSKRIT		ENGLISH
धार्मिकी	**dhārmikī** (fem. adj.)	virtuous
नदी	**nadī** (fem.)	river
पत्नी	**patnī** (fem.)	wife
मित्रम्	**mitram** (n.)	friend
यद्	**yad** (pro.)	who, what, which
वापी	**vāpī** (fem.)	pond
सुन्दरी	**sundarī** (fem. adj.)	beautiful

SANSKRIT		ENGLISH	SANSKRIT		ENGLISH
(relative adverbs)			(correlative adverbs)		
यतः	**yataḥ**	since, when	ततः	**tataḥ**	therefore
यत्र	**yatra**	where	तत्र	**tatra**	there
यथा	**yathā**	since, as	तथा	**tathā**	so, therefore
यदा	**yadā**	when	तदा	**tadā**	then
यदि	**yadi**	if	तदा	**tadā**	then

EXERCISES

1. Translate the following:

a. यत्र शान्तिस्तत्र सिद्धिः ।१।

b. या मम पत्न्याः पुत्रिकास्ति सा बालात्र वसति ।२।

c. सीता सुन्दरी नृपस्य पुत्रिकास्तीति रामो वदति ।३।

d. यथाश्वा अत्र नागच्छन्ति तथा नरा बालाश्च तत्र गच्छन्ति ।४।

e. नदीं गत्वा मित्रे पुस्तकानि पठतः ।५।

f. यदा सेना नृपं सेवते तदा धार्मिको नृपो जयति ।६।

g. यदि नरः सिद्धिं लभते तदा स ऋषिर्भवते ।७।

h. यस्तस्यातिथिर्भवति तस्मै बालाय कविः कथां पठति ।८।

i. नरो मित्रेण सह सुन्दरीं नदीं गच्छति ।९।

j. यस्मादहमागच्छामि तं ग्रामं वीरः स्मरति ।१०।

2. Translate the following into Sanskrit:

   a. The boy obtains water from the river.

   b. The wife sees the fruit which is in the pond.

   c. Having obtained a garland, our guest goes to the village.

   d. He lives like a king when his wife serves him.

   e. Sītā, who is the wife of Rāma, obtains fame on earth.

   f. The virtuous king sees the boy who is coming.

   g. The student, having thought, asks the poet about the river.

   h. That beautiful wife lives without suffering.

   i. Ignorance is like a shadow for the man who sees.

   j. When the daughter of the king comes, then the subjects stand.

14

LESSON FOURTEEN

Alphabet:	The **sandhi** rules for final ḥ
Grammar:	Verb prefixes and the imperfect active
Vocabulary:	More verbs

j. The hero remembers that village from which [village] I came.

i. The man goes with his friends to the beautiful river

h. The poet narrates the story to the boy

ALPHABET: SANDHI RULES FOR FINAL ḥ

Now we will memorize the **sandhi** rules for words ending in **ḥ**. These rules were presented in charts in Lesson 9. Both charts in Lesson 9 present the same rules, but it will be easier to follow the structure of the second chart on page 111. While the first word ends in **ḥ**, the second word may begin with any letter of the alphabet. Notice that the chart breaks the alphabet into three parts. The chart is arranged according to which section of the alphabet the second word begins. Here is one way of dividing the alphabet in order to learn these rules:

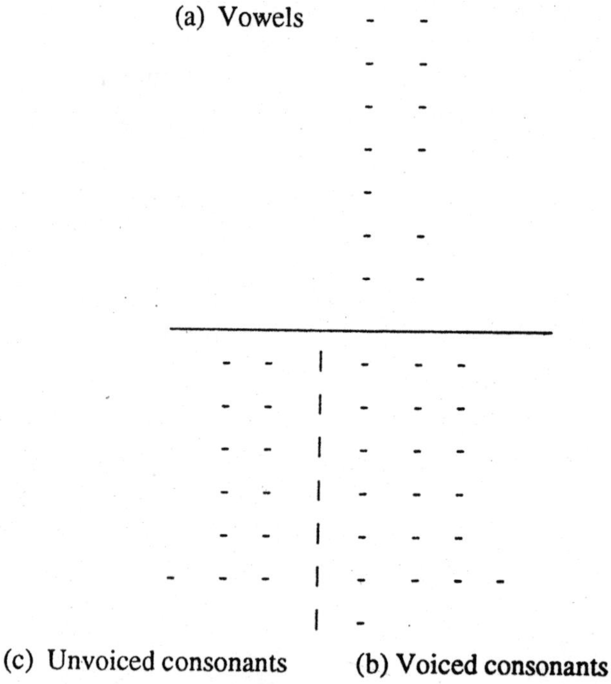

(a) If the second word begins in a vowel, there are four rules:

Second word begins in any of the following:

a	**ā**		
i	**ī**		
u	**ū**		
ṛ	**ṝ**		
ḷ			
e	**ai**	**o**	**au**

(1) If the first word ends in **aḥ** and the second begins in **a**, the **aḥ** changes to **o**, and **a** is deleted (marked by an apostrophe in roman script or **avagraha** in **devanāgarī**). For example:

aḥ + a = o ’

रामः + अत्र = रामोऽत्र
rāmaḥ + atra = rāmo ’tra

(2) If the first word ends in **aḥ** and the second word begins in any vowel (except **a**), **aḥ** changes to **a**:

aḥ + vowel = **a** vowel

रामः + आगच्छति = राम आगच्छति
rāmaḥ + āgacchati = rāma āgacchati

(3) If the first word ends in **āḥ** and the second word begins in any vowel, **āḥ** changes to **ā**:

āḥ + vowel = **ā** + vowel

नराः + इति = नरा इति

narāḥ + iti = narā iti

(4) If the first word ends in any other vowel before the final **ḥ**, and the second word begins in a vowel, then the **ḥ** changes to **r**. For example:

oḥ + vowel = **or**vowel

नद्योः + अत्र = नद्योरत्र

nadyoḥ + atra = nadyor atra

(b) If the second word begins in a voiced consonant, there are three rules:

Second word begins in :

ga	**gha**	**ṅa**		
ja	**jha**	**ña**		
ḍa	**ḍha**	**ṇa**		
da	**dha**	**na**		
ba	**bha**	**ma**		
ya	**ra**	**la**	**va**	**ha**

(1) If the first word ends in **aḥ**, it becomes **o**:

aḥ + voiced consonant = **o** voiced consonant

रामः + गच्छति = रामो गच्छति

rāmaḥ + gacchati = rāmo gacchati

(2) If the first word ends in **āḥ**, it becomes **ā**:

āḥ + voiced consonant = **ā** voiced consonant

नराः + गच्छन्ति = नरा गच्छन्ति

narāḥ + gacchanti = narā gacchanti

(3) If the first word ends in any other vowel before the final **ḥ**, the **ḥ** becomes **r** (unless the second word begins with an **r**). For example:

oḥ + voiced consonant = **or**voiced consonant

नरयोः + गच्छति = नरयोर्गच्छति

narayoḥ + gacchati = narayor gacchati

A double **r** does not occur. If the second word begins in **r**, the first **r** is dropped and the preceding vowel made long, if it is short.

Note that the last two rules (2 and 3) are the similar to the rules (3 and 4) for second words beginning in a vowel.

(c) For the third group, the second word begins in an **unvoiced** consonant. For this group, the rules are the same when the first word ends in **aḥ**, **āḥ**, or any other vowel before the **ḥ**. There are four rules:

Second word begins in:

ka	**kha**		
ca	**cha**		
ṭa	**ṭha**		
ta	**tha**		
pa	**pha**		
śa	**ṣa**	**sa**	end of line

(1) If the second word begins in **ca** or **cha**, the **ḥ** (with any vowel preceding it) changes to **ś**. For example:

aḥ + ca = aśca

रामः + च = रामश्च
rāmaḥ + ca = rāmaś ca

(2) If the second word begins in **ṭa** or **ṭha**, the **ḥ** changes to **ṣ**:

aḥ + ṭ = aṣṭ

रामः + टीका = रामष्टीका
rāmaḥ + ṭīkā = rāmaṣ ṭīkā

(3) If the second word begins in **ta** or **tha**, the **ḥ** becomes **s**:

aḥ + ta = asta

रामः + तत्र = रामस्तत्र

rāmaḥ + tatra = rāmas tatra

The above three rules might best be learned visually, using the **devanāgarī** script. In each case the **ḥ** becomes the sibilant that corresponds with the following letter, whether palatal (**ca, cha**), retroflex (**ṭa, ṭha**), or dental (**ta, tha**):

श्च	श्छ	ष्ट	ष्ठ	स्त	स्थ
śca	**ścha**	**ṣṭa**	**ṣṭha**	**sta**	**stha**

(4) All other unvoiced consonants (**ka, kha, pa, pha, śa, ṣa,** and **sa**) cause the **ḥ** to stay **ḥ**. The end of the line also causes the **ḥ** to stay **ḥ**. For example:

aḥ + k = aḥ k

रामः + कुत्र = रामः कुत्र

rāmaḥ + kutra = rāmaḥ kutra

GRAMMAR: VERB PREFIXES

1. Verb prefixes (**upasarga**) are placed before verbs to modify the basic meaning of the verb. They are used much like verb prefixes in English, such as "receive" and "perceive." We have already learned one prefix, **ā**, which changes "he goes" (**gacchati**) to "he comes" (**āgacchati**).

2. Here are two additional prefixes:

upa	towards, near
upagacchati	he goes toward, he approaches
prati	back to, against
pratigacchati	he goes back to, he returns.

THE IMPERFECT

3. The imperfect (**laṅ**) indicates past action. It is traditionally described as action done "not of today," (**anadyatana**), or in the past. It is formed by putting an augment (**āgama**), **a**, before the present stem. The **a** is called "maker of the past tense" (**bhūta-karaṇa**). The imperfect uses slightly different endings, called secondary endings, or the imperfect endings. For example:

a +	**gaccha**	**+ t**	becomes	**agacchat**	he went
a +	**vada**	**+ t**	becomes	**avadat**	he spoke
augment	stem	ending		imperfect	

IMPERFECT ACTIVE VERBS

4. Here is the formation for the imperfect:

	Singular	Dual	Plural
3rd	अगच्छत् **agacchat**	अगच्छताम् **agacchatām**	अगच्छन् **agacchan**
2nd	अगच्छः **agacchaḥ**	अगच्छतम् **agacchatam**	अगच्छत **agacchata**
1st	अगच्छम् **agaccham**	अगच्छाव **agacchāva**	अगच्छाम **agacchāma**

Note that the imperfect active endings are listed on p. 317.

5. Here are the endings for the present indicative that we have already learned. Notice that the imperfect has similar endings, but shorter:

	Singular	Dual	Plural
3rd	गच्छति **gacchati**	गच्छतः **gacchataḥ**	गच्छन्ति **gacchanti**
2nd	गच्छसि **gacchasi**	गच्छथः **gacchathaḥ**	गच्छथ **gacchatha**
1st	गच्छामि **gacchāmi**	गच्छावः **gacchāvaḥ**	गच्छामः **gacchāmaḥ**

6. The imperfect puts the augment, **a**, after the prefix but before the stem. The **sandhi** rules apply here. Study these examples:

प्रति + अ + गच्छ + त् = प्रत्यगच्छत्

prati + a + gaccha + t = pratyagacchat
he returned

prefix augment stem ending imperfect

उप + अ + गच्छ + त् = उपागच्छत्

upa + a + gaccha + t = upāgacchat
he approached

आ + अ + गच्छ - अ + अम् = आगच्छम्

ā + a + gaccha - a + am = āgaccham
I came

7. Often a prefix may affect whether a verb takes active or middle endings. The dictionary will indicate which endings should be used.

VOCABULARY

SANSKRIT		ENGLISH
आ + नी ā + √**nī** (active)*	आनयति **ānayati**	he brings
उप + गम् **upa** + √**gam** (active)	उपगच्छति **upagacchati**	he goes toward, approaches
गुप् √**gup** (active)	गोपायति **gopāyati**	he protects
नी √**nī** (**ubhayapada**)*	नयति **nayati -te**	he leads
पा √**pā** (active)	पिबति **pibati**	he drinks
प्रति + गम् **prati** + √**gam** (active)	प्रतिगच्छति **pratigacchati**	he goes back, returns
बुध् √**budh** (**ubhayapada**)	बोधति **bodhati -te**	he knows
हस् √**has** (active)	हसति **hasati**	he laughs

The gerund forms for each of these verbs is listed in the back of the text (pages 312-314). Remember that if a verb has a prefix, it forms a gerund with **-ya** rather than **-tvā**.

*Note that √**nī** and √**budh** are **ubhayapada**, but **ā** + √**nī** is active.

EXERCISES

1. Memorize the **sandhi** rules that take place when the first word ends in **ḥ**.

2. Memorize the endings for the imperfect active.

3. Translate the following sentences into English:

a. यदा शिष्यो जलमानयति तदाचार्यस्तत्पिबति ।१।

b. बालो वापीं गजाननयत् ।२।

c. यो नरो ग्राममुपगच्छति तं कविर्वदति ।३।

d. वीरः कुपितान्नृपाद्ग्रामं गोपायतीति रामोऽवदत् ।४।

e. वाप्यां गजं दृष्ट्वर्षिरहसदहसच्च ।५।

f. सुन्दरीं तव पत्नीं बोधामीति कन्या वीरमवदत् ।६।

in what house wife
patnyava

how settler

g. यस्मिन्गृहे पत्न्यवसत्तत्सा प्रत्यगच्छत् ।७।

yasmin ho patnyavashtatava pratyagacchāt
graho *wife* *Returned*

h. ऋषिः शान्तिं सत्यं सिद्धिममृतं सुखं च बोधति ।८।

rsih shandin satyam siddhimmat mrtam ca bodhati
sabjam

i. वीरः सेनाया ग्राममगोपायत् ।९।

virah senaya gramamgopayat
Gen

j. सुन्दरं नृपं दृष्ट्वा बालोऽहसत् ।१०।

sundra nrpam dristra balo' hasat

4. Translate the following into Sanskrit:

patat
kavih pustakam ~~tea~~ jalā apibat.iva

a. The poet read the book as if he were drinking water.

katham gramam agopayam iti viro prcchat
senaya

b. The hero asked, "How do I protect the village from the army?"

c. How did sages live without fire?

Katham rsayah agneh vina avasan ।

d. If the horses go back to the river, then the boy leads them to the forest. (Use double accusative.)

yadi asvāh nadim pratigacchanti, tadi balo tān vanam nayati.

e. When a man does not know suffering, then he approaches perfection.

f. The king, named Rāma, brought his wife, Sītā, a garland.

g. By means of knowledge, a man conquers ignorance.

h. The child drank the water which came from the river.

balo yat jalam apibat tat nadyat pratyagacchat.

i. Having seen the river, the girl returned to her house.

Nadim drstvā, bālā grham tasya pratyāgacchat

j. The boy led the horses from the forest to the river. (double accusative)

15

LESSON FIFTEEN

Alphabet: The **sandhi** rules for final **m**

Grammar: More verb prefixes and the imperfect middle

Vocabulary: More verbs

ALPHABET: SANDHI RULES FOR FINAL M

1. If the first word ends in **m**, there are only two rules:

   (a) If the next word begins in a consonant, the **m** becomes **ṃ** and is pronounced (and could be written) as the nasal corresponding to the first letter of the next word. For example:

   पुत्रम् + गच्छामि = पुत्रं गच्छामि

   putram + gacchāmi = putraṃ gacchāmi

   (b) If the next word begins in a vowel or the **m** is at the end of a line, the **m** remains the same. The **m** remains the same because the mouth is not preparing to close at a specific point of contact as it would if the next word began with a consonant. For example:

   पुत्रम् + आगच्छामि = पुत्रमागच्छामि

   putram + āgacchāmi = putram āgacchāmi

वाद् vad - -ism
apavad - exception

GRAMMAR: VERB PREFIXES

1. Here are two more verb prefixes. Some prefixes hardly change the meaning of the original stem, while others change the meaning:

ud	up, up out
uttiṣṭhati	he stands up
(The **d** changes to **t** because of **sandhi**.)	
udbhavati	he is born
ava	down, away, off
avagacchati	he goes down, understands

2. Here is a list of the major prefixes (given in **Pāṇini** 1.4.58). Prefixes can also be used in front of nouns.

अति	**ati**	across, beyond, surpassing, past (**atīndriya**, beyond the senses; **atyanta**, beyond the end, infinite)
अधि	**adhi**	above, over, on (**adhyātma**, pertaining to the Self; **adhiviśva**, above all, responsible for the universe)
अनु	**anu**	after, following (**anusvāra**, "after sound")
अप	**apa**	away, off (**apāna**, downward breath, elimination)
अपि	**api**	on, close on (**apihita**, placed into)
अभि	**abhi**	to, against (**abhyaṅga**, rubbing against)
अव	**ava**	down, away, off (**avatāra**, crossing down)
आ	**ā**	back, return, to, fully (**ācāra**, to go toward, conduct; **ācārya**, teacher of conduct

3द्   udbhava (existence)
      origination

उद्	ud	up, up out (**udāna**, upward breath) (ur —)
उप	upa	towards, near, subordinate (**upaniṣad**, sit down near; **upasarga**, "discharged near," prefix)

su pryat — praise of
good things
dus pryat — telling
hero's bad side in poem

दुस्	dus	ill, bad, difficult, hard (**duṣkṛta**, badly done; NEGATIVE **duḥkham**, suffering) (usually used with nouns)

निःकृप inactive

नि	ni	down, into (**upaniṣad**, sit down near)

पूर्व →

पराफूर्व longer
              now

निस्	nis	out from, forth, without, entirely (**nistraiguṇya**, NOT without the three **guṇas**) features
परा	parā	away, forth, along, off (**parāśara**, "crusher")
परि	pari	around, about (**pariṇāma**, transformation)
प्र	pra	forward, onward, forth (**prāṇa**, vital breath; **prakṛti**, nature)
प्रति	prati	back to, in reverse direction, every (**pratyāhāra**, food from the reverse direction)
वि	vi	apart, away, out (**vyāna**, moving breath, circulation)
सम्	sam	together (**samāna**, even breath, digestion; **saṃskṛta**, put together, perfected)
सु	su	well, very, good, right, easy (**sukṛta**, well-done; **sukham**, happiness) (usually used with nouns)

Note a as augment

IMPERFECT MIDDLE

3. Here is the imperfect middle, which is also used as a past tense:

Root: √**bhāṣ** (middle) speak

	Singular	Dual	Plural
3rd	अभाषत **abhāṣata**	अभाषेताम् **abhāṣetām**	अभाषन्त **abhāṣanta**
2nd	अभाषथाः **abhāṣathāḥ**	अभाषेथाम् **abhāṣethām**	अभाषध्वम् **abhāṣadhvam**
1st	अभाषे **abhāṣe**	अभाषावहि **abhāṣāvahi**	अभाषामहि **abhāṣāmahi**

Note that the endings are given on page 317.

4. Compare the imperfect endings with the present indicative endings:

	Singular	Dual	Plural
3rd	भाषते **bhāṣate**	भाषेते **bhāṣete**	भाषन्ते **bhāṣante**
2nd	भाषसे **bhāṣase**	भाषेथे **bhāṣethe**	भाषध्वे **bhāṣadhve**
1st	भाषे **bhāṣe**	भाषावहे **bhāṣāvahe**	भाषामहे **bhāṣāmahe**

VOCABULARY

SANSKRIT		ENGLISH
अव + गम् **ava + √gam** (active)	अवगच्छति **avagacchati**	he understands
उद् + भू **ud + √bhū** (active)	उद्भवति **udbhavati**	he is born
उद् + स्था **ud + √sthā** (active)	उत्तिष्ठति **uttiṣṭhati**	he stands up
रम् **√ram** (middle)	रमते **ramate**	he enjoys
शुभ् **√śubh** (middle)	शोभते **śobhate**	he shines
स्मि **√smi** (middle)	स्मयते **smayate**	he smiles

The gerund forms for each of these verbs is listed at the back of the text (pages 312–314).

EXERCISES

1. Memorize the **sandhi** rules that take place when the first word ends in **m**.

2. Memorize the endings for the imperfect middle.

3. Translate the following sentences into English:

   a. कथामवगत्य कविरस्मयत ।१।

   b. रामः सीता च नद्यां जलमरमेताम् ।२।

   c. यदातिथिरुपगच्छति तदा बाला उत्तिष्ठन्ति ।३।

   d. यदातिथिरुपागच्छत्तदा बाला उदतिष्ठन् ।४।

   e. यत्र शान्तिस्तत्र सुखं ।५।

   f. पुत्रिका नृपस्य गृह उद्भवति ।६।

   g. विद्ययाविद्यां जित्वा सूर्य इवर्षिः शोभते ।७।

h. अहो राम कथं तस्मिन्गज उत्तिष्ठसीति बालो
aho rama kathaṃ tasmin gaja upatiṣṭhasīti balo
ऽपृच्छत् ।८।
apṛcchat

i. वने फलानि रत्वा वीरस्य पत्नी गृहं प्रत्यगच्छत् ।९।
vane phalāni rajtvā vīrasya patnī gṛhaṃ pratyagacchat

j. यो बालस्तस्य पुत्रस्तं रामोऽस्मयत ।१०।
yo bālastasya putrstaṃ smayata ramo

k. यदाचार्योऽवदत्तदा शिष्या उदतिष्ठन् ।११। *plur*
yadā ācāryo 'vadata tadā śiṣyā udatiṣṭhan

4. Translate the following sentences into Sanskrit:

a. Since the guest enjoyed the fruit, (therefore) he returns to the
   house again. *yathā atithi ... phalaṃ aromata*
   tathā grihaṃ punar prati gacchati

b. Having smiled, Sītā spoke to the beautiful girl.

c. Having come from the elephant, the boy approached that
   village.

d. He understands that the man has a son.

e. After drinking the water from the fruit, the girl stands up.

f. When the moon shines, then you see shadows in the forest.

g. When the boy sees the elephant, then he smiles and laughs.

h. The man and his wife enjoy that beautiful house.

i. When his son was born, the hero smiled.

j. The girl obtained fruit from the man who is standing.

k. When the sun shines on the moon, then the moon shines on us.

सु प्रभातम् good morning.

16

LESSON SIXTEEN

Alphabet:	The **sandhi** rules for final **n**
Grammar:	Nouns in **an**
	The imperfect for √ **as**
	The **dvandva** compound
Vocabulary:	Nouns in **an**
	More adjectives

ALPHABET: SANDHI RULES FOR FINAL N

1. Now we will learn the **sandhi** rules for when the first word ends in **n**. In the majority of cases it remains unchanged. The chart below contains eight rules (a - h) in which **n** changes.

2. For each rule, those letters in the alphabet that are in bold represent the first letter of the second word, which causes the change. The letters outside the alphabet are the change the **n** undergoes. See the examples on the following pages.

preceding **n** becomes								preceding **n** becomes
				a	**ā**			
				i	**ī**			
				u	**ū**			**nn** (e)
				ṛ	**ṝ**			(if preceded by
				ḷ				a short vowel)
				e	**ai**			
				o	**au**			
		ka	kha	ga	gha	ṅa		
(a) ṃś		**ca**	**cha**	**ja**	**jha**	ña		**ñ** (f)
(b) ṃṣ		**ṭa**	**ṭha**	**ḍa**	**ḍha**	ṇa		**ṇ** (g)
(c) ṃs		**ta**	**tha**	da	dha	na		
		pa	pha	ba	bha	ma		
				ya	ra	**la**	va	**ṃl** (h)
(d) **ñ (ch)**	**śa**	ṣa	sa	ha				
		end of line						

3. Here are examples for each of these eight rules:

(a) तस्मिन् + च = तस्मिंश्च
tasmin + ca = tasmiṃś ca

नरान् + च = नरांश्च
narān + ca = narāṃś ca

(b) नरान् + ट = नरांष्ट
narān + ṭa = narāṃṣ ṭa

(c) नरान् + तत्र = नरांस्तत्र
narān + tatra = narāṃs tatra

(d) नरान् + शोभन्ते = नराञ्छोभन्ते
narān + śobhante = narāñ chobhante

or (rarely)
नरान् + शोभन्ते = नराञ्शोभन्ते
narān + śobhante = narāñ śobhante

(e) राजन् + अत्र = राजन्नत्र
rājan + atra = rājann atra

= usual, but both are OK (metrical)

नरान् + अत्र = नरानत्र
narān + atra = narān atra

(f) नरान् + जयति = नराञ्जयति

narān + jayati = narāñ jayati

(g) नरान् + ड = नराण्ड

narān + ḍa = narāṇ ḍa

(h) नरान् + लभते = नरांल्लभते

narān + labhate = narāṃl labhate

GRAMMAR: NOUNS IN AN

1. Here is the declension for nouns ending in **an**:

Stem: **rājan** (masculine) king; **ātman** (masculine) Self

	Singular	Dual	Plural
Nom.	राजा **rājā**	राजानौ **rājānau**	राजानः **rājānaḥ**
Acc.	राजानम् **rājānam**	राजानौ **rājānau**	राज्ञः आत्मनः **rājñaḥ/ātmanaḥ**
Inst.	राज्ञा आत्मना **rājñā/ātmanā**	राजभ्याम् **rājabhyām**	राजभिः **rājabhiḥ**
Dat.	राज्ञे आत्मने **rājñe/ātmane**	राजभ्याम् **rājabhyām**	राजभ्यः **rājabhyaḥ**
Abl.	राज्ञः आत्मनः **rājñaḥ/ātmanaḥ**	राजभ्याम् **rājabhyām**	राजभ्यः **rājabhyaḥ**
Gen.	राज्ञः आत्मनः **rājñaḥ / ātmanaḥ**	राज्ञोः आत्मनोः **rājñoḥ / ātmanoḥ**	राज्ञाम् आत्मनाम् **rājñām / ātmanām**
Loc.	राज्ञि आत्मनि **rājñi/ātmani**	राज्ञोः आत्मनोः **rājñoḥ/ātmanoḥ**	राजसु **rājasu**
Voc.	राजन् **rājan**	राजानौ **rājānau**	राजानः **rājānaḥ**

2. Note that the only difference between **rājan** and **ātman** is that since the **tmn** combination cannot occur, **ātman** always keeps the **a** before the **n**. Sometimes that **a** may be long. If so, the form is considered strong. The neuter is similar to the masculine:

Stem: **nāman** (neuter) name

	Singular	Dual	Plural
Nom.	नाम **nāma**	नाम्नी नामनी **nāmnī/nāmanī**	नामानि **nāmāni**
Acc.	नाम **nāma**	नाम्नी नामनी **nāmnī/nāmanī**	नामानि **nāmāni**
Inst.	नाम्ना **nāmnā**	नामभ्याम् **nāmabhyām**	नामभिः **nāmabhiḥ**
Dat.	नाम्ने **nāmne**	नामभ्याम् **nāmabhyām**	नामभ्यः **nāmabhyaḥ**
Abl.	नाम्नः **nāmnaḥ**	नामभ्याम् **nāmabhyām**	नामभ्यः **nāmabhyaḥ**
Gen.	नाम्नः **nāmnaḥ**	नाम्नोः **nāmnoḥ**	नाम्नाम् **nāmnām**
Loc.	नाम्नि नामनि **nāmni/nāmani**	नाम्नोः **nāmnoḥ**	नामसु **nāmasu**
Voc.	नामन् नाम **nāman/nāma**	नाम्नी नामनी **nāmnī/nāmanī**	नामानि **nāmāni**

THE IMPERFECT FOR √AS

3. Here is the imperfect for √**as**:

	Singular	Dual	Plural
3rd	आसीत् **āsīt**	आस्ताम् **āstām**	आसन् **āsan**
2nd	आसीः **āsīḥ**	आस्तम् **āstam**	आस्त **āsta**
1st	आसम् **āsam**	आस्व **āsva**	आस्म **āsma**

Remember that these are not the endings, but the entire verb.

THE DVANDVA COMPOUND

4. Now we will begin our study of compounds (**samāsa**). Sanskrit has several different types of compounds, which are members joined together to create one unit. In **devanāgarī**, compounds are written without a break. With transliteration, in this text the members of a compound are joined by a hyphen, when **sandhi** permits. For example:

एकवचन **eka-vacana** (singular number)

5. Nominal compounds join nouns, adjectives, or pronouns. They are usually formed by taking the base form (**nara**, **phala**, etc.) and putting them together, using **sandhi** rules. Generally only the last member is declined, and prior members have loss (**luk**) of case ending (**sup**).

6. The first type of compound that we will study is the **dvandva** compound. A **dvandva** (related to the word "dual") is a series of

John susan + o
susajan o

S - R order

equal items that would normally be joined by "and." For example, "Sītā and Rāma" could be written as a **dvandva** compound:

सीतारामौ
sītā-rāmau

7. All compounds may undergo an analysis (**vigraha**), which is how the words would appear if the compound were dissolved. For example:

Sitaramo

सीतारामौ	vigraha:	सीता रामश्च
sītā-rāmau		sītā rāmaś ca
"Sītā-Rāma"	analysis:	Sītā and Rāma

8. This **dvandva** (above) is called an **itaretara-dvandva**, because it names its members in a distributive sense. (See #13.) In it, the last member is in the dual because two persons are named.

9. If more than two persons are named, the last member is in the plural. For example:

आचार्यशिष्याः	vigraha:	आचार्यः शिष्याश्च
ācārya-śiṣyāḥ		ācāryaḥ śiṣyāś ca
"teacher-students"	analysis:	the teacher and students

10. A **dvandva** with three members is always plural. For example:

अश्वगजमृगाः	vigraha:	अश्वो गजो मृगाश्च
aśva-gaja-mṛgāḥ		aśvo gajo mṛgāś ca
"horse-elephant-deer"	analysis:	horse, elephant and deer

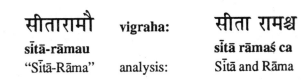

11. The gender is determined by the last item named. For example:

रामसीते	**vigraha:**	रामः सीता च
rāma-sīte		**rāmaḥ sītā ca**
"Rāma-Sīte"	analysis:	Rāma and Sītā

12. The first member is in its stem form even if it refers to something plural. Because of this, there is sometimes ambiguity concerning whether a member is singular, dual, or plural. For example:

आचार्यशिष्याः	could be analyzed as:
"teacher-students"	teacher and students (or)
	teachers and student (or)
	teachers and students

You must judge the correct translation by the context, and in most contexts, the first example would be what is meant: "the teacher and the students."

13. There is an additional kind of **dvandva**, called **samāhāra,** in which the ending is always singular and neuter. The members are referred to collectively as a single unit. The meaning of the individual members is not as important as the collective sense of the whole compound. Often pairs of opposites are put in **samāhāra-dvandva** form. For example:

सुखदुःखम्	**vigraha:**	सुखं दुःखं च
sukha-duḥkham		**sukhaṃ duḥkhaṃ ca**
"happiness-suffering"	analysis:	happiness and suffering

14. Words ending in **-an** usually act in compounds like words that end in **-a**. For example, **ātman** is often reduced to **ātma**, when it is

prior to the last member of the compound. Some words, such as **rājan**, take the **-a** ending as a prior member and also as the last member of the compound. For example:

राजरामौ
rāja-rāmau The king and Rāma

रामराजौ
rāma-rājau Rāma and the king

THE NEGATIVE COMPOUND

15. Another type of compound is negating, or the negative compound (**nañ**, or negative **samāsa**). A noun can be negated by placing **a** before it. For example:

विद्या	अविद्या
vidyā	**avidyā**
knowledge	ignorance

16. A gerund is also negated with **a**. If the gerund begins with **a**, and there is no prefix, the ending is **-tvā**. For example:

अगत्वा
agatvā not having gone

a nāgatva not having come

17. If the word begins with a vowel, then it is negated with **an**. For example:

अनुदित्वा
anuditvā not having spoken

VOCABULARY	SANSKRIT	ENGLISH
	आत्मा **ātmā** (mas.)	Self (usually has capital "S") (follows the **an** declension)
	कर्म **karma** (n.)	action (**an** declension)
	कृष्ण **kṛṣṇa** mf(**ā**)n (adj.)	black
	कृष्णः **kṛṣṇaḥ** (mas. noun)	Kṛṣṇa
	नाम **nāma** (n.)	name (**an** declension)
	प्रिय **priya** mf(**ā**)n (adj.)	dear, beloved
	रमणीय **ramaṇīya** mf(**ā**)n (adj.)	pleasant
	राजा **rājā** (mas.)	king (**an** declension)
	शुक्ल **śukla** mf(**ā**)n (adj.)	white
	शोभन **śobhana** mf(**ā** or **ī**)n (adj.)	shining, bright, beautiful

EXERCISES

1. Memorize the **sandhi** rules for final **n**.

2. Memorize the masculine and neuter for the **an** declension.

3. Memorize the imperfect of √ **as**.

4. Review the formation of **dvandva** compounds.

5. Translate the following sentences into English:

a. कृष्णोऽश्वमृगगजानगोपायत् ।१।

b. प्रियो राजा रामो ग्रामस्य बालानस्मयत ।२।

c. कन्या प्रजां सूर्यात्तस्याश्छाययागोपायत् ।३।

d. य आत्मानं बोधति स कर्माणि रमते ।४।

e. प्रजा कृष्णस्याश्वस्य कर्माहसत् ।५।

f. यदा सा तस्य नामावदत्तदा बाल उदतिष्ठत् ।६।

g. प्रियं तस्य पुत्रमुपगत्य वीरोऽस्मयत ।७।

h. बालबाले शोभनस्य राज्ञः प्रजे स्तः ।८।

i. शुक्ला अश्वा वन आसन् ।९।

j. आसीद्राजा रामो नाम ग्रामे ।१०।

6. Translate the following sentences into Sanskrit:

a. The black horse drinks the water from the river.

b. He who knows the Self enjoys action and inaction.

c. The king's name was Kṛṣṇa.

d. The king enjoys the pleasant actions of the son.

e. The beloved hero understood perfection and imperfection (success and failure).

f. The boy comes from the elephant and returns to the house.

g. That which neither comes nor goes is the Self.

h. When the king approached, the boys and girls stood up.

i. The man who was king came from the black forest.

j. Knowledge of the Self is knowledge also of the sun and the moon.

17

LESSON SEVENTEEN

Alphabet: The **sandhi** rules for final **t**

Grammar: Nouns ending in **ṛ** and the future tense

Vocabulary: Nouns in **ṛ**

calendar

nepale

moon

new → full

śukla (wax)

kṛṣṇa pakṣya

1 parerva 1st day of month

14 chaturdasi

15 aũsi

Purnima full moon

ALPHABET: SANDHI RULES FOR FINAL T

1. When the first word ends in **t**, in the majority of cases it remains the same if the following letter is unvoiced, and it changes to **d** if the following letter is voiced. Those letters which are in bold are exceptions. See the examples that follow.

t remains **t** except: | **t** changes to **d** except:

				a	ā			
				i	ī			
				u	ū			
				ṛ	ṝ			
				ḷ				
				e	ai			(before all nasals)
				o	au			**n** (d)
		ka	kha	ga	gha	**ṅa**		
(a) **c**		**ca**	**cha**	**ja**	**jha**	**ña**		**j** (e)
(b) ṭ		**ṭa**	**ṭha**	**ḍa**	**ḍha**	**ṇa**		**ḍ** (f)
		ta	tha	da	dha	**na**		
		pa	pha	ba	bha	**ma**		
				ya	ra	**la**	va	**l** (g)
(c) **c (ch)**	**śa**	ṣa	sa	**ha**				**d (dh)** (h)
		end of line						

2. Here are examples for each of these eight rules:

(a) रामात् + च = रामाच्च
rāmāt + ca = rāmāc ca

(b) रामात् + ट = रामाट्ट
rāmāt + ṭa = rāmāṭ ṭa

(c) रामात् + शास्त्रम् = रामाच्छास्त्रम्
rāmāt + śāstram = rāmāc chāstram

(d) रामात् + मन्यते = रामान्मन्यते
rāmāt + manyate = rāmān manyate

(e) रामात् + जलम् = रामाज्जलम्
rāmāt + jalam = rāmāj jalam

(f) रामात् + ड = रामाड्ड
rāmāt + ḍa = rāmāḍ ḍa

(g) रामात् + लभते = रामाल्लभते
rāmāt + labhate = rāmāl labhate

(h) रामात् + हस्तः = रामाद्धस्तः
rāmāt + hastaḥ = rāmād dhastaḥ

GRAMMAR: NOUNS IN Ṛ

1. Here is the declension for nouns ending in **ṛ**. These nouns are usually an agent of action or a relation, such as father or mother.

Stem: **dātṛ** (masculine) giver; **svasṛ** (feminine) sister

	Singular	Dual	Plural
Nom.	दाता **dātā**	दातारौ **dātārau**	दातारः **dātāraḥ**
Acc.	दातारम् **dātāram**	दातारौ **dātārau**	दातॄन् स्वसॄः **dātṝn / svasṝḥ**
Inst.	दात्रा **dātrā**	दातृभ्याम् **dātṛbhyām**	दातृभिः **dātṛbhiḥ**
Dat.	दात्रे **dātre**	दातृभ्याम् **dātṛbhyām**	दातृभ्यः **dātṛbhyaḥ**
Abl.	दातुः **dātuḥ**	दातृभ्याम् **dātṛbhyām**	दातृभ्यः **dātṛbhyaḥ**
Gen.	दातुः **dātuḥ**	दात्रोः **dātroḥ**	दातॄणाम् **dātṝṇām**
Loc.	दातरि **dātari**	दात्रोः **dātroḥ**	दातृषु **dātṛṣu**
Voc.	दातर् **dātar**	दातारौ **dātārau**	दातारः **dātāraḥ**

2. Father, mother, and brother have a weaker form (looking at the second syllable) in the nominative and vocative (dual and plural), and the accusative (singular and dual):

Stem: **pitṛ** (mas.) father; **mātṛ** (fem.) mother; **bhrātṛ** (mas.) brother

	Singular	Dual	Plural
Nom.	पिता **pitā**	पितरौ **pitarau**	पितरः **pitaraḥ**
Acc.	पितरम् **pitaram**	पितरौ **pitarau**	पितॄन् भ्रातॄन् मातॄः **pitṝn bhrātṝn mātṝḥ**
Voc.	पितर् **pitar**	पितरौ **pitarau**	पितरः **pitaraḥ**

3. In a few but frequently used **dvandva** compounds of pairs, such as "mother and father," the first word usually ends in **ā**, the nominative singular. For example:

मातापितरौ
mātā-pitarau mother and father

THE FUTURE TENSE

4. Now we will study the future tense. Sometimes the present indicative may indicate the immediate future. For example:

गच्छामि
gacchāmi I will go

5. More often, the simple future is used. The future tense (**lṛṭ**) is used for any future action. It is formed by adding **sya** or **iṣya** to the

strengthened root. (Remember that **s** becomes **ṣ** when immediately preceded by any vowel except **a** or **ā**. See internal **sandhi**, p. 142.)

6. Most roots are strengthened by adding **guṇa** changes to the vowel. (See page 167.) The standard active and middle endings are then added.

7. Here is the third person singular future for some of the verbs we have learned:

upa + √gam	**upagamiṣyati**	he will approach
√gam	**gamiṣyati**	he will go
√gup	**gopsyati**	he will protect
√cint	**cintayiṣyati -te**	he will think
√ji	**jeṣyati**	he will conquer
√dṛś	**drakṣyati**	he will see
√nī	**neṣyati -te**	he will lead
√paṭh	**paṭhiṣyati**	he will read
√paś	**drakṣyati**	he will see
√pā	**pāsyati**	he will drink

√prach	**prakṣyati**	he will ask
√budh	**bodhiṣyati -te**	he will know
√bhū	**bhaviṣyati**	he will be
√man	**maṃsyate**	he will think
√ram	**raṃsyate**	he will enjoy
√labh	**lapsyate**	he will obtain
√vad	**vadiṣyati**	he will speak
√vas	**vatsyati**	he will live
√śubh	**śobhiṣyate**	he will shine
√sev	**seviṣyate**	he will serve
√sthā	**sthāsyati**	he will stand
√smi	**smeṣyate**	he will smile
√smṛ	**smariṣyati**	he will remember
√has	**hasiṣyati**	he will laugh

VOCABULARY: NOUNS IN Ṛ	SANSKRIT		ENGLISH
	कदा	**kadā** (indeclinable)	when (used like **kutra**)
	कर्ता	**kartā** (mas.)	maker, doer (follows the ṛ declension)
	कर्त्री	**kartrī** (fem.)	maker, doer (follows long ī declension)
	कुलम्	**kulam** (n.)	family
	दाता	**dātā** (mas.)	giver (follows the ṛ declension)
	दात्री	**dātrī** (fem.)	giver (ī declension)
	पिता	**pitā** (mas.)	father (ṛ declension)
	भ्राता	**bhrātā** (mas.)	brother (ṛ declension)
	माता	**mātā** (fem.)	mother (ṛ declension)
	स्वसा	**svasā** (fem.)	sister (ṛ declension)

EXERCISES

1. Memorize the **sandhi** rules for final **t**.

2. Memorize the declension for nouns ending in **ṛ**.

3. Make yourself familiar with the future third person singular forms.

4. Translate the following sentences into English:

a. मम पिता तत्र गमिष्यतीति बालस्तस्य

मातरमवदत् ।१।

b. कदा तव भ्राता जलं लप्स्यत इति पितापृच्छत् ।२।

c. पितामातरौ जलात्कुलं गोप्स्यतः ।३।

d. कदा वनादागमिष्यसीति रामस्तस्य

भ्रातरमपृच्छत् ।४।

e. तस्य पितरं सेवित्वा रामो राजा भविष्यति ।५।

f. यदा तस्या भ्रातरं मन्यते तदा सा स्मयते ।६।

g. माता तस्याः प्रजायै सुखस्य दात्री भवति ।७।

h. य आत्मानं जयति स शान्तेः कर्ता ।८।

i. जलं पीत्वा तस्य मातुः पुस्तकं पठिष्यति ।९।

j. भ्रात्रा सह रामो वने वत्स्यति ।१०।

5. Translate the following sentences into Sanskrit:

a. When my sister was born, she smiled at my mother.

b. My family's name is from the name of a seer.

c. "When will I speak to the king?" her father thought.

d. Her father's wife is her mother.

e. My father is the maker of peace in our family.

f. The brother and sister will obtain fruit from the forest.

g. The hero will protect the king from the fire in the forest.

h. The son of the king has no brothers.

i. When will the students obtain knowledge from the virtuous teacher?

j. "I have seen you in the pond," the king says to the beautiful son.

18

LESSON EIGHTEEN

Alphabet:	All remaining **sandhi** rules
Grammar:	Nouns in **u**
	The **karmadhāraya** and **tatpuruṣa** compound
	Summary of compounds
Vocabulary:	Nouns in **u**, more adjectives

ALPHABET: ALL REMAINING SANDHI RULES

1. We will now study the remaining **sandhi** rules, which include final **r**, **p**, **ṭ**, **k**, **ṅ**, **ṇ**, and initial **ch**.

2. Here are the rules for final **r**:

   (a) Before a word beginning with a voiced letter, the **r** remains the same. For example:

   पुनर् + गच्छति = पुनर्गच्छति
   punar + gacchati = punar gacchati

   पुनर् + आगच्छति = पुनरागच्छति
   punar + āgacchati = punar āgacchati

   (b) Before an unvoiced letter or the end of a line, **r** follows the same rules as final **s**. For example:

   पुनर् + पुनर् = पुनः पुनः
   punar + punar = punaḥ punaḥ

   पुनर् + तत्र = पुनस्तत्र
   punar + tatra = punas tatra

   (c) Final **r**, whether original or derived from **s**, cannot stand before another **r**. The final **r** is dropped and the vowel before it made long if it is short. For example:

   पुनर् + रामः = पुना रामः
   punar + rāmaḥ = punā rāmaḥ

3. Here are the rules for final **p**, **ṭ**, and **k:**
   (a) Before a voiced sound these letters become voiced, and before an unvoiced sound they remain the same. For example:

ऋक् + वेद = ऋग्वेद

ṛk + veda = ṛg veda

ऋक् + संहिता = ऋक्संहिता

ṛk + saṃhitā = ṛk saṃhitā

   (b) Before a nasal these letters become the nasal of their row (**varga**). For example:

सुप् + नाम = सुम्नाम

sup + nāma = sumnāma

   (c) Before **h** these letters become voiced and the **h** becomes their voiced aspirated counterpart. For example:

वाक् + हसति = वाग्घसति

vāk + hasati = vāg ghasati

4. Here is the rule for final **ṅ** and **ṇ**:
   (a) Like final **n**, final **ṅ** becomes **ṅṅ** before vowels if the **ṅ** is preceded by a short vowel. Also, final **ṇ** becomes **ṇṇ** if the **ṇ** is preceded by a short vowel.

5. Here is the rule for initial **ch**:
   (a) Initial **ch** becomes **cch** if the first word ends in a short vowel. The **ch** also becomes **cch** after **ā** and **mā**. For example:

कुत्र + छाया = कुत्र च्छाया

kutra + chāyā = kutra cchāyā

6. Ambiguities can sometimes be created by **sandhi**. Two different sets of words could appear the same after **sandhi** has been applied. For example:

रामः + एव = राम एव

rāmaḥ + eva = rāma eva

रामे + एव = राम एव

rāme + eva = rāma eva

बालाः + न = बाला न

bālāḥ + na = bālā na

बाला + न = बाला न

bālā + na = bālā na

You can usually judge from the context of the sentence which words are correct.

GRAMMAR: NOUNS IN U

1. Here is the declension for final **u**:

Stem: **hetu** (masculine) cause; **dhenu** (feminine) cow

	Singular	Dual	Plural
Nom.	हेतुः **hetuḥ**	हेतू **hetū**	हेतवः **hetavaḥ**
Acc.	हेतुम् **hetum**	हेतू **hetū**	हेतून् धेनूः **hetūn / dhenūḥ**
Inst.	हेतुना धेन्वा **hetunā / dhenvā**	हेतुभ्याम् **hetubhyām**	हेतुभिः **hetubhiḥ**
Dat.	हेतवे धेन्वै **hetave (dhenvai)**	हेतुभ्याम् **hetubhyām**	हेतुभ्यः **hetubhyaḥ**
Abl.	हेतोः धेन्वाः **hetoḥ (dhenvāḥ)**	हेतुभ्याम् **hetubhyām**	हेतुभ्यः **hetubhyaḥ**
Gen.	हेतोः धेन्वाः **hetoḥ (dhenvāḥ)**	हेत्वोः **hetvoḥ**	हेतूनाम् **hetūnām**
Loc.	हेतौ धेन्वाम् **hetau (dhenvām)**	हेत्वोः **hetvoḥ**	हेतुषु **hetuṣu**
Voc.	हेतो **heto**	हेतू **hetū**	हेतवः **hetavaḥ**

The singular dative, ablative, genitive, and locative have an optional feminine form. For example, the feminine dative singular is **dhenave** or **dhenvai**. This entire declension is the same as the declension ending in **i** (page 160). The only differences are due to **sandhi**.

e.g. adj – noun

COMPOUNDS

2. Now we will study another kind of compound: the **tatpuruṣa** compound. Unlike the **dvandva**, whose members are considered equal, in the **tatpuruṣa** the last member is usually principal (**pradhāna**) and the prior member is subordinate (**upasarjana**). The **tatpuruṣa** is sometimes called a "determinative compound," because the subordinate member qualifies or determines the sense of the principal member, which could stand alone.

KARMADHĀRAYA

3. One type of **tatpuruṣa** is the **karmadhāraya**. In a **karmadhāraya** compound, both members refer to the same object, and if separated, would be in the same case (**samānādhikaraṇa**).

4. The simplest kind of **karmadhāraya** is the adjective and noun:

शुक्लमाला	**vigraha:**	शुक्ला माला
śukla-mālā		**śuklā mālā**
"white-garland"	analysis:	the white garland
प्रियबालः	**vigraha:**	प्रियो बालः
priya-bālaḥ		**priyo bālaḥ**
"the dear-boy"	analysis:	the dear boy

Note that even if the second member of the compound is a feminine noun (**mālā**), the adjective often takes the form of a masculine stem (**a**). (Feminine nouns keep their gender in these compounds.)

5. Another type of **karmadhāraya** is the noun and noun:

राजर्षिः	**vigraha:**	राजर्षिः
rāja-ṛṣiḥ		**rāja ṛṣiḥ**
"king-seer"	analysis:	the king seer

TATPURUṢA

6. In other **tatpuruṣa** compounds (here usually referred to as **tatpuruṣa**), the members refer to different objects and would be in different cases (**vyadhikaraṇa**) if the compound were dissolved and the last member is put in the nominative. The compound is further named after the case of the first member, which would be in cases two through seven if the compound were analyzed. For example, if the first member is genitive, the compound is called a genitive **tatpuruṣa**. Here are two genitive **tatpuruṣa** compounds:

राजपुरुषः	**vigraha:**	राज्ञः पुरुषः
rāja-puruṣaḥ		**rājñaḥ puruṣaḥ**
"king-man"	analysis:	the king's man
नरपुस्तकम्	**vigraha:**	नरस्य पुस्तकम्
nara-pustakam		**narasya pustakam**
"man-book"	analysis:	the man's book

7. A compound, like a simple word, may become a member in another compound. In these cases, in India, the analysis usually begins with the smaller pieces. For example:

रामपुत्रपुस्तकम्
rāma-putra-pustakam
"Rāma-son-book"

(1) रामस्य पुत्रः
rāmasya putraḥ
the son of Rāma

(2) रामस्य पुत्रस्य पुस्तकम्

rāmasya putrasya pustakam

the book of the son of Rāma

In the West, analysis of a compound begins at the right and goes to the left. In India, analysis begins with the smaller units. Rather than "taking apart" a compound, the analysis starts with smaller units and shows how the compound is "built up."

SUMMARY OF COMPOUNDS

8. Compounds may be classified into four groups. The following is a generalized description, for background information, to which exceptions may be added later:

(1) **dvandva.** In this compound, each member is considered principal. There are two types:

(a) **itaretara.** The members are viewed separately. For example, **rāma-sīte**, "Rāma and Sītā."

(b) **samāhāra.** The members are viewed as a whole. For example, **sukha-duḥkham**, "happiness and suffering."

(2) **tatpuruṣa.** In this compound, the first member qualifies and is subordinate to the second member. There are several types:

(a) **tatpuruṣa (vyadhikaraṇa-tatpuruṣa).** This name is normally used for the compound that refers to different objects. The first member would be in a different case than the second if the compound were dissolved. This compound has six types, corresponding to cases two through seven. For example, **rāja-puruṣaḥ**, "the king's man."

(b) **karmadhāraya (samānādhikaraṇa-tatpuruṣa)**. Both members refer to the same object and therefore would be in the same case if the compound were dissolved. For example, **śukla-mālā**, "the white garland." If the first member is a number, it is called a **dvigu**. For example, **dvi-vacana**, "dual number."

(c) **upapada**. The second member is an adjusted verbal root. For example, **brahma-vit**, "the knower of **brahman**."

(d) **nañ**. This is a **tatpuruṣa** compound in which **na** is reduced to **a** or **an**, used to negate. For example, **avidyā**, "ignorance." (See p. 213.)

(e) **prādi**. The first member is one of the twenty **upasargas** given by Pāṇini, which he listed as beginning with **pra**. (See pps.197–199.) The entire compound is used as a nominal. For example, **anusvāra**, "after-sound."

(f) **gati**. The first member is another type of prefix, called **gati**, and the entire compound is used as a nominal. For example, **antaryāmin**, "inner ruler."

(3) **bahuvrīhi**. In this compound, the actual principal is outside of the compound. The compound serves as an adjective, describing something else. The members may be in the same or different cases. For example, **mahā-rathaḥ**, "having a great chariot," means one whose chariot is great, or a "great hero." To use an example in English, "redcoat," meaning "having a red coat," refers to a person whose coat is red, or a British soldier.

(4) **avyayībhāva**. This compound usually begins with an indeclinable. The entire compound is used as an adverb. For example, **yathānāma**, "by name."

9. These four groups of compounds may be understood from the perspective of which member is principal:

(1) **dvandva**	Both members are principal.
(2) **tatpuruṣa**	Second member is principal.
(3) **bahuvrīhi**	Neither member is principal.
(4) **avyayībhāva**	First member is principal.

10. If pronouns are used as prior members of a compound, they are put in base forms, which are used regardless of the case, gender, or number of the pronoun:

mad	I
asmad	we
tvad	you
yuṣmad	you (plural)
tad	he, she, it, they

For example:

मद्बालः

mad-bālaḥ

my boy (genitive **tatpuruṣa**)

तत्पुरुषः

tat-puruṣaḥ

his man (genitive **tatpuruṣa**)

VOCABULARY	SANSKRIT	ENGLISH
	अल्प **alpa** mf(ā)n (adj.)	little
	गुरु **guru** mf(vī)n (adj.)	heavy
	गुरुः **guruḥ** (mas. noun)	teacher
	धेनुः **dhenuḥ** (fem.)	cow
	पूर्ण **pūrṇa** mf(ā)n (adj.)	full
	बहु **bahu** mf(**vī** or **u**)n (adj.)	much, many
	शत्रुः **śatruḥ** (mas.)	enemy
	शीघ्र **śīghra** mf(ā)n (adj.)	swift
	हेतुः **hetuḥ** (mas.)	cause, motive

EXERCISES

1. Memorize the last of the **sandhi** rules.

2. Memorize the declension for **u.**

3. Review how to form **karmadhāraya** and **tatpuruṣa** compounds and memorize the short forms of the pronouns used in those compounds.

4. Translate the following sentences into English:

   a. शुक्लधेनुर्वाप्यां तिष्ठति जलं च पिबति ।१।

   b. ऋषिः शत्रुमजयत् ।२।

   c. यदि वनं फलस्य पूर्णमस्ति तदा धेनवस्तत्र गच्छन्ति ।३।

   d. मन्माताल्पं पुस्तकं पठति तत्रमते च ।४।

   e. बहुसुखस्य दाता गुरुः ।५।

   f. अल्पबालः शुक्लसूर्य इव शोभते ।६।

g. यदात्मानमवगच्छसि तदा त्वं बहुसुखस्य हेतुरसि ।७।

h. कदा रमणीयराजा शत्रोरस्माकं कुलं गोप्स्यति ।८।

i. शीघ्रा बाला फलेन सह वनादागच्छति ।९।

j. गुरोः सुखस्य हेतुस्तस्य शिष्याणां सिद्धयो भवति ।१०।

k. विद्यायाः शत्रुरविद्या भवतीति बालोऽवदत् ।११।

5. Translate the following sentences into Sanskrit:

a. The beautiful little cow drank water from the pond.

b. The swift black horse stands in the little village.

c. Having conquered the enemy, the army will enjoy peace and happiness.

d. Ignorance is the enemy of truth.

e. Having known the Self, he understood the cause of action and inaction.

f. The child was born in a little house in the beautiful forest.

g. The student will bring the beautiful garland for his teacher.

h. The forest is full of fruit and the pond is full of water.

i. Seeing his family, the father went to the forest for water.

j. When will the beautiful cow come here from the swift river?

k. Having seen the cow, the beautiful boy enjoys the water in the pond.

ANSWERS TO EXERCISES

LESSON ONE

5. a. You ask and he goes.

   b. I go and I ask. (or) I go and ask.

   c. He asks and he goes. (or) He asks and goes.

   d. You go and I ask.

   e. He asks and I ask. (or) He and I ask.

   f. You go and he goes. (or) You and he go.

   g. I ask and you go.

   h. He asks and I go.

6. a. **gacchāmi pṛcchāmi ca** (or) **gacchāmi ca pṛcchāmi ca**

   b. **pṛcchasi gacchati ca** (**ca** may also go in the middle.)

   c. **pṛcchati gacchasi ca**

   d. **gacchati pṛcchati ca**

   e. **pṛcchasi**

   f. **pṛcchāmi ca gacchasi ca** (or) **pṛcchāmi gacchasi ca**

   g. **gacchāmi gacchasi ca**

   h. **gacchati gacchasi ca**

LESSON TWO

5. a. Where do we two live?
   b. You are and we two are.
   c. I live and those two remember.
   d. You two ask and he remembers.
   e. Where are we two going?
   f. Where am I?
   g. Where am I going? (or) Where do I go?
   h. I ask and he remembers.
   i. You live and we two go.
   j. Where are you going? (or) Where do you go?

6. Use only one verb. The auxiliary verb "are" need not be translated when there is another verb.

   (Just observe the sentences in parentheses, written with the sandhi included.)

   a. **kutra gacchathaḥ**
      (kutra gacchathaḥ)
   b. **vasāmi vasataḥ ca**
      (vasāmi vasataś ca)
   c. **pṛcchāvaḥ smarataḥ ca**
      (pṛcchāvaḥ smarataś ca)
   d. **gacchasi gacchati ca**
      (gacchasi gacchati ca)

LESSON TWO (CONTINUED)

e. **kutra gacchāmi**

(kutra gacchāmi)

f. **bhavāmi ca bhavathaḥ ca**

(bhavāmi ca bhavathaś ca)

g. **kutra bhavasi**

(kutra bhavasi)

h. **kutra gacchati**

(kutra gacchati)

LESSON THREE

5. a. He speaks and I do not speak. (or) He says and I do not say.
   b. You two speak and those two remember.
   c. They do not go.
   d. We all stand and go.
   e. You two are and you two live. (or) You two are and live.
   f. Where are you?
   g. They stand and go. (or) They stand and they go.
   h. He does not ask and he does not speak.

6. (All the following sentences are written the same with **sandhi.**)

   a. **kutra gacchanti**
   b. **na vadāmaḥ**
   c. **pṛcchati ca vadanti ca**
   d. **kutra tiṣṭhāmaḥ**
   e. **kutra vasataḥ**
   f. **na gacchāmaḥ**
   g. **pṛcchāmi smaranti ca**
   h. **kutra bhavāmaḥ**

LESSON FOUR

4. a. The men remember the deer.

   b. Rāma goes to the two horses.

   c. Where do the elephants live?

   d. The two men speak to Rāma.

   e. The son remembers or asks.

   f. Rāma goes to the deer.

   g. The two horses do not speak.

   h. Rāma speaks to the son.

5. (The sentences in parentheses are with **sandhi.**)

   a. **narāḥ mṛgam vadanti**

      (narā mṛgaṃ vadanti)

   b. **rāmaḥ aśvān vadati**

      (rāmo 'śvān vadati)

   c. **putraḥ aśvam gacchati tiṣṭhati ca**

      (putro 'śvaṃ gacchati tiṣṭhati ca)

   d. **gajāḥ na smaranti**

      (gajā na smaranti)

   e. **kutra aśvāḥ tiṣṭhanti**

      (kutra aśvās tiṣṭhanti)

   f. **kutra gajaḥ bhavati**

      (kutra gajo bhavati)

LESSON FOUR

(CONTINUED)

g. **rāmaḥ vadati putraḥ ca smarati**

(rāmo vadati putraś ca smarati)

h. **tiṣṭhanti vā gacchanti vā**

(tiṣṭhanti vā gacchanti vā)

i. **kutra rāmaḥ tiṣṭhati**

(kutra rāmas tiṣṭhati)

j. **rāmaḥ putraḥ vā gacchati**

(rāmaḥ putro vā gacchati)

k. **rāmaḥ putraḥ ca gacchataḥ**

(rāmaḥ putraś ca gacchataḥ)

6. a. The two men speak to the son.
   b. Where are the horses and elephants going?
   c. The horse or the deer goes.
   d. Rāma speaks to the two sons.
   e. The deer, horse and elephant are going.
   f. The sons do not remember the deer. (Deer is plural.)
   g. Where do the two men live?
   h. I ask Rāma.
   i. The two men do not speak to the sons.
   j. Where are the deer?

LESSON FOUR

(CONTINUED)

7. a. **kutra rāmaḥ gacchati**

   (kutra rāmo gacchati)

   b. **rāmaḥ aśvam gacchati**

   (rāmo 'śvaṃ gacchati)

   c. **putraḥ aśvān na vadati**

   (putro 'śvān na vadati)

   d. **gajau naram smarataḥ**

   (gajau naraṃ smarataḥ)

   e. **kutra mṛgau vasataḥ**

   (kutra mṛgau vasataḥ)

   f. **aśvam gacchasi**

   (aśvaṃ gacchasi)

   g. **kutra tiṣṭhāmaḥ**

   (kutra tiṣṭhāmaḥ)

   h. **putraḥ aśvān gajān ca gacchati**

   (putro 'śvān gajāṃś ca gacchati)

   i. **gajam vadatha**

   (gajaṃ vadatha)

   j. **gajaḥ na smarati**

   (gajo na smarati)

LESSON FIVE

4. a. Where do the heroes stand?
   b. There, together with the elephant, are the two boys.
   c. The king goes to the horse.
   d. With the horse, the hero goes to the kings.
   e. Rāma lives with the deer.
   f. The boys go together with the elephants.
   g. The men speak to the son.
   h. The heroes ask Rāma about all the deer.
   i. The boy goes there for the king.

5. a. **bālāḥ aśvān gacchanti**
   (bālā aśvān gacchanti)
   b. **putraḥ mṛgam nṛpam pṛcchati**
   (putro mṛgaṃ nṛpaṃ pṛcchati)
   c. **nṛpaḥ naram smarati**
   (nṛpo naraṃ smarati)
   d. **putreṇa saha vīraḥ vasati**
   (putreṇa saha vīro vasati)
   e. **bālaḥ nṛpam pṛcchati nṛpaḥ ca smarati**
   (bālo nṛpaṃ pṛcchati nṛpaś ca smarati)
   f. **putreṇa saha tatra gajāḥ na bhavanti**
   (putreṇa saha tatra gajā na bhavanti)

LESSON FIVE (CONTINUED)

g. **kutra rāmaḥ vasati**

(kutra rāmo vasati)

h. **nṛpaḥ vīraḥ vā bālam vadati**

(nṛpo vīro vā bālaṃ vadati)

i. **vīraḥ bālāya gacchati**

(vīro bālāya gacchati)

j. **tatra gajāḥ aśvaiḥ saha bhavanti**

(tatra gajā aśvaiḥ saha bhavanti)

k. **nṛpam smarāmi**

(nṛpaṃ smarāmi)

l. **tatra bālena saha gacchasi**

(tatra bālena saha gacchasi)

6. a. The hero goes with the horses.
   b. The men go there for the king.
   c. The two heroes stand and speak.
   d. All the deer live there.
   e. Where does the king go with the two boys?
   f. Rāma asks the son about the horse.
   g. The elephants are not standing there.
   h. The hero speaks to the boy about the king.
   i. The elephant lives with the deer and the horses.
   j. Where are we standing?

LESSON FIVE (CONTINUED)

7. a. **tatra bālābhyām saha nṛpaḥ vasati**

   (tatra bālābhyāṃ saha nṛpo vasati)

   b. **kutra gajaiḥ saha gacchasi**

   (kutra gajaiḥ saha gacchasi)

   c. **tatra naraḥ aśvāya gacchati**

   (tatra naro 'śvāya gacchati)

   d. **bālaḥ nṛpam na smarati**

   (bālo nṛpaṃ na smarati)

   e. **gajau nṛpam vadāmi**

   (gajau nṛpaṃ vadāmi)

   f. **nṛpaḥ putrāya aśvam gacchati**

   (nṛpaḥ putrāyāśvaṃ gacchati)

   g. **kutra tiṣṭhāmaḥ**

   (kutra tiṣṭhāmaḥ)

   h. **naraḥ aśvam bālam pṛcchati**

   (naro 'śvaṃ bālaṃ pṛcchati)

   i. **tatra rāmaḥ narāya gacchati**

   (tatra rāmo narāya gacchati)

   j. **kutra mṛgāḥ bhavanti**

   (kutra mṛgā bhavanti)

LESSON SIX

3. a. इति g. भवावः m. ऋषि
   b. नर h. वदसि n. देवता
   c. राम i. नृपः o. गुण
   d. गज j. न p. जय
   e. वीर k. वा q. गुरु
   f. वसति l. च r. देव

4. a. The boy's elephant goes to the village.
   b. The son of Rāma goes to the horse.
   c. "Here is the horse," the king says.
   d. The son comes from the village.
   e. "Where are the elephants standing?" the king asks.
   f. The boy goes to the village of the king.
   g. "The heroes live here," the men say.
   h. "Where are you going?" asks Rāma.

5. a. **atra vasāmi iti putraḥ vadati**
   (atra vasāmīti putro vadati)
   b. **aśvāḥ gajāḥ ca grāmāt āgacchanti**
   (aśvā gajāś ca grāmād āgacchanti)

LESSON SIX

(CONTINUED)

c. **narān smarasi iti nṛpaḥ bālam pṛcchati**

(narān smarasīti nṛpo bālaṃ pṛcchati)

(The question is understood.)

d. **grāmam gacchāmi iti rāmaḥ vadati**

(grāmaṃ gacchāmīti rāmo vadati)

e. **bālāya grāmam gacchāmi iti rāmaḥ vadati**

(bālāya grāmaṃ gacchāmīti rāmo vadati)

f. **kutra vīraḥ gacchati**

(kutra vīro gacchati)

g. **vīraḥ grāmam gacchati iti nṛpaḥ vadati**

(vīro grāmaṃ gacchatīti nṛpo vadati)

h. **atra nṛpasya putraḥ vasati**

(atra nṛpasya putro vasati)

i. **nṛpasya putrāḥ grāmāt āgacchanti**

(nṛpasya putrā grāmād āgacchanti)

j. **naraḥ gajān rāmam vadati**

(naro gajān rāmaṃ vadati)

6. a. The two men come from the village.

b. "Here I am," the boy says to the king.

c. "Where do you live?" the hero asks the son.

d. "I live here with Rāma," the son says.

e. The sons of the man are standing there.

LESSON SIX

(CONTINUED)

f. Here is the hero's elephant.

g. "Do you remember Rāma?" the boys ask the man.

h. "Where is the village?" the man asks the son.

i. "The village is there," the son says to the man.

j. "I am going to the village for the elephant," the man says.

7. a. **kutra gacchasi iti nṛpaḥ bālam pṛcchati**
(kutra gacchasīti nṛpo bālaṃ pṛcchati)

b. **aśvam gacchāmi iti bālaḥ vadati**
(aśvaṃ gacchāmīti bālo vadati)

c. **grāmāṇām nṛpaḥ narān vadati**
(grāmāṇāṃ nṛpo narān vadati)

d. **aśvāt gajāt ca bālau āgacchataḥ**
(aśvād gajāc ca bālāvāgacchataḥ)

e. **rāmeṇa saha bālaḥ vasati**
(rāmeṇa saha bālo vasati)

f. **atra rāmasya putrāḥ bhavanti iti vīraḥ vadati**
(atra rāmasya putrā bhavantīti vīro vadati)

g. **tatra bālāḥ tiṣṭhanti iti nṛpaḥ vadati**
(tatra bālās tiṣṭhantīti nṛpo vadati)

h. **grāmam gacchāmi iti vīrasya putraḥ vadati**
(grāmaṃ gacchāmīti vīrasya putro vadati)

i. **atra mṛgābhyām saha aśvau āgacchataḥ**
(atra mṛgābhyāṃ sahāśvāvāgacchataḥ)

j. **tatra nṛpasya aśvau bhavataḥ**
(tatra nṛpasyāśvau bhavataḥ)

LESSON SEVEN

1. a. **purāṇa** e. **gacchati** i. **aśva**
   b. **gandharva** f. **candra** j. **putrasya**
   c. **chandaḥ** g. **jyotiṣa** k. **śiṣyaḥ**
   d. **vyākaraṇa** h. **kalpa** l. **tiṣṭhanti**

3. a. the men (mas., nom., pl.)
   b. the hands (mas., nom., dual or mas., acc., dual)
   c. of the boys (mas., gen., pl.)
   d. from the king (mas., abl., sing.)
   e. for Rāma (mas., dat., sing.)
   f. with the deer (mas., inst., sing.)
   g. with the elephants (mas., inst., pl.)
   h. the heroes (mas., acc., pl.)
   i. in the villages (mas., loc., pl.)
   j. for the teacher (mas., dat., sing.)

4. a. The student sees the moon and the sun.
   b. O Rāma! The elephants are standing in the village.
   c. "The hero lives in the village," the teacher tells the student.
   d. "Where is the moon?" the son asks.
   e. The two boys are standing there on the elephant.
   f. "Son, where is the moon?" the hero asks the boy.
   g. The student of the teacher stands and speaks.
   h. Without Rāma the heroes come from the village.
   i. The hero's boy thinks that he lives in the village.

LESSON SEVEN (CONTINUED)

5. a. **bālāḥ grāmam gacchanti iti nṛpaḥ vīram vadati**
   (bālā grāmaṃ gacchantīti nṛpo vīraṃ vadati)

   b. **nṛpeṇa vinā bālāḥ āgacchanti**
   (nṛpeṇa vinā bālā āgacchanti)

   c. **vīrasya haste putraḥ bhavati**
   (vīrasya haste putro bhavati)

   d. **kutra bhavāmi iti bālaḥ cintayati**
   (kutra bhavāmīti bālaś cintayati)

   e. **kutra narāḥ bhavanti iti vīrasya putram pṛcchati**
   (kutra narā bhavantīti vīrasya putraṃ pṛcchati)

   f. **sūryaḥ candraḥ na bhavati iti ācāryaḥ śiṣyam vadati**
   (sūryaś candro na bhavatītyācāryaḥ śiṣyaṃ vadati)

   g. **grāme nṛpaḥ vasati**
   (grāme nṛpo vasati)

   h. **tatra nṛpasya gajāḥ bhavanti**
   (tatra nṛpasya gajā bhavanti)

6. a. The boy goes to the village without Rāma.
   b. Where are the king's elephants?
   c. "Here I am," the boy says to the man.
   d. Without the sun you cannot see the moon.
   e. The teacher speaks to the students.

LESSON SEVEN

(CONTINUED)

f. "I see the moon," the boy thinks.

g. Here comes the king of the villages.

h. The king sees the horse of the hero.

i. "Where are the sun and the moon?" the boy asks.

j. The students do not remember the man.

7. a. कुत्र गच्छसि इति बालः नृपस्य पुत्रम् पृच्छति ।

kutra gacchasi iti bālaḥ nṛpasya putram pṛcchati
(kutra gacchasīti bālo nṛpasya putraṃ pṛcchati)

b. मृगौ ग्रामे भवतः ।

mṛgau grāme bhavataḥ
(mṛgau grāme bhavataḥ)

c. आचार्यः वीरस्य पुत्रम् वदति ।

ācāryaḥ vīrasya putram vadati
(ācāryo vīrasya putraṃ vadati)

d. नृपः सूर्यम् चन्द्रम् च पश्यति ।

nṛpaḥ sūryam candram ca paśyati
(nṛpaḥ sūryaṃ candraṃ ca paśyati)

e. सूर्येण विना चन्द्रम् न पश्यामः ।

sūryeṇa vinā candram na paśyāmaḥ
(sūryeṇa vinā candraṃ na paśyāmaḥ)

LESSON SEVEN
(CONTINUED)

f. वीरः नृपस्य गजे भवति ।
vīraḥ nṛpasya gaje bhavati
(vīro nṛpasya gaje bhavati)

g. ग्रामेषु वसामः इति बालाः वदन्ति ।
grāmeṣu vasāmaḥ iti bālāḥ vadanti
(grāmeṣu vasāma iti bālā vadanti)

h. रामः अश्वेभ्यः गजान् गच्छति ।
rāmaḥ aśvebhyaḥ gajān gacchati
(rāmo 'śvebhyo gajān gacchati)

i कुत्र गच्छावः इति बालः नृपम् पृच्छति ।
kutra gacchāvaḥ iti bālaḥ nṛpam pṛcchati
(kutra gacchāva iti bālo nṛpaṃ pṛcchati)

j. शिष्यैः सह ग्रामे आचार्यः वसति ।
śiṣyaiḥ saha grāme ācāryaḥ vasati
(śiṣyaiḥ saha grāma ācāryo vasati)

LESSON SEVEN (CONTINUED)

8.
1. **ṛṣi** (seer)
2. **āsana** (seat)
3. **ahaṃkāra** (ego, "I maker")
4. **guṇa** (quality)
5. **jñāna** (knowledge)
6. **kuru-kṣetra** (field of the Kurus)
7. **karma** (action)
8. **dhyāna** (meditation)
9. **darśana** (vision, or system of philosophy)
10. **duḥkha** (pain)
11. **veda** (knowledge)
12. **citta** (mind)
13. **citta-vṛtti** (impulse of the mind)
14. **avidyā** (ignorance)
15. **avyakta** (unseen)
16. **dhāraṇā** (steadiness)
17. **ātman** (the Self)
18. **ānanda** (bliss)
19. **aṣṭāṅga-yoga** (eight limbs of yoga)
20. **tat tvam asi** (thou art that)
21. **nāma-rūpa** (name and form)
22. **upaniṣad** (sit down near)
23. **nitya** (eternal)
24. **dharma** (duty, or that which upholds)

LESSON EIGHT

2. a. पुत्रेणात्र
   b. सहाचार्यः
   c. तत्रेति
   d. इत्यत्र
   e. इत्याचार्यः
   f. देवावागच्छतः
   g. नरेऽत्र
   h. वन इति
   i. फलानीति
   j. स्मरत्यत्र

3. a. **gacchati iti**
   b. **gajau āgacchataḥ**
   c. **pṛcchati āgacchati ca**
   d. **gacchāmi iti**
   e. **haste iti**
   f. **nṛpasya aśvaḥ**
   g. **aśve atra**
   h. **kutra aśvaḥ**
   i. **kutra iti**
   j. **gacchati atra**

5. a. Rāma goes from the village to the forest.
   b. Immortality is the fruit of knowledge.
   c. "Knowledge is truth," the boys read in the scripture.
   d. "You are the sons of immortality," the teacher tells the students.
   e. How do the teachers remember the hymns?
   f. Rāma says that he sees the truth in the scriptures.

LESSON EIGHT (CONTINUED)

g. "Where is the knowledge of the hymns?" the hero asks the son.

h. The king reads the book to the boy.

6. a. **gajaḥ vanasya nṛpaḥ na bhavati**
gajaḥ vanasya nṛpaḥ na bhavati (with vowel **sandhi)**

गजः वनस्य नृपः न भवति । (with vowel **sandhi)**

(गजो वनस्य नृपो न भवति ।) (complete **sandhi)**

b. **katham candram paśyasi**
katham candram paśyasi

कथम् चन्द्रम् पश्यसि ।

(कथं चन्द्रं पश्यसि ।) (with complete **sandhi)**

c. **mṛgam paśyāmi iti rāmaḥ cintayati**
mṛgam paśyāmīti rāmaḥ cintayati

मृगम् पश्यामीति रामः चिन्तयति ।

(मृगं पश्यामीति रामश्चिन्तयति ।)

d. **phalam bālasya hastayoḥ bhavati** (or **phalāni)**
phalam bālasya hastayoḥ bhavati

फलम् बालस्य हस्तयोः भवति ।

(फलं बालस्य हस्तयोर्भवति ।)

LESSON EIGHT (CONTINUED)

e. **katham rāmeṇa vinā nṛpaḥ vasati**
katham rāmeṇa vinā nṛpaḥ vasati

कथम् रामेण विना नृपः वसति ।

(कथं रामेण विना नृपो वसति ।)

f. **rāmaḥ nṛpaḥ bhavati**
rāmaḥ nṛpaḥ bhavati

रामः नृपः भवति ।

(रामो नृपो भवति ।)

g. **nṛpaḥ rāmaḥ bhavati**
nṛpaḥ rāmaḥ bhavati

नृपः रामः भवति ।

(नृपो रामो भवति ।)

h. **vīraḥ amṛtānām grāme vasati**
vīraḥ amṛtānām grāme vasati

वीरः अमृतानाम् ग्रामे वसति ।

(वीरोऽमृतानां ग्रामे वसति ।)

7. a. How can the men see the king without the sun?

   b. The students' teacher reads the book.

LESSON EIGHT (CONTINUED)

c. "Here in the forest is fruit," the boy says to the hero.

d. The deer lives in the forest and the elephant lives in the village.

e. "Knowledge is not in the book," the teacher says.

f. Without the book the student remembers the knowledge.

g. "Rāma, where are you going with the deer?" the son asks.

h. The man reads the book to the boy.

8. a. **kutra amṛtasya jñānam paṭhasi**
kutrāmṛtasya jñānam paṭhasi (with vowel **sandhi**)

कुत्रामृतस्य ज्ञानम् पठसि । (with vowel **sandhi**)

(कुत्रामृतस्य ज्ञानं पठसि ।) (with complete **sandhi**)

b. **katham aśvaiḥ vinā rāmaḥ vanam gacchati**
katham aśvaiḥ vinā rāmaḥ vanam gacchati

कथम् अश्वैः विना रामः वनम् गच्छति ।

(कथमश्वैर्विना रामो वनं गच्छति ।)

c. **pustake sūktāni bhavanti iti ācāryaḥ śiṣyān vadati**
pustake sūktāni bhavantīty ācāryaḥ śiṣyān vadati

पुस्तके सूक्तानि भवन्तीत्याचार्यः शिष्यान् वदति ।

(पुस्तके सूक्तानि भवन्तीत्याचार्यः शिष्यान्वदति ।)

LESSON EIGHT (CONTINUED)

d. rāmaḥ satyam paśyati satyam ca vadati
rāmaḥ satyam paśyati satyam ca vadati

रामः सत्यम् पश्यति सत्यम् च वदति ।

(रामः सत्यं पश्यति सत्यं च वदति ।)

e. sūryam candram ca paśyāmi iti nṛpasya putraḥ vadati
sūryam candram ca paśyāmīti nṛpasya putraḥ vadati

सूर्यम् चन्द्रम् च पश्यामीति नृपस्य पुत्रः वदति ।

(सूर्यं चन्द्रं च पश्यामीति नृपस्य पुत्रो वदति ।)

f. jñānena vinā tatra ācāryāḥ śiṣyāḥ vā na bhavanti
jñānena vinā tatrācāryāḥ śiṣyāḥ vā na bhavanti

ज्ञानेन विना तत्राचार्याः शिष्याः वा न भवन्ति ।

(ज्ञानेन विना तत्राचार्याः शिष्या वा न भवन्ति ।)

g. vīraḥ amṛtam bālān vadati
vīraḥ amṛtam bālān vadati

वीरः अमृतम् बालान् वदति ।

(वीरोऽमृतं बालान्वदति ।)

LESSON EIGHT (CONTINUED)

h. **grāmāt aśvāḥ gajāḥ bālāḥ ca āgacchanti**
grāmāt aśvāḥ gajāḥ bālāḥ cāgacchanti

ग्रामात् अश्वाः गजाः बालाः चागच्छन्ति ।

(ग्रामादश्वा गजा बालाश्चागच्छन्ति ।)

9. 1. **purāṇa** (ancient)
2. **rāma** (**Rāma**, hero of the Rāmāyaṇa)
3. **puruṣa** (man, or consciousness)
4. **prakṛti** (nature)
5. **prajñā** (intellect)
6. **sītā** (Sītā, Rāma's wife)
7. **sukham** (happiness)
8. **saṃyama** (last three of the eight limbs of yoga)
9. **saṃsāra** (creation)
10. **saṃskāra** (impression)
11. **saṃskṛta** (perfected, put together)
12. **satyam** (truth)
13. **rāma-rājya** (kingdom of Rāma)
14. **rāmāyaṇa** (life of Rāma)
15. **śiṣya** (student)
16. **sthita-prajña** (man of established intellect)
17. **bhagavad-gītā** (Song of the Lord)
18. **samādhi** (even intelligence)
19. **yoga** (union)
20. **buddha** (Buddha)
21. **mahābhārata** (Great India)
22. **prajñāparādha** (mistake of the intellect)
23. **vedānta** (culmination of the Veda)
24. **veda-līlā** (play of knowledge)

THE MONKEY AND THE CROCODILE

1. **tatra gaṅgāyām kumbhīraḥ bhavati**
   (tatra gaṅgāyāṃ kumbhīro bhavati)

2. **vānaraḥ taṭe vasati**
   (vānaras taṭe vasati)

3. **vānaraḥ phalāni kumbhīrāya nikṣipati**
   (vānaraḥ phalāni kumbhīrāya nikṣipati)

4. **kumbhīraḥ phalāni khādati**
   (kumbhīraḥ phalāni khādati)

5. **bhāryā vānarasya hṛdayam icchati**
   (bhāryā vānarasya hṛdayam icchati)

6. **hṛdayam vṛkṣe bhavatīti vānaraḥ vadati**
   (hṛdayaṃ vṛkṣe bhavatīti vānaro vadati)

7. **kaścit hṛdayam corayatīti vānaraḥ vadati**
   (kaścid dhṛdayaṃ corayatīti vānaro vadati)

8. **evam kumbhīraḥ vānaraḥ ca mitre tiṣṭhataḥ**
   (evaṃ kumbhīro vānaraś ca mitre tiṣṭhataḥ)

1. There is a crocodile in the Ganges.

2. A monkey lives on the bank (of the river).

3. The monkey throws down fruit for the crocodile.

4. The crocodile eats the fruit.

5. The wife wants (to eat) the monkey's heart.

6. "The heart is in the tree!" the monkey says.

7. "Someone steals the heart," the monkey says.

8. Therefore, the crocodile and the monkey remain friends (stand in friendship).

LESSON NINE

1. a. रामो गच्छति
   b. बाला आगच्छन्ति
   c. वीरावागच्छतः
   d. शिष्योऽत्र
   e. राम इति
   f. देवाः स्मरन्ति
   g. पुत्रः पश्यति
   h. अश्वो वदति

2. a. रामः गच्छति
   b. कुत्र आगच्छसि
   c. सूर्यः चन्द्रः च
   d. गजैः वीरः
   e. अश्वाः आगच्छन्ति
   f. रामः पुत्रः च
   g. गजैः सह
   h. फलयोः जलम्

3. a. The hero has a boy. (Of the hero a boy is.)
   b. Happiness is the fruit of knowledge.
   c. The students obtain water from the house for the teacher.
   d. "Rāma goes there for the water," the hero says.
   e. The student serves the teacher.
   f. The students obtain knowledge from the teacher.
   g. O Rāma! How do you conquer suffering?

LESSON NINE (CONTINUED)

h. The son goes from the house on the king's horses.

i. "Immortality is the fruit of happiness," he thinks.

j. The teacher reads the book of knowledge to the student.

4. a. जलम् रामस्य हस्तयोः भवति । (without **sandhi**)

जलम् रामस्य हस्तयोर्भवति । (with vowel and final **ḥ sandhi**)

(जलं रामस्य हस्तयोर्भवति ।) (with complete **sandhi**)

b. बालः पुस्तकम् पठति ।

बालः पुस्तकम् पठति ।

(बालः पुस्तकं पठति ।)

c. वीरः नृपस्य गृहे एव तिष्ठति ।

वीरो नृपस्य गृह एव तिष्ठति ।

(वीरो नृपस्य गृह एव तिष्ठति ।)

LESSON NINE

(CONTINUED)

d. बालाः वनात् फलानि लभन्ते ।

बाला वनात् फलानि लभन्ते ।

(बाला वनात्फलानि लभन्ते ।)

e. ज्ञानेन दुःखम् जयसि इति आचार्यः वदति ।

ज्ञानेन दुःखम् जयसीत्याचार्यो वदति ।

(ज्ञानेन दुःखं जयसीत्याचार्यो वदति ।)

f. फलात् बालः जलम् लभते ।

फलात् बालो जलम् लभते ।

(फलाद्बालो जलं लभते ।)

g. सूर्ये चन्द्रे च सत्यम् पश्यामि इति रामः वदति ।

सूर्ये चन्द्रे च सत्यम् पश्यामीति रामो वदति ।

(सूर्ये चन्द्रे च सत्यं पश्यामीति रामो वदति ।)

LESSON NINE

(CONTINUED)

h. ज्ञानेन विना दुःखम् भवति ।

ज्ञानेन विना दुःखम् भवति ।

(ज्ञानेन विना दुःखं भवति ।)

i. ग्रामात् न आगच्छामि इति नृपस्य पुत्रः वदति ।

ग्रामात् नागच्छामीति नृपस्य पुत्रो वदति ।

(ग्रामान्नागच्छामीति नृपस्य पुत्रो वदति ।)

j. वीरः बालः च वने वसतः ।

वीरो बालश्च वने वसतः ।

(वीरो बालश्च वने वसतः ।)

RĀMĀYAṆA

1. **ayodhyāyām daśaratho nāma nṛpo vasati**
   (ayodhyāyāṃ daśaratho nāma nṛpo vasati)
2. **daśarathasya catvāraḥ putrā bhavanti**
   (daśarathasya catvāraḥ putrā bhavanti)
3. **putrā rāmo bharato lakṣmaṇaḥ śatrughno bhavanti**
   (putrā rāmo bharato lakṣmaṇaḥ śatrughno bhavanti)
4. **rāmaḥ sundaraḥ śānto vīraś ca bhavati**
   (rāmaḥ sundaraḥ śānto vīraś ca bhavati)
5. **nṛpo rāme snihyati**
   (nṛpo rāme snihyati)
6. **rāmo mithilām lakṣmaṇena saha gacchati**
   (rāmo mithilāṃ lakṣmaṇena saha gacchati)
7. **tatra rāmaḥ sītām paśyati**
   (tatra rāmaḥ sītāṃ paśyati)
8. **sītāyām snihyāmīti rāmo vadati**
   (sītāyāṃ snihyāmīti rāmo vadati)

1. In Ayodhyā lives a king named Daśaratha.
2. Daśaratha has four sons.
3. The sons are Rāma, Bharata, Lakṣmaṇa, and Śatrughna.
4. Rāma is beautiful, peaceful, and strong.
5. The king loves Rāma.
6. Rāma goes to Mithilā with Lakṣmaṇa.
7. There Rāma sees Sītā.
8. "I love Sītā," Rāma says.

LESSON TEN

1. a. मम पुत्रो गच्छति ।

   My son goes.

   b. तव गजो मत्तवां गच्छति ।

   Your elephant goes from me to you.

   c. मम हस्तौ पुस्तकेषु स्तः ।

   My hands are on the books.

   d. अहं नृपोऽस्मि ।

   I am the king.

   e. वयमश्वे तिष्ठामः ।

   We are standing on the horse.

   f. त्वं मम पुस्तकं पठसि ।

   You are reading my book.

   g. रामस्तव नृपोऽस्ति ।

   Rāma is your king.

   h. यूयं गृहे स्थ ।

   You are all in the house.

   i. अस्माकं नृपः कुपितोऽस्ति ।

   Our king is angry.

   j. त्वया सहाहं गच्छामि ।

   I am going with you.

LESSON TEN
(CONTINUED)

k. धार्मिको नृपो भीतोऽस्ति ।

The virtuous king is afraid.

l. सुन्दरस्त्वम् ।

You are beautiful.

2. a. The king has a son.

b. Aha! Rāma is speaking again.

c. I am very afraid.

d. Even teachers read books.

e. There is a king named Rāma in the forest.

f. "How do I go to your house?" the student asks.

g. The hero conquers my village.

h. The son obtains water from the beautiful fruit.

i. Without happiness there is suffering.

j. The son thinks that the elephant is beautiful.

3. a. शिष्यः आचार्यात् भीतः न अस्ति ।

शिष्य आचार्याद्भीतो नास्ति ।

LESSON TEN

(CONTINUED)

b. त्वम् शास्त्रेभ्यः ज्ञानम् लभसे ।

त्वं शास्त्रेभ्यो ज्ञानं लभसे ।

c. तत्र बालः अस्ति इति वीरः आचार्यम् वदति ।

तत्र बालोऽस्तीति वीर आचार्यं वदति ।

d. अहम् मृगम् आचार्यम् पृच्छामि ।

अहं मृगमाचार्यं पृच्छामि ।

e. कुत्र गच्छसि इति बालः पृच्छति ।

कुत्र गच्छसीति बालः पृच्छति ।

f. पुनर् वीरः मम गृहम् आगच्छति ।

पुनर्वीरो मम गृहमागच्छति ।

g. तव आचार्यः सत्यम् वदति ।

तवाचार्यः सत्यं वदति ।

LESSON TEN

(CONTINUED)

h. अस्माकम् अश्वाः ग्रामे तिष्ठन्ति ।

अस्माकमश्वा ग्रामे तिष्ठन्ति ।

i. अस्ति नृपः रामः नाम अस्माकम् ग्रामे ।

अस्ति नृपो रामो नामास्माकं ग्रामे ।

j. कथम् त्वत् नृपस्य अश्वान् लभे ।

कथं त्वन्नृपस्याश्वांल्लभे ।

LESSON ELEVEN

1. a. रामेण सह — with Rāma

   b. शास्त्राणि — scriptures

   c. फले अश्वे स्तः। — The two fruits are on the horse. (The dual ends in a **pragṛhya** vowel. See page 91.)

   d. स गच्छति। — He goes.

   e. स बाल आगच्छति। — That boy comes.

   f. बालो मामागच्छति। — The boy comes to me.

   g. सा बाला मामागच्छति। — That girl comes to me.

   h. तां गच्छति। — He goes to her.

   i. स बालो गच्छति। — That boy goes.

   j. सा बाला गच्छति। — That girl goes.

   k. स बाल इव गच्छामि। — Like that boy, I go.

   l. अहो राम — Hey Rāma!

   m. तस्मिन्वने स वसति। — He lives in that forest.

   n. सीताया माला — Sītā's garland

LESSON ELEVEN

(CONTINUED)

2. a. That army conquers the king.
   b. Like Rāma, the boy is virtuous.
   c. Your child reads the story.
   d. The children stand in the shadow of the elephant.
   e. Sītā is the daughter of the king.
   f. He serves the teacher's wife.
   g. The king has a daughter.
   h. With knowledge the student obtains immortality.
   i. Like that girl, Sītā goes to the house.

3. a. अस्ति कन्या सीता नाम तस्मिन् ग्रामे ।

   अस्ति कन्या सीता नाम तस्मिन्ग्रामे ।

   b. धार्मिकस्य नृपस्य पुत्रिका अतीव भीता भवति ।

   धार्मिकस्य नृपस्य पुत्रिकातीव भीता भवति ।

   c. पुनर् माम् वदति इति सा प्रजा वदति ।

   पुनर्मां वदतीति सा प्रजा वदति ।

LESSON ELEVEN

(CONTINUED)

d. अहो अहम् ताम् कथाम् स्मरामि इति कन्या वदति ।

अहो अहं तां कथां स्मरामीति कन्या वदति ।

e. विद्यया अमृतम् लभसे । अविद्यया दुःखम् लभसे ।

विद्ययामृतं लभसे । अविद्यया दुःखं लभसे ।

f. ताः कन्याः इव सीता पुस्तकानि पठति ।

ताः कन्या इव सीता पुस्तकानि पठति ।

g. कुत्र आवयोः पुत्रिका अस्ति इति वीरः तस्य भार्याम् पृच्छति । ("Our" is dual.)

कुत्रावयोः पुत्रिकास्तीति वीरस्तस्य भार्यां पृच्छति ।

h. रामस्य भार्या सीता अस्ति ।

रामस्य भार्या सीतास्ति ।

LESSON ELEVEN

(CONTINUED)

i. वीरः मालाम् लभते एवम् च भार्याम् लभते ।

वीरो मालां लभत एवं च भार्यां लभते ।

j. सीतया विना सूर्येन विना इव अस्मि इति रामः वदति ।

सीतया विना सूर्येण विनेवास्मीति रामो वदति ।

THE MONKEY AND THE CROCODILE

4. a. There is in the Ganges a crocodile.
   b. His friend, a monkey, lives on the bank of the Ganges.
   c. Everyday the monkey throws down ripe fruits.
   d. The crocodile eats the fruits.
   e. "The heart of the monkey is sweet!" says the wife of the crocodile.
   f. The wife wants to eat the heart.
   g. "Hey monkey! Come to my house!" the crocodile says to the monkey.
   h. "OK" the monkey says.
   i. The crocodile carries the monkey on his back.
   j. In the middle of the Ganges the crocodile tells the truth.
   k. "My heart is in the tree!" the monkey says.
   l. "Take me there again," the monkey says.
   m. The crocodile takes the monkey to the bank of the Ganges.
   n. The monkey jumps up to the tree.
   o. The monkey looks in the hole of the tree.
   p. "Someone has stolen my heart!" the monkey says.
   q. Therefore the crocodile and the monkey remain friends.

LESSON TWELVE

1. a. Having seen the fire, the horse goes from the house.
   b. The student lives in the village.
   c. The seers see the hymns of the scriptures.
   d. The king serves the tenth guest.
   e. Having conquered the village, the hero obtains fame.
   f. The siddha lives in the village.
   g. "Hey Rāma! Where are you going?" the second hero asks.
   h. Having read the book, the poet thinks about it.
   i. With truth comes peace.
   j. "We live on the earth," the people say.

2. a. सेनाम् जित्वा वीरः भूमौ कीर्तिम् लभते ।१।

   सेनां जित्वा वीरो भूमौ कीर्तिं लभते ।१।

   b. सीता रामः च इव शिष्यः वनम् गच्छति ।२।

   सीता रामश्चेव शिष्यो वनं गच्छति ।२।

   c. तृतीयम् तस्याः अतिथिम् सेवित्वा सीता रामम् वदति ।३।

LESSON TWELVE

(CONTINUED)

तृतीयं तस्या अतिथिं सेवित्वा सीता रामं

वदति ।३।

d. कथायाम् रामः कीर्तिम् लभते ।४।

कथायां रामः कीर्तिं लभते ।४।

e. वीरः अविद्याम् न जयते ।५।

वीरोऽविद्यां न जयते ।५।

f. नृपः रामः नाम अतीव धार्मिकः अस्ति ।६।

नृपो रामो नामातीव धार्मिकोऽस्ति ।६।

g. कथम् सिद्धिम् लभसे इति द्वितीयः शिष्यः

पृच्छति ।७।

कथं सिद्धिं लभस इति द्वितीयः शिष्यः

पृच्छति ।७।

LESSON TWELVE

(CONTINUED)

h. तस्य भार्यया सह वने उषित्वा नृपः रामः नाम ग्रामम् गच्छति ।८।

तस्य भार्यया सह वन उषित्वा नृपो रामो नाम ग्रामं गच्छति ।८।

i. शान्तिम् सिद्धिम् कीर्तिम् च लब्ध्वा ऋषिः सुन्दरम् वनम् गच्छति ।९।

शान्तिं सिद्धिं कीर्तिं च लब्ध्वर्षिः सुन्दरं वनं गच्छति ।९।

j. गजे एवम् तस्य भार्याम् दृष्ट्वा वीरः ताम् गच्छति ।१०।

गज एवं तस्य भार्यां दृष्ट्वा वीरस्तां गच्छति ।१०।

LESSON THIRTEEN

1. a. Where there is peace, there is perfection.
   b. The girl who is my wife's daughter lives here.
   c. "Sītā is the beautiful daughter of the king," Rāma says.
   d. Since the horses are not coming here, the men and the boys are going there.
   e. Having gone to the river, the two friends read books.
   f. When the army serves the king, then the virtuous king conquers.
   g. If a man obtains perfection, then he becomes a sage.
   h. The poet reads the story to the boy who is his guest.
   i. With the friend, the man goes to the beautiful river.
   j. The hero remembers the village from which I come.

2. a. नद्याः जलम् बालः लभते ।१।

   नद्या जलं बालो लभते ।१।

   b. यत् वाप्याम् अस्ति तत् फलम् पत्नी पश्यति ।२।

   यद्वाप्यामस्ति तत्फलं पत्नी पश्यति ।२।

   c. मालाम् लब्ध्वा अस्माकम् अतिथिः ग्रामम् गच्छति ।३।

   मालां लब्ध्वास्माकमतिथिर्ग्रामं गच्छति ।३।

LESSON THIRTEEN

(CONTINUED)

d. यदा तस्य पत्नी तम् सेवते तदा सः नृपः इव

वसति ।४।

यदा तस्य पत्नी तं सेवते तदा स नृप इव

वसति ।४।

e. या रामस्य भार्या भवति सा सीता भूमौ कीर्तिम्

लभते ।५।

या रामस्य भार्या भवति सा सीता भूमौ कीर्तिं

लभते ।५।

f. यः बालः आगच्छति तम् धार्मिकः नृपः

पश्यति ।६।

यो बाल आगच्छति तं धार्मिको नृपः पश्यति ।६।

g. शिष्यः मत्वा नदीम् कविम् पृच्छति ।७।

शिष्यो मत्वा नदीं कविं पृच्छति ।७।

LESSON THIRTEEN

(CONTINUED)

h. सा सुन्दरी पत्नी दुःखेन विना वसति ।८।

सा सुन्दरी पत्नी दुःखेन विना वसति ।८।

i. यः नरः पश्यति तस्मै अविद्या छाया इव भवति ।९।

यो नरः पश्यति तस्मा अविद्या छायेव भवति ।९।

j. यदा नृपस्य पुत्रिका आगच्छति तदा प्रजाः तिष्ठन्ति ।१०।

यदा नृपस्य पुत्रिकागच्छति तदा प्रजास्तिष्ठन्ति ।१०।

LESSON FOURTEEN

3. a. When the student brings water, then the teacher drinks it.
   b. The boy led the elephants to the pond. (A double accusative is a common formation in Sanskrit.)
   c. The poet speaks to the man who is approaching the village.
   d. Rāma said that the hero protects the village from the angry king.
   e. After seeing the elephant in the pond, the seer laughed and laughed.
   f. "I know your beautiful wife," the girl said to the hero.
   g. The wife returned to the house in which she lived.
   h. The sage knows peace, truth, perfection, immortality, and happiness.
   i. The hero protected the village from the army.
   j. Having seen the beautiful king, the boy laughed.

4. a. कविः पुस्तकम् अपठत् जलम् अपिबत् इव ।१।

   कविः पुस्तकमपठज्जलमपिबदिव ।१।

   b. कथम् सेनायाः ग्रामम् गोपायामि इति वीरः अपृच्छत् ।२।

   कथं सेनाया ग्रामं गोपायामीति वीरोऽपृच्छत् ।२।

LESSON FOURTEEN

(CONTINUED)

c. कथम् ऋषयः अग्निना विना अवसन् ।३।

कथमृषयोऽग्निना विनावसन् ।३।

d. यदि अश्वाः नदीम् प्रतिगच्छन्ति तदा बालः

तान् वनम् नयति ।४।

यद्यश्वा नदीं प्रतिगच्छन्ति तदा बालस्तान्वनं

नयति ।४।

e. यदा नरः दुःखम् न बोधते तदा

सिद्धिम् उपगच्छति ।५।

यदा नरो दुःखं न बोधते तदा

सिद्धिमुपगच्छति ।५।

f. नृपः रामः नाम तस्य भार्यायै सीतायै मालाम्

आनयत् ।६।

नृपो रामो नाम तस्य भार्यायै सीतायै

मालामानयत् ।६।

LESSON FOURTEEN

(CONTINUED)

g. नरः अविद्याम् विद्यया जयति ।७।

नरोऽविद्यां विद्यया जयति ।७।

h. यत् जलम् नद्याः आगच्छत् तत् प्रजा अपिबत् ।८।

यज्जलं नद्या आगच्छत्तत्प्रजापिबत् ।८।

i. कन्या नदीम् दृष्ट्वा तस्याः गृहम् प्रत्यगच्छत् ।९।

कन्या नदीं दृष्ट्वा तस्या गृहं प्रत्यगच्छत् ।९।

j. बालः वनात् नदीम् अश्वान् अनयत् ।१०।

बालो वनान्नदीमश्वाननयत् ।१०।

LESSON FIFTEEN

3. a. Having understood the story, the poet smiled.
   b. Rāma and Sītā enjoyed the water in the river.
   c When the guest approaches, then the boys stand up.
   d. When the guest approached, then the boys stood up.
   e. Where there is peace, there is happiness.
   f. A daughter is born in the house of the king.
   g. Having conquered ignorance with knowledge, the sage shines like the sun.
   h. "Hey Rāma! How do you stand up on that elephant?" the boy asked.
   i. Having enjoyed the fruit in the forest, the wife of the hero returned to the house.
   j. Rāma smiled at the boy who is his son.
   k. When the teacher spoke, then the students stood up.

4. Sentences will be given with **sandhi**. If the **sandhi** is difficult, the sentence will be given without **sandhi** first.

   a. यथातिथिः फलमरमत तथा गृहं पुनः प्रतिगच्छति ।१।

   b. स्मित्वा सीता सुन्दरीं बालामवदत् ।२।

   c. गजादागत्य बालस्तं ग्राममुपागच्छत् ।३।

LESSON FIFTEEN

(CONTINUED)

d. नरस्य पुत्रोऽस्तीत्यवगच्छति ।४।

e. फलाज्जलं पीत्वा कन्योत्तिष्ठति ।५।

f. यदा चन्द्रः शोभते तदा वने छायाः पश्यसि ।६।

g. यदा बालो गजं पश्यति तदा स्मयते हसति च ।७।

h. नरस्तस्य पत्नी च तत्सुन्दरं गृहं रमेते ।८।

i. यदा तस्य पुत्रः उदभवत् तदा वीरः

अस्मयत ।९।

यदा तस्य पुत्र उदभवत्तदा वीरोऽस्मयत ।९।

j. यः नरः तिष्ठति तस्मात् कन्या फलानि

अलभत ।१०।

यो नरस्तिष्ठति तस्मात्कन्या फलान्यलभत ।१०।

k. यतः सूर्यश्चन्द्रे शोभते ततश्चन्द्रोऽस्मासु शलभते

।११।

LESSON SIXTEEN

5\. a. Kṛṣṇa protected the horses, deer, and elephants. (This could be written in other ways, such as "horse, deer, and elephant.")

b. The beloved king, Rāma, smiled to the boys of the village.

c. The girl protected the child from the sun with her shadow.

d. He who knows the Self, (he) enjoys action. ("Action" is sometimes put in the plural when it is used in this way.)

e. The child laughed at the black horse's action.

f. The boy stood up when she said his name.

g. Having approached his dear son, the hero smiled.

h. The boy and girl are the children of the shining king.

i. The white horses were in the forest.

j. In the village there was a king, named Rāma.

6\. a. कृष्णोऽश्वो नद्या जलं पिबति ।१।

b. य आत्मानं बोधति स कर्माकर्म रमते ।२।

c. राज्ञो नाम कृष्ण आसीत् ।३।

d. राजा रमणीयानि पुत्रस्य कर्माणि रमते ।४।

e. प्रियः वीरः सिद्धि असिद्धी अवागच्छत् ।५।

प्रियो वीरः सिद्ध्यसिद्ध्यवागच्छत् ।५।

LESSON SIXTEEN

(CONTINUED)

f. बालो गजादागच्छति गृहं च प्रतिगच्छति ।६।

g. यो नागच्छति न गच्छति स आत्मा ।७।

h. यदा राजोपागच्छत्तदा बालबाला उदतिष्ठन् ।८।

i. यः नरः राजा आसीत् सः कृष्णात् वनात्

आगच्छत् ।९।

यो नरो राजासीत्स कृष्णाद्वनादागच्छत् ।९।

j. आत्मनः ज्ञानम् सूर्यचन्द्रयोः ज्ञानम् अपि

अस्ति ।१०।

आत्मनो ज्ञानं सूर्यचन्द्रयोर्ज्ञानमप्यस्ति ।१०।

LESSON SEVENTEEN

4. a. "My father will go there," the boy said to his mother.
   b. "When will your brother obtain the water?" the father asked.
   c. The father and mother will protect the family from the water.
   d. "When will you come from the forest?" Rāma asked his brother.
   e. After serving his father, Rāma will be the king.
   f. She smiles when she thinks of her brother.
   g. A mother is the giver of happiness to her child.
   h. He who conquers the Self is a maker of peace.
   i. After drinking the water, he will read his mother's book.
   h. Rāma will live in the forest with the brother.

5. a. यदा मम स्वसा उदभवत् तदा सा मम

   मातरम् अस्मयत ।१।

   यदा मम स्वसोदभवत्तदा सा मम

   मातरमस्मयत ।१।

   b. मम कुलस्य नाम ऋषेः नाम्नः भवति ।२।

   मम कुलस्य नामर्षेर्नाम्नो भवति ।२।

   c. कदा राजानं वदिष्यामीति तस्याः पितामन्यत ।३।

LESSON SEVENTEEN

(CONTINUED)

d. तस्याः पितुः पत्नी तस्या माता भवति ।४।

e. मम पितास्माकं कुले शान्तेः कर्तास्ति ।५।

f. भ्रातास्वसारौ वनात्फलानि लप्स्येते ।६।

g. वीरः वने अग्नेः राजानम् गोप्स्यति ।७।

वीरो वनेऽग्ने राजानं गोप्स्यति ।७।

h. राज्ञः पुत्रस्य भ्रातरो न भवन्ति ।८।

i. कदा शिष्याः धार्मिकात् आचार्यात् ज्ञानम् लप्स्यन्ते ।९।

कदा शिष्या धार्मिकादाचार्याज्ज्ञानं लप्स्यन्ते ।९।

j. वाप्याम् त्वाम् अपश्यम् इति राजा सुन्दरम् पुत्रम् वदति ।१०।

वाप्यां त्वामपश्यमिति राजा सुन्दरं पुत्रं वदति ।१०।

LESSON EIGHTEEN

4. a. The white cow stands in the pond and drinks water.
   b. The sage has conquered the enemy.
   c. If the forest is full of fruit, then the cows go there.
   d. My mother reads the little book and enjoys it.
   e. A teacher is the giver of much happiness.
   f. The little boy shines like the white sun.
   g. When you understand the Self, then you are the cause of much happiness.
   h. When will the pleasant king protect our family from the enemy?
   i. The swift girl comes from the forest with fruit.
   j. The cause of the teacher's happiness is the attainments of his students.
   k. "The enemy of knowledge is ignorance," the boy said.

5. a. सुन्दराल्पधेनुर्वाप्या जलमपिबत् ।१।
   b. शीघ्रकृष्णाश्वोऽल्पे ग्रामे तिष्ठति ।२।
   c. शत्रुं जित्वा सेना शान्तिसुखे रंस्यते ।३।
   d. अविद्या सत्यशत्रुः ।४।
   e. आत्मानं बुद्ध्वा स कर्माकर्मस्य हेतुमवागच्छत् ।५।

LESSON EIGHTEEN

(CONTINUED)

f. प्रजा सुन्दरे वनेऽल्पगृह उदभवत् ।६।

g. शिष्यस्तस्य गुरवे सुन्दरमालामानेष्यति ।७।

h. वनं फलपूर्णं भवति वापी च जलपूर्णा भवति ।८।

i. तस्य कुलं दृष्ट्वा पिता जलाय वनमगच्छत् ।९।

j. कदा सुन्दरी धेनुरत्र शीघ्रनद्या

आगमिष्यति ।१०।

k. धेनुं दृष्ट्वा रमणीयो बालो वाप्यां जलं रमते ।११।

a

MASCULINE

TABLES

Stem: **nara** (masculine) man (given on p. 74)

	Singular	Dual	Plural
Nom.	नरः	नरौ	नराः
Acc.	नरम्	नरौ	नरान्
Inst.	नरेण *	नराभ्याम्	नरैः
Dat.	नराय	नराभ्याम्	नरेभ्यः
Abl.	नरात्	नराभ्याम्	नरेभ्यः
Gen.	नरस्य	नरयोः	नराणाम् *
Loc.	नरे	नरयोः	नरेषु
Voc.	नर	नरौ	नराः

*The instrumental singular for **gaja** is **gajena**, and the genitive plural for **gaja** is **gajānām**. The **r** in **nareṇa** and **narāṇām** causes the **n** to become **ṇ**. (See page 142, 143.)

a
NEUTER

Stem: **phala** (neuter) fruit (given on p. 92)

	Singular	Dual	Plural
Nom.	फलम्	फले	फलानि
Acc.	फलम्	फले	फलानि
Inst.	फलेन	फलाभ्याम्	फलैः
Dat.	फलाय	फलाभ्याम्	फलेभ्यः
Abl.	फलात्	फलाभ्याम्	फलेभ्यः
Gen.	फलस्य	फलयोः	फलानाम्
Loc.	फले	फलयोः	फलेषु
Voc.	फल	फले	फलानि

ā
FEMININE

Stem: **senā** (feminine) army (given on p. 145)

	Singular	Dual	Plural
Nom.	सेना	सेने	सेनाः
Acc.	सेनाम्	सेने	सेनाः
Inst.	सेनया	सेनाभ्याम्	सेनाभिः
Dat.	सेनायै	सेनाभ्याम्	सेनाभ्यः
Abl.	सेनायाः	सेनाभ्याम्	सेनाभ्यः
Gen.	सेनायाः	सेनयोः	सेनानाम्
Loc.	सेनायाम्	सेनयोः	सेनासु
Voc.	सेने	सेने	सेनाः

i

MASCULINE

FEMININE

Stem: **agni** (masculine) fire; **kīrti** (feminine) glory (given on p. 160)

	Singular	Dual	Plural
Nom.	अग्निः	अग्नी	अग्नयः
Acc.	अग्निम्	अग्नी	अग्नीन् कीर्तीः
Inst.	अग्निना कीर्त्या	अग्निभ्याम्	अग्निभिः
Dat.	अग्नये कीर्त्यै	अग्निभ्याम्	अग्निभ्यः
Abl.	अग्नेः कीर्त्याः	अग्निभ्याम्	अग्निभ्यः
Gen.	अग्नेः कीर्त्याः	अग्न्योः	अग्नीनाम्
Loc.	अग्नौ कीर्त्याम्	अग्न्योः	अग्निषु
Voc.	अग्ने	अग्नी	अग्नयः

The singular dative, ablative, genitive, and locative have an optional feminine form. For example,the feminine dative singular is **kīrtaye** or **kīrtyai**. The feminine instrumental singular is **kīrtyā**.

ī

FEMININE

Stem: **nadī** (feminine) river (given on p. 171)

	Singular	Dual	Plural
Nom.	नदी	नद्यौ	नद्यः
Acc.	नदीम्	नद्यौ	नदीः
Inst.	नद्या	नदीभ्याम्	नदीभिः
Dat.	नद्यै	नदीभ्याम्	नदीभ्यः
Abl.	नद्याः	नदीभ्याम्	नदीभ्यः
Gen.	नद्याः	नद्योः	नदीनाम्
Loc.	नद्याम्	नद्योः	नदीषु
Voc.	नदि	नद्यौ	नद्यः

an

MASCULINE

Stem: **rājan** (mas.) king; **ātman** (mas.) Self (given on p. 208)

	Singular	Dual	Plural
Nom.	राजा	राजानौ	राजानः
Acc.	राजानम्	राजानौ	राज्ञः आत्मनः
Inst.	राज्ञा आत्मना	राजभ्याम्	राजभिः
Dat.	राज्ञे आत्मने	राजभ्याम्	राजभ्यः
Abl.	राज्ञः आत्मनः	राजभ्याम्	राजभ्यः
Gen.	राज्ञः	राज्ञोः	राज्ञाम्
	आत्मनः	आत्मनोः	आत्मनाम्
Loc.	राज्ञि आत्मनि	राज्ञोः आत्मनोः	राजसु
Voc.	राजन्	राजानौ	राजानः

an
NEUTER

Stem: **nāman** (neuter) name (given on p. 209)

	Singular	Dual	Plural
Nom.	नाम	नाम्नी नामनी	नामानि
Acc.	नाम	नाम्नी नामनी	नामानि
Inst.	नाम्ना	नामभ्याम्	नामभिः
Dat.	नाम्ने	नामभ्याम्	नामभ्यः
Abl.	नाम्नः	नामभ्याम्	नामभ्यः
Gen.	नाम्नः	नाम्नोः	नाम्नाम्
Loc.	नाम्नि नामनि	नाम्नोः	नामसु
Voc.	नामन् नाम	नाम्नी नामनी	नामानि

ṛ
MASCULINE

FEMININE

Stem: **dātṛ** (mas.) giver; **svasṛ** (fem.) sister (given on p. 220)

Nom.	दाता	दातारौ	दातारः
Acc.	दातारम्	दातारौ	दातॄन् स्वसॄः
Inst.	दात्रा	दातृभ्याम्	दातृभिः
Dat.	दात्रे	दातृभ्याम्	दातृभ्यः
Abl.	दातुः	दातृभ्याम्	दातृभ्यः
Gen.	दातुः	दात्रोः	दातॄणाम्
Loc.	दातरि	दात्रोः	दातृषु
Voc.	दातर्	दातारौ	दातारः

Stem: **pitṛ** (mas.) father; **mātṛ** (fem.) mother; **bhrātṛ** (mas.) brother

(These nouns follow **dātṛ** in all other cases.)

Nom.	**pitā**	**pitarau**	**pitaraḥ**
Acc.	**pitaram**	**pitarau**	**pitṝn / bhrātṝn / mātṝḥ**

u

MASCULINE

FEMININE

Stem: **hetu** (mas.) cause; **dhenu** (fem.) cow (given on p. 232)

	Singular	Dual	Plural
Nom.	हेतुः	हेतू	हेतवः
Acc.	हेतुम्	हेतू	हेतून् धेनूः
Inst.	हेतुना धेन्वा	हेतुभ्याम्	हेतुभिः
Dat.	हेतवे धेन्वै	हेतुभ्याम्	हेतुभ्यः
Abl.	हेतोः धेन्वाः	हेतुभ्याम्	हेतुभ्यः
Gen.	हेतोः धेन्वाः	हेत्वोः	हेतूनाम्
Loc.	हेतौ धेन्वाम्	हेत्वोः	हेतुषु
Voc.	हेतो	हेतू	हेतवः

The singular dative, ablative, genitive, and locative have an optional feminine form. For example, the feminine dative singular is **dhenave** or **dhenvai**.

mad asmad

Stem: **mad** (singular) I; **asmad** (plural) we (given on p. 128)

	Singular	Dual	Plural
Nom. I, we	अहम्	आवाम्	वयम्
Acc. me, us	माम् मा	आवाम् नौ	अस्मान् नः
Inst. with me, us	मया	आवाभ्याम्	अस्माभिः
Dat. for me, us	मह्यम् मे	आवाभ्याम् नौ	अस्मभ्यम् नः
Abl. from me, us	मत्	आवाभ्याम्	अस्मत्
Gen. my, our	मम मे	आवयोः नौ	अस्माकम् नः
Loc. on me, us	मयि	आवयोः	अस्मासु

tvad yuṣmad

Stem: **tvad** (singular) you; **yuṣmad** (plural) you (given on p. 129)

	Singular	Dual	Plural
Nom. you (subject)	त्वम्	युवाम्	यूयम्
Acc. you (object)	त्वाम् त्वा	युवाम् वाम्	युष्मान् व
Inst. with you	त्वया	युवाभ्याम्	युष्माभिः
Dat. for you	तुभ्यम् ते	युवाभ्याम् वाम्	युष्मभ्यम् वः
Abl. from you	त्वत्	युवाभ्याम्	युष्मत्
Gen. of you, your	तव ते	युवयोः वाम्	युष्माकम् वः
Loc. on you	त्वयि	युवयोः	युष्मासु

tad

MASCULINE

Stem: **tad** (masculine) he

	Singular	Dual	Plural
Nom. he, they	सः	तौ	ते
Acc. him, them	तम्	तौ	तान्
Inst. with him, them	तेन	ताभ्याम्	तैः
Dat. for him, them	तस्मै	ताभ्याम्	तेभ्यः
Abl. from him, them	तस्मात्	ताभ्याम्	तेभ्यः
Gen. his, their	तस्य	तयोः	तेषाम्
Loc. on him, them	तस्मिन्	तयोः	तेषु

Remember that **saḥ**, the nominative singular, usually appears as **sa**. (See #5, p. 147.)

tad

NEUTER

Stem: **tad** (neuter) it

	Singular	Dual	Plural
Nom. it (subject)	तत्	ते	तानि
Acc. it (object)	तत्	ते	तानि
Inst. with it	तेन	ताभ्याम्	तैः
Dat. for it	तस्मै	ताभ्याम्	तेभ्यः
Abl. from it	तस्मात्	ताभ्याम्	तेभ्यः
Gen. of it, its	तस्य	तयोः	तेषाम्
Loc. on it	तस्मिन्	तयोः	तेषु

tad

FEMININE

Stem: **tad** (feminine) she

	Singular	Dual	Plural
Nom. she, they	सा	ते	ताः
Acc. her, them	ताम्	ते	ताः
Inst. with her, them	तया	ताभ्याम्	ताभिः
Dat. for her, them	तस्यै	ताभ्याम्	ताभ्यः
Abl. from her, them	तस्याः	ताभ्याम्	ताभ्यः
Gen. her, their	तस्याः	तयोः	तासाम्
Loc. on her, them	तस्याम्	तयोः	तासु

VERBS

ROOT	PRESENT	GERUND	FUTURE	ENGLISH
अव गम्	अवगच्छति	अवगत्य	अवगमिष्यति	understand
		अवगम्य		
आ गम्	आगच्छति	आगत्य	आगमिष्यति	come
		आगम्य		
आ नी	आनयति	आनीय	आनेष्यति	bring
उद् भू	उद्भवति	उद्भूय	उद्भविष्यति	born
उद् स्था	उत्तिष्ठति	उत्स्थाय	उत्स्थास्यति	stand up
उप गम्	उपगच्छति	उपगत्य	उपगमिष्यति	approach
		उपगम्य		
गम्	गच्छति	गत्वा	गमिष्यति	go
गुप्	गोपायति	गोपित्वा	गोप्स्यति	protect
चिन्त्	चिन्तयति	चिन्तयित्वा	चिन्तयिष्यति	think
	चिन्तयते		चिन्तयिष्यते	
जि	जयति	जित्वा	जेष्यति	conquer

ROOT	PRESENT	GERUND	FUTURE	ENGLISH
दृश्	पश्यति	दृष्ट्वा	द्रक्ष्यति	see
नी	नयति	नीत्वा	नेष्यति	lead
	नयते		नेष्यते	
पठ्	पठति	पठित्वा	पठिष्यति	read
पश्	पश्यति	दृष्ट्वा	द्रक्ष्यति	see
पा	पिबति	पीत्वा	पास्यति	drink
प्रछ्	पृच्छति	पृष्ट्वा	प्रक्ष्यति	ask
प्रति गम्	प्रतिगच्छति	प्रतिगत्य	प्रतिगमिष्यति	return
		प्रतिगम्य		
बुध्	बोधति	बुद्ध्वा	बोधिष्यति	know
	बोधते		बोधिष्यते	
भाष्	भाषते	भाषित्वा	भाषिष्यते	speak
भू	भवति	भूत्वा	भविष्यति	be
मन्	मन्यते	मत्वा	मंस्यते	think

ROOT	PRESENT	GERUND	FUTURE	ENGLISH
रम्	रमते	रत्वा	रंस्यते	enjoy
लभ्	लभते	लब्ध्वा	लप्स्यते	obtain
वद्	वदति	उदित्वा	वदिष्यति	speak
वस्	वसति	उषित्वा	वत्स्यति	live
शुभ्	शोभते	शोभित्वा	शोभिष्यति	shine
सेव्	सेवते	सेवित्वा	सेविष्यते	serve
स्था	तिष्ठति	स्थित्वा	स्थास्यति	stand
स्मि	स्मयते	स्मित्वा	स्मेष्यते	smile
स्मृ	स्मरति	स्मृत्वा	स्मरिष्यति	remember
हस्	हसति	हसित्वा	हसिष्यति	laugh

√as

PRESENT INDICATIVE

	Singular	Dual	Plural
3rd	अस्ति	स्तः	सन्ति
2nd	असि	स्थः	स्थ
1st	अस्मि	स्वः	स्मः

IMPERFECT

	Singular	Dual	Plural
3rd	आसीत्	आस्ताम्	आसन्
2nd	आसीः	आस्तम्	आस्त
1st	आसम्	आस्व	आस्म

PRESENT ACTIVE

Root: √**gam** (active) go

	Singular	Dual	Plural
3rd	गच्छति	गच्छतः	गच्छन्ति
2nd	गच्छसि	गच्छथः	गच्छथ
1st	गच्छामि	गच्छावः	गच्छामः

PRESENT MIDDLE

Root: √**bhāṣ** (middle) speak

	Singular	Dual	Plural
3rd	भाषते	भाषेते	भाषन्ते
2nd	भाषसे	भाषेथे	भाषध्वे
1st	भाषे	भाषावहे	भाषामहे

ENDINGS

	PRESENT ACTIVE			PRESENT MIDDLE		
	Singular	Dual	Plural	Singular	Dual	Plural
3rd	ति	तस्	अन्ति	ते	इते	अन्ते
2nd	सि	थस्	थ	से	इथे	ध्वे
1st	मि	वस्	मस्	इ	वहे	महे

Note that when a word is formed, final **s** becomes **ḥ** due to **sandhi**.

IMPERFECT ACTIVE

Root: √**gam** (active) go

	Singular	Dual	Plural
3rd	अगच्छत्	अगच्छताम्	अगच्छन्
2nd	अगच्छः	अगच्छतम्	अगच्छत
1st	अगच्छम्	अगच्छाव	अगच्छाम

IMPERFECT MIDDLE

Root: √**bhāṣ** (middle) speak

	Singular	Dual	Plural
3rd	अभाषत	अभाषेताम्	अभाषन्त
2nd	अभाषथाः	अभाषेथाम्	अभाषध्वम्
1st	अभाषे	अभाषावहि	अभाषामहि

ENDINGS

	IMPERFECT ACTIVE			IMPERFECT MIDDLE		
	Singular	Dual	Plural	Singular	Dual	Plural
3rd	त्	ताम्	अन्	त	इताम्	अन्त
2nd	स्	तम्	त	थास्	इथाम्	ध्वम्
1st	अम्	व	म	इ	वहि	महि

Note that when a word is formed, final **s** becomes **ḥ** due to **sandhi**.

PREFIXES

(given on pp.197-199)

अति	across, beyond, surpassing, past
अधि	above, over, on
अनु	after, following
अप	away, off
अपि	on, close on
अभि	to, against
अव	down, away, off
आ	back, return, to, fully
उद्	up, up out
उप	towards, near, subordinate
दुस्	ill, bad, difficult, hard
नि	down, into
निस्	out from, forth, without, entirely
परा	away, forth, along, off
परि	around, about
प्र	forward, onward, forth
प्रति	back to, in reverse direction
वि	apart, away, out
सम्	together
सु	well, very, good, right, easy

NUMERALS

CARDINAL NUMBERS

(given on pp.157-159)

Numerals		Cardinal Numbers	
1.	१	one	एक
2.	२	two	द्वि
3.	३	three	त्रि
4.	४	four	चतुर्
5.	५ (५)	five	पञ्च
6.	६	six	षष्
7.	७	seven	सप्त
8.	८ (८)	eight	अष्ट
9.	९ (९)	nine	नव
10.	१०	ten	दश

ORDINAL NUMBERS

First	प्रथम	Sixth	षष्ठ
Second	द्वितीय	Seventh	सप्तम
Third	तृतीय	Eighth	अष्टम
Fourth	चतुर्थ or तुरीय	Ninth	नवम
Fifth	पञ्चम	Tenth	दशम

SANDHI VOWELS

FINAL VOWELS

ă̄	ĭ̄	ŭ̄	ṛ	e		ai		au	INITIAL VOWELS
ā	ya	va	ra	e	'	ā	a	āva	**a**
ā	yā	vā	rā	a	ā	ā	ā	āvā	**ā**
e	ī	vi	ri	a	i	ā	i	āvi	**i**
e	ī	vī	rī	a	ī	ā	ī	āvī	**ī**
o	yu	ū	ru	a	u	ā	u	āvu	**u**
o	yū	ū	rū	a	ū	ā	ū	āvū	**ū**
ar	yṛ	vṛ	ṝ	a	ṛ	ā	ṛ	āvṛ	**ṛ**
ai	ye	ve	re	a	e	ā	e	āve	**e**
ai	yai	vai	rai	a	ai	ā	ai	āvai	**ai**
au	yo	vo	ro	a	o	ā	o	āvo	**o**
au	yau	vau	rau	a	au	ā	au	āvau	**au**

SANDHI
FINAL ḥ

Final letters of first word:

Any vowel **ḥ** or **r** (except **aḥ** and **āḥ**)	**āḥ**	**aḥ**	Initial letter of second word:	
r	**ā**	**a** [2]	**vowels**	(a)
r	**ā**	**o**	**g/gh**	
r	**ā**	**o**	**j/jh**	
r	**ā**	**o**	**ḍ/ḍh**	
r	**ā**	**o**	**d/dh**	
r	**ā**	**o**	**b/bh**	(b)
r	**ā**	**o**	**nasals (n/m)**	
r	**ā**	**o**	**y/v**	
- [1]	**ā**	**o**	**r**	
r	**ā**	**o**	**l**	
r	**ā**	**o**	**h**	
ḥ	**āḥ**	**aḥ**	**k/kh**	
ś	**āś**	**aś**	**c/ch**	
ṣ	**āṣ**	**aṣ**	**ṭ/ṭh**	
s	**ās**	**as**	**t/th**	
ḥ	**āḥ**	**aḥ**	**p/ph**	(c)
ḥ	**āḥ**	**aḥ**	**ś**	
ḥ	**āḥ**	**aḥ**	**ṣ/s**	
ḥ	**āḥ**	**aḥ**	**end of line**	

(1) The **ḥ** disappears, and if **i** or **u** precedes, it becomes **ī** or **ū**.

The **r** disappears, and if **a**, **i**, or **u** precedes, it becomes **ā**, **ī**, or **ū**.

(2) Except that **aḥ** + **a** = **o '** For example:

रामः + अत्र = रामोऽत्र

rāmaḥ + atra = rāmo 'tra

Remember that final **s** follows the same rules as final **ḥ**.

SANDHI
FINAL Ḥ

					a	ā			
					i	ī			
					u	ū	(a)		
					ṛ	ṝ	Vowels		
					ḷ				
					e	ai			
					o	au			
ḥ		ka	kha	|	ga	gha	ṅa		
ś		ca	cha	|	ja	jha	ña		
ṣ		ṭa	ṭha	|	ḍa	ḍha	ṇa		
s		ta	tha	|	da	dha	na		
ḥ		pa	pha	|	ba	bha	ma		
				|	ya	ra	la	va	
ḥ	śa	ṣa	sa	|	ha				
ḥ	end of line			|					
	(c) Unvoiced consonant			|		(b) Voiced consonant			

(a) If the second word begins in a vowel:

aḥ becomes **a** (except **aḥ + a = o '**)

āḥ becomes **ā**

vowel **ḥ** becomes **r**

(b) If the first letter of the second word is a voiced consonant:

aḥ becomes **o**

āḥ becomes **ā**

vowel **ḥ** becomes **r** (except before a word beginning in **r**)

(c) If the first letter of the second word is an unvoiced consonant, the **ḥ** (with any vowel in front of it) changes to the letter in the far left column.

SANDHI
FINAL M, N, T

Final letter of first word: t	n	m	Initial letter of second word:
d	n[1]	m	vowels
d	n	ṃ	g/gh
j	ñ	ṃ	j/jh
ḍ	ṇ	ṃ	ḍ/ḍh
d	n	ṃ	d/dh
d	n	ṃ	b/bh
n	n	ṃ	nasals (n/m)
d	n	ṃ	y/v
d	n	ṃ	r
l	ṃl	ṃ	l
d(dh)[3]	n	ṃ	h
t	n	ṃ	k/kh
c	ṃś	ṃ	c/ch
ṭ	ṃṣ	ṃ	ṭ/ṭh
t	ṃs	ṃ	t/th
t	n	ṃ	p/ph
c(ch)[4]	ñ(ch)[2]	ṃ	ś
t	n	ṃ	ṣ/s
t	n	m	end of line

1. If the vowel before the **n** is short, the **n** becomes **nn**.

2. The following **ś** may become **ch**.

3. The following **h** becomes **dh**.

4. The following **ś** becomes **ch**

SANDHI FINAL N

Final **n** remains unchanged unless the following letter is in bold. Then:

n becomes							**n** becomes
			a	**ā**			
			i	**ī**			
			u	**ū**			**nn** (e)
			ṛ	**ṝ**			(if preceded by
			ḷ				a short vowel)
			e	**ai**			
			o	**au**			
	ka	kha	ga	gha	ṅa		
(a) **ṃś**	**ca**	**cha**	**ja**	**jha**	ña		**ñ** (f)
(b) **ṃṣ**	**ṭa**	**ṭha**	**ḍa**	**ḍha**	ṇa		**ṇ** (g)
(c) **ṃs**	**ta**	**tha**	da	dha	na		
	pa	pha	ba	bha	ma		
			ya	ra	**la**	va	**ṃl** (h)
(d) **ñ (ch)** **śa**	ṣa	sa	ha				
	end of line						

(a) **n + ca = ṃśca ; n + cha = ṃścha**
(b) **n + ṭa = ṃṣṭa ; n + ṭha = ṃṣṭha**
(c) **n + ta = ṃsta ; n + tha = ṃstha**
(d) **n + śa = ñśa** or **ñcha**
(e) **an + a = anna**
an + i = anni
ān + u = ānu
(f) **n + ja = ñja ; n + jha = ñjha**
(g) **n + ḍa = ṇḍa ; n + ḍha = ṇḍha**
(h) **n + la = ṃlla**

SANDHI
FINAL T

t remains t except:			t changes to d except:				
			a	ā			
			i	ī			
			u	ū			
			ṛ	ṝ			
			ḷ				
			e	ai			
			o	au			(before all nasals)
							n (d)
	ka	kha	ga	gha	**ṅa**		
(a) **c**	**ca**	**cha**	**ja**	**jha**	**ña**		**j** (e)
(b) **ṭ**	**ṭa**	**ṭha**	**ḍa**	**ḍha**	**ṇa**		**ḍ** (f)
	ta	tha	da	dha	**na**		
	pa	pha	ba	bha	**ma**		
			ya	ra	**la**	va	**l** (g)
(c) **c (ch) śa**	ṣa	sa	**ha**				**d (dh)** (h)
	end of line						

(a) **t + ca = cca ; t + cha = ccha**
(b) **t + ṭa = ṭṭa ; t + ṭha = ṭṭha**
(c) **t + śa = ccha**
(d) **t** + all nasals = **n**nasal
(e) **t + ja = jja ; t + jha = jjha**
(f) **t + ḍa = ḍḍa ; t + ḍha = ḍḍha**
(g) **t + la = lla**
(h) **t + ha = ddha** (**ha** becomes **dha**.)

SANDHI FINAL M

(a) If the next word begins in a consonant, the **m** becomes **ṃ** and is pronounced (and could be written) as the nasal corresponding to the first letter of the next word.

(b) If the next word begins in a vowel or the **m** is at the end of a line, the **m** remains the same. The **m** remains the same because the mouth is not preparing to close at a specific point of contact as it would if the next word began with a consonant.

SANDHI FINAL R

(a) Before a word beginning with a voiced letter (other than **r**), the **r** remains the same.

(b) Before an unvoiced letter or the end of a line, **r** follows the same rules as final **ḥ**.

(c) Final **r**, whether original or derived from **ḥ**, cannot stand before another **r**. The final **r** is dropped and the vowel before it made long if it is short.

FINAL P, Ṭ, K

(a) Before a voiced sound these letters become voiced, and before an unvoiced sound they remain the same.

(b) Before a nasal these letters become the nasal of their row (**varga**).

(c) Before **h** these letters become voiced and the **h** becomes their voiced aspirated counterpart.

FINAL Ṅ AND Ṇ

(a) Like final **n**, final **ṅ** becomes **ṅṅ** before vowels if the **ṅ** is preceded by a short vowel. Also, final **ṇ** becomes **ṇṇ** before vowels if the **ṇ** is preceded by a short vowel.

INITIAL CH

(a) Initial **ch** becomes **cch** if the first word ends in a short vowel. The **ch** also becomes **cch** after the preposition **ā** and **mā**.

INTERNAL SANDHI S TO Ṣ

any vowel (but **a** or **ā**), **k**, or **r**	in spite of intervening **ṃ** or **ḥ**	changes s to ṣ	unless final or followed by **r**

N TO Ṇ

r **ṛ** **ṝ** or **ṣ**	unless **c, ch, j, jh, ñ, ṭ, ṭh, ḍ, ḍh, ṇ, t, th, d, dh, l, ś, s** interferes	changes **n** to **ṇ**	if followed by vowels, **m, y, v**, or **n**

VOCABULARY

अग्निः	**agniḥ** (mas.)	fire
अति	**ati** (prefix)	across, beyond, surpassing
अतिथिः	**atithiḥ** (mas.)	guest
अतीव	**atīva** (ind.)	very
अत्र	**atra** (ind.)	here
अधि	**adhi** (prefix)	above, over, on
अनु	**anu** (prefix)	after, following
अप	**apa** (prefix)	away, off
अपि	**api** (prefix)	on, close on
अपि	**api** (ind.)	also, too
अभि	**abhi** (prefix)	to, against
अमृतम्	**amṛtam** (n.)	immortality
अल्प	**alpa** mf(ā)n (adj.)	little
अव	**ava** (prefix)	down, away, off

अव गम्	**ava + √gam avagacchati**	he understands
अविद्या	**avidyā** (fem.)	ignorance
अश्वः	**aśvaḥ** (mas.)	horse
अष्ट	**aṣṭa**	eight
अष्टम	**aṣṭama** mf(ī)n (adj.)	eighth
अस्	**√as asti**	he, she, it is
असिद्धिः		**asiddhiḥ** (fem.) failure
अस्मद्	**asmad** (pro.)	we (used in compounds)
अहो	**aho** (ind.)	aha, hey!
आ	**ā** (prefix)	back, return
आ गम्	**ā + √gam āgacchati**	he comes
आ नी	**ā + √nī ānayati**	he brings
आचार्यः	**ācāryaḥ** (mas.)	teacher
आत्मन्	**ātman** (mas.)	Self

इति	**iti** (ind.)	(end of quote)
इव	**iva** (ind.)	as if, like
उद्	**ud** (prefix)	up, up out
उद् भू	**ud + √bhū udbhavati**	he is born
उद् स्था	**ud + √sthā uttiṣṭhati**	he stands up
उप	**upa** (prefix)	towards
उप गम्	**upa + √gam upagacchati**	he goes toward, approaches
ऋषिः	**ṛṣiḥ** (mas.)	seer, sage
एक	**eka**	one
एव	**eva** (ind.)	only, ever
एवम्	**evam** (ind.)	thus, in this way
कथम्	**katham** (ind.)	how
कथा	**kathā** (fem.)	story
कदा	**kadā** (ind.)	when

कन्या	**kanyā** (fem.)	girl
कर्ता	**kartā** (mas.)	maker, doer (**ṛ** declension)
कर्म	**karma** (n.)	action (**an** declension)
कविः	**kaviḥ** (mas.)	poet
कुत्र	**kutra** (ind.)	where
कुपित	**kupita** mf(**ā**)n (adj.)	angry
कुलम्	**kulam** (n.)	family
कीर्तिः	**kīrtiḥ** (fem.)	glory, fame
कृष्ण	**kṛṣṇa** mf(**ā**)n (adj.)	black
कृष्णः	**kṛṣṇaḥ** (mas.)	Kṛṣṇa
गजः	**gajaḥ** (mas.)	elephant
गम्	√**gam gacchati**	he goes
गुप्	√**gup gopāyati**	he protects
गुरु	**guru** mf(**vī**)n (adj.)	heavy

गुरुः	**guruḥ** (mas.)	teacher
गृहम्	**gṛham** (n.)	house
ग्रामः	**grāmaḥ** (mas.)	village
च	**ca** (ind.)	and
चतुर्	**catur**	four
चतुर्थ	**caturtha** mf(ī)n (adj.)	fourth
चन्द्रः	**candraḥ** (mas.)	moon
चिन्त्	**√cint cintayati -te**	he thinks
छाया	**chāyā** (fem.)	shadow
जलम्	**jalam** (n.)	water
जि	**√ji jayati**	he conquers
ज्ञानम्	**jñānam** (n.)	knowledge
ततः	**tataḥ** (ind.)	therefore
तत्र	**tatra** (ind.)	there

तथा	**tathā** (ind.)	so, therefore
तद्	**tad** (pro.)	he, she, it (used in compounds)
तदा	**tadā** (ind.)	then
तुरीय	**turīya** mf(ā)n (adj.)	fourth
तृतीय	**tṛtīya** mf(ā)n (adj.)	third
त्वद्	**tvad** (pro.)	you (used in compounds)
त्रि	**tri**	three
दश	**daśa**	ten
दशम	**daśama** mf(ī)n (adj.)	tenth
दाता	**dātā** (mas.)	giver (ṛ declension)
दात्री	**dātrī** (fem.)	giver
दुस्	**dus** (prefix)	ill, bad, difficult, hard

दुःखम्	**duḥkham** (n.)	suffering
दृश्	**√dṛś paśyati**	he sees
द्वि	**dvi**	two
द्वितीय	**dvitīya** mf(ā)n (adj.)	second
धार्मिक	**dhārmika** mf(ī)n (adj.)	virtuous
धेनुः	**dhenuḥ** (fem.)	cow
न	**na** (ind.)	not
नदी	**nadī** (fem.)	river
नरः	**naraḥ** (mas.)	man
नव	**nava**	nine
नवम	**navama** mf(ī)n (adj.)	ninth
नाम	**nāma** (ind.)	by name
नाम	**nāman** (n.)	name (**an** declension)
नि	**ni** (prefix)	down, into

निस्	**nis** (prefix)	out, forth, without, entirely
नी	**√nī nayati -te**	he leads
नृपः	**nṛpaḥ** (mas.)	king
पञ्च	**pañca**	five
पञ्चम	**pañcama** mf(**ī**)n (adj.)	fifth
पठ्	**√paṭh paṭhati**	he reads
पत्नी	**patnī** (fem.)	wife
परा	**parā** (prefix)	away, forth
परि	**pari** (prefix)	around, about
पश्	**√paś paśyati**	he sees
पा	**√pā pibati**	he drinks
पिता	**pitā** (mas.)	father (ṛ declension)
पुत्रः	**putraḥ** (mas.)	son
पुत्रिका	**putrikā** (fem.)	daughter

पुनर्	**punar** (ind.)	again
पुस्तकम्	**pustakam** (n.)	book
पूर्ण	**pūrṇa** mf(**ā**)n (adj.)	full
प्र	**pra** (prefix)	forward, onward, forth
प्रछ्	**√prach pṛcchati**	he asks
प्रजा	**prajā** (fem.)	child, subject (of a king)
प्रति	**prati** (prefix)	back to, in reverse direction, every
प्रति गम्	**prati** + **√gam pratigacchati**	he goes back, returns
प्रथम	**prathama** mf(**ā**)n (adj.)	first
प्रिय	**priya** mf(**ā**)n (adj.)	dear, beloved
फलम्	**phalam** (n.)	fruit
बहु	**bahu** mf(**vī** or **u**)n (adj.)	much, many

बालः	**bālaḥ** (mas.)	boy
बाला	**bālā** (fem.)	girl
बुध्	**√budh bodhati -te**	he knows
भार्या	**bhāryā** (fem.)	wife
भाष्	**√bhāṣ bhāṣate**	he speaks
भीत	**bhīta** mf(**ā**)n (adj.)	afraid
भू	**√bhū bhavati**	he is
भूमिः	**bhūmiḥ** (fem.)	earth
भ्राता	**bhrātā** (mas.)	brother (**ṛ** declension)
मद्	**mad** (pro.)	I (used in compounds)
मन्	**√man manyate**	he thinks
माता	**mātā** (fem.)	mother (**ṛ** declension)
माला	**mālā** (fem.)	garland
मित्रम्	**mitram** (n.)	friend

मृगः	**mṛgaḥ** (mas.)	deer
यतः	**yataḥ** (ind.)	since
यत्र	**yatra** (ind.)	where
यथा	**yathā** (ind.)	since
यद्	**yad** (rel pro.)	who, what, which (declined like **tad**)
यदा	**yadā** (ind.)	when
यदि	**yadi** (ind.)	if
युष्मद्	**yuṣmad** (pro.)	you (used in compounds)
रम्	**√ram ramate**	he enjoys
रमणीय	**ramaṇīya** mf(ā)n (adj.)	pleasant
राजा	**rājā** (mas.)	king (**an** declension)
रामः	**rāmaḥ** (mas.)	Rāma
लभ्	**√labh labhate**	he obtains

वद्	√**vad vadati**	he speaks
वनम्	**vanam** (n.)	forest
वस्	√**vas vasati**	he lives
वा	**vā** (ind.)	or
वापी	**vāpī** (fem.)	pond
वि	**vi** (prefix)	apart, away, out
विद्या	**vidyā** (fem.)	knowledge
विना	**vinā** (ind.)	without
वीरः	**vīraḥ** (mas.)	hero
शत्रुः	**śatruḥ** (mas.)	enemy
शान्तिः	**śāntiḥ** (fem.)	peace
शास्त्रम्	**śāstram** (n.)	scripture
शिष्यः	**śiṣyaḥ** (mas.)	student
शीघ्र	**śīghra** mf(ā)n (adj.)	swift

शुभ्	√**śubh śobhate**	he shines
शोभन	**śobhana** mf(ā or ī)n (adj.)	shining, bright, beautiful
षष्	**ṣaṣ**	six
षष्ठ	**ṣaṣṭha** mf(ī)n (adj.)	sixth
सत्यम्	**satyam** (n.)	truth
सप्त	**sapta**	seven
सप्तम	**saptama** mf(ī)n (adj.)	seventh
सम्	**sam** (prefix)	together
सह	**saha** (ind.)	with
सिद्धः	**siddhaḥ** mf(**siddhā**)	one who attains perfection
सिद्धिः	**siddhiḥ** (fem.)	perfection, attainment, proof
सीता	**sītā** (fem.)	Sītā
सु	**su** (prefix)	well, very, good, right, easy

सुखम्	**sukham** (n.)	happiness
सुन्दर	**sundara** mf(ī)n (adj.)	beautiful
सूक्तम्	**sūktam** (n.)	hymn
सूर्यः	**sūryaḥ** (mas.)	sun
सेना	**senā** (fem.)	army
सेव्	**√sev sevate**	he serves
स्था	**√sthā tiṣṭhati**	he stands
स्मि	**√smi smayate**	he smiles
स्मृ	**√smṛ smarati**	he remembers
स्वसृ	**svasṛ** (fem.)	sister
हस्	**√has hasati**	he laughs
हस्तः	**hastaḥ** (mas.)	hand
हेतुः	**hetuḥ** (mas.)	cause, motive

ENGLISH-SANSKRIT VOCABULARY

above, over, on	अधि	**adhi** (prefix)
across, beyond, surpassing	अति	**ati** (prefix)
action (**an** declension)	कर्म	**karma** (n.)
afraid	भीत	**bhīta** mf(ā)n (adj.)
after, following	अनु	**anu** (prefix)
again	पुनर्	**punar** (ind.)
aha, hey!	अहो	**aho** (ind.)
also, too	अपि	**api** (ind.)
and	च	**ca** (ind.)
angry	कुपित	**kupita** mf(ā)n (adj.)
apart, away, out	वि	**vi** (prefix)
army	सेना	**senā** (fem.)
around, about	परि	**pari** (prefix)
as if, like	इव	**iva** (ind.)
ask	प्रछ्	**√prach pṛcchati**
away, forth	परा	**parā** (prefix)
away, off	अप	**apa** (prefix)
back, return	आ	**ā** (prefix)
back to, in reverse direction, every	प्रति	**prati** (prefix)
beautiful	सुन्दर	**sundara** mf(ī)n (adj.)

black	कृष्ण	**kṛṣṇa** mf(ā)n (adj.)
book	पुस्तकम्	**pustakam** (n.)
born	उद् भू	**ud + √bhū udbhavati**
boy	बालः	**bālaḥ** (mas.)
bring	आ नी	**ā + √nī ānayati**
brother (ṛ declension)	भ्राता	**bhrātā** (mas.)
by name, named	नाम	**nāma** (ind.)
cause, motive	हेतुः	**hetuḥ** (mas.)
child, subject (of a king)	प्रजा	**prajā** (fem.)
come	आ गम्	**ā + √gam āgacchati**
conquer	जि	**√ji jayati**
cow	धेनुः	**dhenuḥ** (fem.)
daughter	पुत्रिका	**putrikā** (fem.)
dear, beloved	प्रिय	**priya** mf(ā)n (adj.)
deer	मृगः	**mṛgaḥ** (mas.)
doer (ṛ declension)	कर्ता	**kartā** (mas.)
down	अव	**ava** (prefix)
down, into	नि	**ni** (prefix)
drink	पा	**√pā pibati**
earth	भूमिः	**bhūmiḥ** (fem.)

eight	अष्ट	**aṣṭi**
eighth	अष्टम	**aṣṭama** mf(ī)n (adj.)
elephant	गजः	**gajaḥ** (mas.)
(end of quote)	इति	**iti** (ind.)
enemy	शत्रुः	**śatruḥ** (mas.)
enjoy	रम्	**√ram ramate**
failure	असिद्धिः	**asiddhiḥ** (fem.)
family	कुलम्	**kulam** (n.)
father	पितृ	**pitṛ** (mas.)
fifth	पञ्चम	**pañcama** mf(ī)n (adj.)
fire	अग्निः	**agniḥ** (mas.)
first	प्रथम	**prathama** mf(ā)n (adj.)
five	पञ्च	**pañca**
forest	वनम्	**vanam** (n.)
forward, onward, forth	प्र	**pra** (prefix)
four	चतुर्	**catur**
fourth	चतुर्थ	**caturtha** mf(ī)n (adj.)
fourth	तुरीय	**turīya** mf(ā)n (adj.)
friend	मित्रम्	**mitram** (n.)

fruit	फलम्	**phalam** (n.)
full	पूर्ण	**pūrṇa** mf(**ā**)n (adj.)
garland	माला	**mālā** (fem.)
girl	कन्या	**kanyā** (fem.)
girl	बाला	**bālā** (fem.)
giver (ṛ declension)	दाता	**dātā** (mas.)
giver	दात्री	**dātrī** (fem.)
glory, fame	कीर्तिः	**kīrtiḥ** (fem.)
go	गम्	**√gam gacchati**
go back, return	प्रति गम्	**prati + √gam pratigacchati**
go toward, approach	उप गम्	**upa + √gam upagacchati**
guest	अतिथिः	**atithiḥ** (mas.)
hand	हस्तः	**hastaḥ** (mas.)
happiness	सुखम्	**sukham** (n.)
he (see declension)	तद्	**tad** (pro.)
heavy	गुरु	**guru** mf(**vī**)n (adj.)
here	अत्र	**atra** (ind.)
hero	वीरः	**vīraḥ** (mas.)
horse	अश्वः	**aśvaḥ** (mas.)
house	गृहम्	**gṛham** (n.)

how	कथम्	**katham** (ind.)
hymn	सूक्तम्	**sūktam** (n.)
I (used in compounds)	मद्	**mad** (pro.)
if	यदि	**yadi** (ind.)
ignorance	अविद्या	**avidyā** (fem.)
ill, bad, difficult, hard	दुस्	**dus** (prefix)
immortality	अमृतम्	**amṛtam** (n.)
is	अस्	**√as asti**
is	भू	**√bhū bhavati**
it (used in compounds)	तद्	**tad** (pro.)
king	नृपः	**nṛpaḥ** (mas.)
king (**an** declension)	राजा	**rājā** (mas.)
know	बुध्	**√budh bodhati -te**
knowledge	ज्ञानम्	**jñānam** (n.)
knowledge	विद्या	**vidyā** (fem.)
Kṛṣṇa	कृष्णः	**kṛṣṇaḥ** (mas.)
laugh	हस्	**√has hasati**
lead	नी	**√nī nayati -te**
little	अल्प	**alpa** mf(**ā**)n (adj.)
live	वस्	**√vas vasati**
maker (ṛ declension)	कर्ता	**kartā** (mas.)

man	नरः	**naraḥ** (mas.)
moon	चन्द्रः	**candraḥ** (mas.)
mother	मातृ	**mātṛ** (fem.)
much, many	बहुः	**bahuḥ** mf(**vī** or **u**)n (adj.)
name	नामन्	**nāman** (n.)
nine	नव	**nava**
ninth	नवम	**navama** mf(**ī**)n
not	न	**na** (ind.)
obtain	लभ्	**√labh labhate**
on, close on	अपि	**api** (prefix)
one	एक	**eka**
one who attains perfection	सिद्धः	**siddhaḥ** (mas.)
one who attains perfection	सिद्धा	**siddhā** (fem.)
only, ever (emphatic)	एव	**eva** (ind.)
or	वा	**vā** (ind.)
out, forth	निस्	**nis** (prefix)
peace	शान्तिः	**śāntiḥ** (fem.)
perfection, attainment, proof	सिद्धिः	**siddhiḥ** (fem.)
pleasant	रमणीय	**ramaṇīya** mf(**ā**)n (adj.)
poet	कविः	**kaviḥ** (mas.)

pond	वापी	**vāpī** (fem.)
protect	गुप्	**√gup gopāyati**
Rāma	रामः	**rāmaḥ** (mas.)
read	पठ्	**√paṭh paṭhati**
remember	स्मृ	**√smṛ smarati**
river	नदी	**nadī** (fem.)
scripture, text	शास्त्रम्	**śāstram** (n.)
second	द्वितीय	**dvitīya** mf(**ā**)n (adj.)
see	दृश्	**√dṛś paśyati**
see	पश्	**√paś paśyati**
seer, sage	ऋषिः	**ṛṣiḥ** (mas.)
Self (**an** declension)	आत्मा	**ātmā** (mas.)
serve	सेव्	**√sev sevate**
seven	सप्त	**sapta**
seventh	सप्तम	**saptama** mf(**ī**)n (adj.)
shadow	छाया	**chāyā** (fem.)
she (see declension)	तद्	**tad** (pro.)
shine	शुभ्	**√śubh śobhate**
shining, bright, beautiful	शोभन	**śobhana** mf(**ā** or **ī**)n (adj.)
since	यतः	**yataḥ** (ind.)

since	यथा	**yathā** (ind.)
sister (ṛ declension)	स्वसा	**svasā** (fem.)
Sītā	सीता	**sītā** (fem.)
six	षष्	**ṣaṣ**
sixth	षष्ठ	**ṣaṣṭha** mf(ī)n (adj.)
smile	स्मि	**√smi smayate**
so, therefore	तथा	**tathā** (ind.)
son	पुत्रः	**putraḥ** (mas.)
speak	भाष्	**√bhāṣ bhāṣate**
speak	वद्	**√vad vadati**
stand	स्था	**√sthā tiṣṭhati**
stand up	उद् स्था	**ud + √sthā uttiṣṭhati**
story	कथा	**kathā** (fem.)
student	शिष्यः	**śiṣyaḥ** (mas.)
subject (of a king)	प्रजा	**prajā** (fem.)
suffering	दुःखम्	**duḥkham** (n.)
sun	सूर्यः	**sūryaḥ** (mas.)
swift	शीघ्र	**śīghra** mf(ā)n (adj.)
teacher	आचार्यः	**ācāryaḥ** (mas.)
teacher	गुरुः	**guruḥ** (mas.)

ten	दश	**daśa**
tenth	दशम	**daśama mf(ī)n** (adj.)
then	तदा	**tadā** (ind.)
there	तत्र	**tatra** (ind.)
therefore	ततः	**tataḥ** (ind.)
think	चिन्त्	**√cint cintayati -te**
think	मन्	**√man manyate**
third	तृतीय	**tṛtīya mf(ā)n (adj.)**
three	त्रि	**tri**
thus, in this way	एवम्	**evam** (ind.)
to, against	अभि	**abhi** (prefix)
together	सम्	**sam** (prefix)
towards	उप	**upa** (prefix)
truth	सत्यम्	**satyam** (n.)
two	द्वि	**dvi**
understand	अव गम्	**ava + √gam avagacchati**
up, up out	उद्	**ud** (prefix)
very	अतीव	**atīva** (ind.)
village	ग्राम	**grāma** (mas.)
virtuous	धार्मिक	**dhārmika mf(ī)n** (adj.)

water	जलम्	**jalam** (n.)
we (used in compounds)	अस्मद्	**asmad** (pro.)
well, very, good, right, easy	सु	**su** (prefix)
when (question)	कदा	**kadā** (ind.)
when	यदा	**yadā** (ind.)
where (question)	कुत्र	**kutra** (ind.)
where	यत्र	**yatra** (ind.)
white	शुक्ल	**śukla** mf(ā)n (adj.)
who, what (declined like **tad**)	यद्	**yad** (rel. pro.)
with	सह	**saha** (ind.)
without	विना	**vinā** (ind.)
wife	पत्नी	**patnī** (fem.)
wife	भार्या	**bhāryā** (fem.)
you (sing., used in compounds)	त्वद्	**tvad** (pro.)
you (plural, used in compounds)	युष्मद्	**yuṣmad** (pro.)

SANSKRIT QUOTATIONS

ऋचो अक्षरे परमे व्योमन्
यस्मिन्देवा अधि विश्वे निषेदुः
यस्तन्न वेद किमृचा करिष्यति
य इत्तद्विदुस्त इमे समासते

ṛco akṣare parame vyoman
yasmin devā adhi viśve niṣeduḥ
yas tan na veda kim ṛcā kariṣyati
ya it tad vidus ta ime samāsate

Ṛk Saṃhitā 1.164.39

The verses of the Veda exist in the collapse of fullness (the kṣara of 'A') in the transcendental field, the Self,
In which reside all the devas, the impulses of creative intelligence, the laws of nature responsible for the whole manifest universe.
He whose awareness is not open to this field, what can the verses accomplish for him?
Those who know this level of reality are established in evenness, wholeness of life.

ṛco	**akṣare**	**parame**	**vyoman**
verses	in the collapse of fullness		in the transcendental
	field		
yasmin	**devā**	**adhi viśve**	**niṣeduḥ**
in which	impulses (laws of nature)	responsible for universe	reside
yas	**tan na veda**	**kim ṛcā kariṣyati**	
who	this (field) not know	what verses will accomplish	
ya	**it tad vidus**	**ta ime samāsate**	
who	this (level) know	they in evenness established	

1. निस्त्रैगुण्यो भवार्जुन

nistraiguṇyo bhavārjuna
without three **guṇas** be O Arjuna
Be without the three guṇas, O Arjuna.

Bhagavad-Gītā 2.45

2. योगस्थः कुरु कर्माणि

yogasthaḥ kuru karmāṇi
yoga established perform actions
Established in Yoga perform actions.

Bhagavad-Gītā 2.48

3. प्रकृतिं स्वामवष्टभ्य विसृजामि पुनः पुनः

prakṛtiṃ svām avaṣṭabhya visṛjāmi punaḥ punaḥ
nature own taking recourse I create again again
Taking recourse to my own nature, I create again and again.

Bhagavad-Gītā 9.8

4. मयाध्यक्षेण प्रकृतिः सूयते सचराचरम्

mayādhyakṣeṇa prakṛtiḥ sūyate sacarācaram
by my presidentship nature creates moving unmoving
Under my presidentship my nature creates all creation.

Bhagavad-Gītā 9.10

Mahāvākyas Great Sayings

1. अहं ब्रह्मास्मि

ahaṃ brahmāsmi

I totality am

I am Totality.

Bṛhadāraṇyaka Upaniṣad 1.4.10

2. तत्त्वमसि

tat tvam asi

that thou art

Thou art that.

Chāndogya Upaniṣad 6.11

3. सर्वं खल्विदं ब्रह्म

sarvaṃ khalv idaṃ brahma

all (emphatic) this (is) Brahman

All this is Totality.

Chāndogya Upaniṣad 3.14.1

4. प्रज्ञानं ब्रह्म

prajñānaṃ brahma

Fully awake self-referral dynamism (of the universe) born of the infinite organizing power of pure knowledge, the Veda—fully awake totality of the individual consciousness is *Brahman*, which comprehends the infinite dynamism of the universe in the infinite silence of the Self.

Aitareya Upaniṣad 3.1.3

1. पूर्णमदः पूर्णमिदं पूर्णात्पूर्णमुदच्यते
पूर्णस्य पूर्णमादाय पूर्णमेवावशिष्यते

pūrṇam adaḥ pūrṇam idaṃ pūrṇāt pūrṇam udacyate
pūrṇasya pūrṇam ādāya pūrṇam evāvaśiṣyate

Īśa Upaniṣad (introductory verse for **Upaniṣads** of the **Śukla Yajur-Veda**)

pūrṇam adaḥ pūrṇam idaṃ pūrṇāt pūrṇam udacyate
full (is) that full (is) this from fullness fullness comes out

pūrṇasya pūrṇam ādāya pūrṇam evāvaśiṣyate
of fullness fullness taking fullness remains

That is full; this is full. From fullness, fullness comes out.
Taking fullness from fullness, what remains is fullness.

2. वसुधैव कुटुम्बकम्

vasudhaiva kuṭumbakam
the world family
The world is my family.

Mahā Upaniṣad 6.71

1. अहं विश्वम्

ahaṃ viśvam

My universe is my Self.

Taittirīya Upaniṣad 3.10

2. हेयं दुःखमनागतम्

heyaṃ duḥkham anāgatam

avert danger not yet come

Avert the danger which has not yet come.

Yoga Sūtra 2.16

3. तत्सृष्ट्वा तदेवानुप्राविशत्

tat sṛṣṭvā tad evānuprāviśat

it having created it entered into

The Creator, having created the creation, entered into it.

Taittirīya Upaniṣad 2.6.1

4. भगवद्गीता किञ्चिदधीता

गङ्गाजललवकणिका पीता

bhagavad-gītā kiñcid adhītā

gaṅgā-jala-lava-kaṇikā pītā

Bhagavad-Gītā a little studied

Ganges-water-drop-particle drank.

Even a little study of the **Bhagavad-Gītā**,

like a drop of the flow of nectar, is sufficient.

Śaṅkara, Bhaja Govindam 20

सह नाववतु

सह नौ भुनक्तु

सह वीर्यं करवावहै

तेजस्वि नावधीतमस्तु

मा विद्विषावहै

saha nāv avatu

saha nau bhunaktu

saha vīryaṃ karavāvahai

tejasvi nāv adhītam astu

mā vidviṣāvahai

Upaniṣads (introductory verse for **Upaniṣads** of the **Kṛṣṇa Yajur-Veda**)

Let us be together,

Let us eat together,

Let us be vital together,

Let us be radiating truth,
radiating the light of life,

Never shall we denounce anyone,
never entertain negativity.

1. सत्यं ब्रूयात्प्रियं ब्रूयात्

satyaṃ brūyāt priyaṃ brūyāt

truth speak sweetness speak

Speak the sweet truth.

Manu Smṛti 4.138

2. ब्रह्मवित् ब्रह्मैव भवति

brahmavit brahmaiva bhavati

Brahman knower Brahman is

The knower of Brahman is Brahman itself.

Muṇḍaka Upaniṣad 3.2.9

3. द्वितीयाद्वै भयं भवति

dvitīyād vai bhayaṃ bhavati

from duality certainly fear is

Certainly fear is born of duality.

Bṛhadāraṇyaka Upaniṣad 1.4.2

4. यो जागार तमृचः कामयन्ते

yo jāgāra tam ṛcaḥ kāmayante

who is awake him hymns seek out

He who is awake, the ṛcas seek him out.

Ṛk Saṃhitā 5.44.14

1. निवर्तध्वम्

nivartadhvam

Return. **Ṛk Saṃhitā** 10.19.1

2. यतीनां ब्रह्मा भवति सारथिः

yatīnām brahmā bhavati sārathiḥ

For those who are established in self-referral consciousness, Brahmā, the Creator, becomes the charioteer of all activity.

Ṛk Saṃhitā 1.158.6

3. आत्मैवेदं सर्वम्

ātmaivedaṃ sarvam

Ātmā is all that there is.

Nṛsiṃhottaratāpanīya Upaniṣad 7

1. एकमेवाद्वितीयम्

ekam evādvitīyam

one no second

One reality without a second.

Chāndogya Upaniṣad 6.2.1

2. अणोरणीयान्महतोमहीयान्

aṇoraṇīyān mahatomahīyān

than small smaller than large larger

Smaller than the smallest, larger than the largest.

Kaṭha Upaniṣad 1.2.20

3. तत्सन्निधौ वैरत्यागः

tat-sannidhau vaira-tyāgaḥ

that-vicinity hostile tendencies-eliminated

In the vicinity of Yoga, hostile tendencies are eliminated.

Yoga Sūtra 2.35

4. सत्यमेव जयते

satyam eva jayate

Truth alone triumphs.

Muṇḍaka Upaniṣad 3.1.6

1. असतो मा सद्गमय

तमसो मा ज्योतिर्गमय

मृत्योर्मा अमृतं गमय

asato mā sad gamaya
tamaso mā jyotir gamaya
mṛtyor mā amṛtaṃ gamaya

Bṛhadāraṇyaka Upaniṣad 1.3.28

From non-existence lead me to existence,
From darkness lead me to light,
From death lead me to immortality.

asato from non-existence lead	**mā** me	**sad**	**gamaya** existence
tamaso from darkness lead	**mā**	**jyotir** me	**gamaya** light
mṛtyor from death lead	**mā** me	**amṛtaṃ**	**gamaya** immortality

2. आयुर्वेदो अमृतानाम्

āyur-vedo amṛtānām
Knowledge of lifespan truly belongs to the custodians of immortality.

Caraka Saṃhitā, Sūtrasthāna 25.40

1. तिलेषु तैलवद्वेदे वेदान्तः सुप्रतिष्ठितः

tileṣu tailavad vede vedāntaḥ supratiṣṭhitaḥ

in a sesame seed oil-like in Veda Vedānta is established

As oil is present in a sesame seed, so is Vedānta present in the Veda

Muktikā Upaniṣad 1.9

2. अयमात्मा ब्रह्म

ayam ātmā brahma

This Ātmā is Brahman.

Māṇḍūkya Upaniṣad 2

3. भूमिरापोऽनलो वायुः

खं मनो बुद्धिरेव च

अहंकार इतीयं मे

भिन्ना प्रकृतिरष्टधा

bhūmir āpo 'nalo vāyuḥ
khaṃ mano buddhir eva ca
ahaṃkāra itīyaṃ me
bhinnā prakṛtir aṣṭadhā

Earth, water, fire, air,
space, mind, intellect, and
ego: Thus is my
prakṛti divided eightfold.

Bhagavad-Gītā 7.4

4. अमृतस्य पुत्राः

amṛtasya putrāḥ

of immortality O sons

O sons of immortality.

Śvetāśvatara Upaniṣad 2.5

1. तत्स्वयं योगसंसिद्धः कालेनात्मनि विन्दति

tat svayaṃ yoga-saṃsiddhaḥ kālenātmani vindati
this himself yoga-perfected with time in himself finds
He who is perfected in Yoga, of himself in time finds this within himself.

Bhagavad-Gītā 4.38

2. समत्वं योग उच्यते

samatvaṃ yoga ucyate
balance yoga is called
Balance of mind is called Yoga.

Bhagavad-Gītā 2.48

3. अत्ता चराचरग्रहणात्

attā carācara-grahaṇāt
devourer movable-immovable-from taking in
Brahman is the devourer of all diversity.

Brahma Sūtra 1.2.9

4. वेदो अखिलो धर्ममूलम्

vedo akhilo dharma-mūlam
Veda is the root of all laws.

Manu Smṛti 2.6

1. यो वै भूमा तत्सुखं नाल्पे सुखमस्ति

yo vai bhūmā tat sukhaṃ nālpe sukham asti

which unbounded that happy not in small joy is

That which is unbounded is happy. There is no happiness in the small.

Chāndogya Upaniṣad 7.23

2. आत्मा वारे द्रष्टव्यः श्रोतव्यो मन्तव्यो निदिध्यासितव्यः

ātmā vāre draṣṭavyaḥ śrotavyo mantavyo nididhyāsitavyaḥ

That Ātmā alone, that simplest form of awareness alone, is worthy of seeing, hearing, contemplating, and realizing.

Bṛhadāraṇyaka Upaniṣad 2.4.5

3. प्रचारः स तु विज्ञेयः

pracāraḥ sa tu vijñeyaḥ

The mind gets expanded in the transcendent.

Gauḍapāda's Māṇḍūkya Kārikā 3.34

4. दूरेदृशं गृहपतिमथर्युम्

dūre-dṛśaṃ gṛha-patim atharyum

distance-seen house-owner reverberating

Far in the distance is seen the owner of the house, reverberating.

Ṛk Saṃhitā 7.1.1

1. शिवं शान्तमद्वैतं चतुर्थं मन्यन्ते स आत्मा स विज्ञेयः

śivaṃ śāntam advaitaṃ caturthaṃ manyante sa ātmā sa vijñeyaḥ

blissful peaceful undivided fourth they regard that Self that to be known

The peaceful, the blissful, the undivided is thought to be the fourth; that is the Self. That is to be known.

Nṛsiṃhottaratāpanīya Upaniṣad 1

2. स्मृतिर्लब्धा

smṛtir labdhā

memory regained

I have regained memory.

Bhagavad-Gītā 18.73

3. अथातो ब्रह्मजिज्ञासा

athāto brahma-jijñāsā

now from here brahman-desire to know

Now, from here, the desire to know Brahman.

Brahma Sūtra 1.1.1

4. पश्य मे योगमैश्वरम्

paśya me yogam aiśvaram

behold my yoga sovereign

Behold the richness of my Yoga.

Bhagavad-Gītā 9.5

1. वेदोऽहम्

vedo 'ham

I am the Veda. **Devī Upaniṣad** 1

2. अथ योगानुशासनम्

atha yogānuśāsanam

now yoga teaching

Now is the teaching on Yoga.

Yoga Sūtra 1.1

3. योगश्चित्तवृत्तिनिरोधः

yogaś citta-vṛtti-nirodhaḥ

yoga mind-activity-complete settling

Yoga is the complete settling of the activity of the mind.

Yoga Sūtra 1.2

4. तदा द्रष्टुः स्वरूपे अवस्थानम्

tadā draṣṭuḥ svarūpe avasthānam

then the observer in himself established

Then the observer is established in himself.

Yoga Sūtra 1.3

5. वृत्तिसारूप्यमितरत्र

vṛtti-sārūpyam itaḥ atra

Tendencies of the observer emerge from here and remain here.

Yoga Sūtra 1.4

1. योगिनः कर्म कुर्वन्ति सङ्गं त्यक्त्वात्मशुद्धये

yoginaḥ karma kurvanti saṅgaṃ tyaktvātma-śuddhaye

yogis action perform attachment abandoning self-purification

Yogis, abandoning attachment, perform action for self-purification.

Bhagavad-Gītā 5.11

2. ज्ञानविज्ञानतृप्तात्मा

jñāna-vijñāna-tṛptātmā

knowledge-experience-contented-Self

Contented in knowledge and experience.

Bhagavad-Gītā 6.8

3. आनन्दाद्ध्येव खल्विमानि भूतानि जायन्ते

आनन्देन जातानि जीवन्ति

आनन्दं प्रयन्त्यभिसंविशन्ति

ānandād dhy eva khalv imāni bhūtāni jāyante
ānandena jātāni jīvanti
ānandaṃ prayanty abhisaṃviśanti

Out of bliss these beings are born,
In bliss they are sustained,
And to bliss they go and merge again.

Taittirīya Upaniṣad 3.6.1

1. भद्रं कर्णेभिः शृणुयाम देवा

भद्रं पश्येमाक्षभिर्यजत्राः

bhadraṃ karṇebhiḥ śṛṇuyāma devā

bhadraṃ paśyemākṣabhir yajatrāḥ

All good I should hear from the ears.

All good I should see through the eyes.

Introduction to **Upaniṣads** of **Atharva Veda**

2. तरति शोकमात्मवित्

tarati śokam ātmavit

crosses suffering Self-knower

Established in the Self, one overcomes sorrows and suffering.

Chāndogya Upaniṣad 7.1.3

3. ब्रह्मसंस्पर्शमत्यन्तं सुखम्

brahma-saṃsparśam atyantaṃ sukham

brahman-contact infinite joy

Contact with Brahman is infinite joy.

Bhagavad-Gītā 6.28

4. समितिः समानी

samitiḥ samānī

assembly even

An assembly is significant in unity.

Ṛk Saṃhitā 10.191.3

1. गहना कर्मणो गतिः

gahanā karmaṇo gatiḥ

unfathomable of action course

Unfathomable is the course of action.

Bhagavad-Gītā 4.17

2. स्वल्पमप्यस्य धर्मस्य त्रायते महतो भयात्

svalpam apy asya dharmasya trāyate mahato bhayāt

little even of this dharma delivers from great fear

Even a little of this dharma delivers from great fear.

Bhagavad-Gītā 2.40

3. आनन्दमयोऽभ्यासात्

ānandamayo 'bhyāsāt

blissful from practice

Brahman becomes blissful through practice.

Brahma Sūtra 1.1.12

4. निमित्तमात्रं भव सव्यसाचिन्

nimitta-mātraṃ bhava savyasācin

instument-only be Arjuna

Be only the instrument, O Arjuna.

Bhagavad-Gītā 11.33

5. प्रत्यवायो न विद्यते

pratyavāyo na vidyate

obstacle not exists

No obstacle exists. **Bhagavad-Gītā** 2.40

1. सर्वभूतस्थमात्मानं सर्वभूतानि चात्मनीक्षते

sarvabhūtastham ātmānaṃ sarvabhūtāni cātmanīkṣate
in all beings established Self all beings and in the Self he sees

He sees the Self in all beings, and all beings in the Self.

Bhagavad-Gītā 6.29

2. ज्ञानाग्निदग्धकर्माणां तमाहुः पण्डितं बुधाः

jñānāgni-dagdha-karmāṇaṃ tam āhuḥ paṇḍitaṃ budhāḥ
knowledge-fire-burnt-action him call wise knowers of reality

Whose action is burnt up in the fire of knowledge, him the knowers of Reality call wise.

Bhagavad-Gītā 4.19

3. वश्यात्मना तु यतता शक्योऽवाप्तुमुपायतः

vaśyātmanā tu yatatā śakyo 'vāptum upāyataḥ
disciplined-man endeavoring possible to gain through proper means

Yoga can be gained through proper means by the man of endeavor who is disciplined.

Bhagavad-Gītā 6.36

4. स तु दीर्घकालनैरंतर्यसत्कारासेवितो दृढभूमिः

sa tu dīrgha-kāla-nairaṃtarya-satkārāsevito dṛdha-bhūmiḥ

Yoga becomes an established state when it has been respectfully and uninterruptedly cultivated for a long time.

Yoga Sūtra 1.14

BHAGAVAD-GĪTĀ

CHAPTER TWO

त्रैगुण्यविषया वेदा निस्त्रैगुण्यो भवार्जुन ।
निर्द्वन्द्वो नित्यसत्त्वस्थो निर्योगक्षेम आत्मवान् ।।४५।।

traiguṇya-viṣayā vedā nistraiguṇyo bhavārjuna

nirdvandvo nitya-sattvastho niryoga-kṣema ātmavān 45

योगस्थः कुरु कर्माणि सङ्गं त्यक्त्वा धनञ्जय ।
सिद्ध्यसिद्ध्योः समो भूत्वा समत्वं योग उच्यते ।।४८।।

yogasthaḥ kuru karmāṇi saṅgaṃ tyaktvā dhanañjaya

siddhy-asiddhyoḥ samo bhūtvā samatvaṃ yoga ucyate 48

दूरेण ह्यवरं कर्म बुद्धियोगाद्धनञ्जय ।
बुद्धौ शरणमन्विच्छ कृपणाः फलहेतवः ।।४९।।

dūreṇa hy avaraṃ karma buddhi-yogād dhanañjaya

buddhau śaraṇam anviccha kṛpaṇāḥ phala-hetavaḥ 49

बुद्धियुक्तो जहातीह उभे सुकृतदुष्कृते ।
तस्माद्योगाय युज्यस्व योगः कर्मसु कौशलम् ।।५०।।

buddhi-yukto jahātīha ubhe sukṛta-duṣkṛte

tasmād yogāya yujyasva yogaḥ karmasu kauśalam 50

कर्मजं बुद्धियुक्ता हि फलं त्यक्त्वा मनीषिणः ।
जन्मबन्धविनिर्मुक्ताः पदं गच्छन्त्यनामयम् ।।५१।।

karmajaṃ buddhi-yuktā hi phalaṃ tyaktvā manīṣiṇaḥ

janma-bandha-vinirmuktāḥ padaṃ gacchanty anāmayam 51

यदा ते मोहकलिलं बुद्धिर्व्यतितरिष्यति ।
तदा गन्तासि निर्वेदं श्रोतव्यस्य श्रुतस्य च ।।५२।।

yadā te moha-kalilaṃ buddhir vyatitariṣyati

tadā gantāsi nirvedaṃ śrotavyasya śrutasya ca 52

श्रुतिविप्रतिपन्ना ते यदा स्थास्यति निश्चला ।
समाधावचला बुद्धिस्तदा योगमवाप्स्यसि ।।५३।।

śruti-vipratipannā te yadā sthāsyati niścalā

samādhāv acalā buddhis tadā yogam avāpsyasi 53

अर्जुन उवाच ।
स्थितप्रज्ञस्य का भाषा समाधिस्थस्य केशव ।
स्थितधीः किं प्रभाषेत किमासीत व्रजेत किम् ।।५४।।

arjuna uvāca
sthita-prajñasya kā bhāṣā samādhi-sthasya keśava

sthita-dhīḥ kiṃ prabhāṣeta kim āsīta vrajeta kim 54

श्रीभगवानुवाच ।
प्रजहाति यदा कामान्सर्वान्पार्थ मनोगतान् ।
आत्मन्येवात्मना तुष्टः स्थितप्रज्ञस्तदोच्यते ।।५५।।

śrī-bhagavān uvāca
prajahāti yadā kāmān sarvān pārtha mano-gatān

ātmany evātmanā tuṣṭaḥ sthita-prajñas tadocyate 55

दुःखेष्वनुद्विग्नमनाः सुखेषु विगतस्पृहः ।
वीतरागभयक्रोधः स्थितधीर्मुनिरुच्यते ।।५६।।

duḥkheṣv anudvigna-manāḥ sukheṣu vigata-spṛhaḥ

vīta-rāga-bhaya-krodhaḥ sthita-dhīr munir ucyate 56

यः सर्वत्रानभिस्नेहस्तत्तत्प्राप्य शुभाशुभम् ।
नाभिनन्दति न द्वेष्टि तस्य प्रज्ञा प्रतिष्ठिता ॥५७॥

yaḥ sarvatrānabhisnehas tat tat prāpya śubhāśubham

nābhinandati na dveṣṭi tasya prajñā pratiṣṭhitā 57

यदा संहरते चायं कूर्मोऽङ्गानीव सर्वशः ।
इन्द्रियाणीन्द्रियार्थेभ्यस्तस्य प्रज्ञा प्रतिष्ठिता ॥५८॥

yadā saṃharate cāyaṃ kūrmo 'ṅgānīva sarvaśaḥ

indriyāṇīndriyārthebhyas tasya prajñā pratiṣṭhitā 58

विषया विनिवर्तन्ते निराहारस्य देहिनः ।
रसवर्जं रसोऽप्यस्य परं दृष्ट्वा निवर्तते ॥५९॥

viṣayā vinivartante nirāhārasya dehinaḥ

rasa-varjaṃ raso 'py asya paraṃ dṛṣṭvā nivartate 59

यततो ह्यपि कौन्तेय पुरुषस्य विपश्चितः ।
इन्द्रियाणि प्रमाथीनि हरन्ति प्रसभं मनः ॥६०॥

yatato hy api kaunteya puruṣasya vipaścitaḥ

indriyāṇi pramāthīni haranti prasabhaṃ manaḥ 60

तानि सर्वाणि संयम्य युक्त आसीत मत्परः ।
वशे हि यस्येन्द्रियाणि तस्य प्रज्ञा प्रतिष्ठिता ॥६१॥

tāni sarvāṇi saṃyamya yukta āsīta mat-paraḥ

vaśe hi yasyendriyāṇi tasya prajñā pratiṣṭhitā 61

ध्यायतो विषयान्पुंसः सङ्गस्तेषूपजायते ।
सङ्गात्संजायते कामः कामात्क्रोधोऽभिजायते ।।६२।।

dhyāyato viṣayān puṃsaḥ saṅgas teṣūpajāyate

saṅgāt saṃjāyate kāmaḥ kāmāt krodho 'bhijāyate 62

क्रोधाद्भवति संमोहः संमोहात्स्मृतिविभ्रमः ।
स्मृतिभ्रंशाद्बुद्धिनाशो बुद्धिनाशात्प्रणश्यति ।।६३।।

krodhād bhavati saṃmohaḥ saṃmohāt smṛti-vibhramaḥ

smṛti-bhraṃśād buddhi-nāśo buddhi-nāśāt praṇaśyati 63

रागद्वेषवियुक्तैस्तु विषयानिन्द्रियैश्चरन् ।
आत्मवश्यैर्विधेयात्मा प्रसादमधिगच्छति ।।६४।।

rāga-dveṣa-viyuktais tu viṣayān indriyaiś caran

ātma-vaśyair vidheyātmā prasādam adhigacchati 64

प्रसादे सर्वदुःखानां हानिरस्योपजायते ।
प्रसन्नचेतसो ह्याशु बुद्धिः पर्यवतिष्ठते ।।६५।।

prasāde sarva-duḥkhānāṃ hānir asyopajāyate

prasanna-cetaso hy āśu buddhiḥ paryavatiṣṭhate 65

नास्ति बुद्धिरयुक्तस्य न चायुक्तस्य भावना ।
न चाभावयतः शान्तिरशान्तस्य कुतः सुखम् ।।६६।।

nāsti buddhir ayuktasya na cāyuktasya bhāvanā

na cābhāvayataḥ śāntir aśāntasya kutaḥ sukham 66

इन्द्रियाणां हि चरतां यन्मनोऽनुविधीयते ।
तदस्य हरति प्रज्ञां वायुर्नावमिवाम्भसि ।।६७।।

indriyāṇāṃ hi caratāṃ yan mano 'nuvidhīyate

tad asya harati prajñāṃ vāyur nāvam ivāmbhasi 67

तस्माद्यस्य महाबाहो निगृहीतानि सर्वशः ।
इन्द्रियाणीन्द्रियार्थेभ्यस्तस्य प्रज्ञा प्रतिष्ठिता ॥६८॥

tasmād yasya mahābāho nigṛhītāni sarvaśaḥ

indriyāṇīndriyārthebhyas tasya prajñā pratiṣṭhitā 68

या निशा सर्वभूतानां तस्यां जागर्ति संयमी ।
यस्यां जाग्रति भूतानि सा निशा पश्यतो मुनेः ॥६९॥

yā niśā sarva-bhūtānāṃ tasyāṃ jāgarti saṃyamī

yasyāṃ jāgrati bhūtāni sā niśā paśyato muneḥ 69

आपूर्यमाणमचलप्रतिष्ठं समुद्रमापः प्रविशन्ति यद्वत् ।
तद्वत्कामा यं प्रविशन्ति सर्वे स शान्तिमाप्नोति न
कामकामी ॥७०॥

āpūryamāṇam acala-pratiṣṭhaṃ samudram āpaḥ praviśanti yadvat

tadvat kāmā yaṃ praviśanti sarve sa śāntim āpnoti na kāma-kāmī 70

विहाय कामान्यः सर्वान्पुमांश्चरति निःस्पृहः ।
निर्ममो निरहङ्कारः स शान्तिमधिगच्छति ॥७१॥

vihāya kāmān yaḥ sarvān pumāṃś carati niḥspṛhaḥ

nirmamo nirahaṅkāraḥ sa śāntim adhigacchati 71

एषा ब्राह्मी स्थितिः पार्थ नैनां प्राप्य विमुह्यति ।
स्थित्वास्यामन्तकालेऽपि ब्रह्मनिर्वाणमृच्छति ॥७२॥

eṣā brāhmī sthitiḥ pārtha naināṃ prāpya vimuhyati

sthitvāsyām anta-kāle 'pi brahma-nirvāṇam ṛcchati 72

INDEX OF GRAMMATICAL TERMS

PAGE

GENERAL INDEX

anusvara मं मः visarga

kantipur.com

nepali font
devanagari font

himali

unicode.com

symbol / insert

priti.com

1. Sanskrit in Devanagari

(2. Transliterate, if needed)

3. Sandhi

4. Translate grammatical

r before a consonant, e.g. rpa र्प rgo र्गो